Dedicated to America's independent farm families
who work the land, care for the soil and the water, plant the seeds,
tend the animals, and gather the harvest

FARM AID
A SONG FOR AMERICA

Featuring the voices of
WILLIE NELSON, NEIL YOUNG, JOHN MELLENCAMP, and DAVE MATTHEWS

Edited by Holly George-Warren

Music essays by Dave Hoekstra

Introduction by Eric Schlosser

Concert photography by Paul Natkin and Ebet Roberts

RODALE

Printed in the United States of America
Rodale Inc. makes every effort to use acid-free ♾, recycled paper ♻.

Book design by Ellen Nygaard
A Jackalope Press Production
Editorial director: Holly George-Warren
Editorial: Nina Pearlman, Robin Aigner, Judy Whitfield, Robert Legault, Andrea Odintz-Cohen

Photo credits and permissions appear on page 236.

Library of Congress Cataloging-in-Publication Data

Farm Aid : a song for America / featuring the voices of Willie Nelson ... [et al.] ; edited by Holly
George-Warren ; essays by Dave Hoekstra ; concert photography by Paul Natkin and Ebet Roberts.
    p.   cm.
ISBN-13 978–1–59486–285–4 hardcover
ISBN-10 1–59486–285–0 hardcover
    1. Farm Aid (Fund raising enterprise)—History.   2. Rock musicians—United States.   3. Country
musicians—United States.   4. Family farms—United States.   I. Hoekstra, Dave.   II. George-Warren,
Holly.
III. Nelson, Willie, date.
ML37.U5F39   2005
781.64'079'73—dc22   2005016655

Distributed to the trade by Holtzbrinck Publishers

2 4 6 8 10 9 7 5 3 1 hardcover

RODALE
LIVE YOUR WHOLE LIFE™

We inspire and enable people to improve their lives and the world around them

For more of our products visit **rodalestore.com** or call 800-848-4735

"We're fighting for the small family farmer, which means that we're fighting for every living American."

—WILLIE NELSON

Contents

1 The Story of Farm Aid

2 Farming in American History and Culture

3

Understanding Farm Policy

4

The Consequences of Industrial Agriculture

5

The Good Food Movement

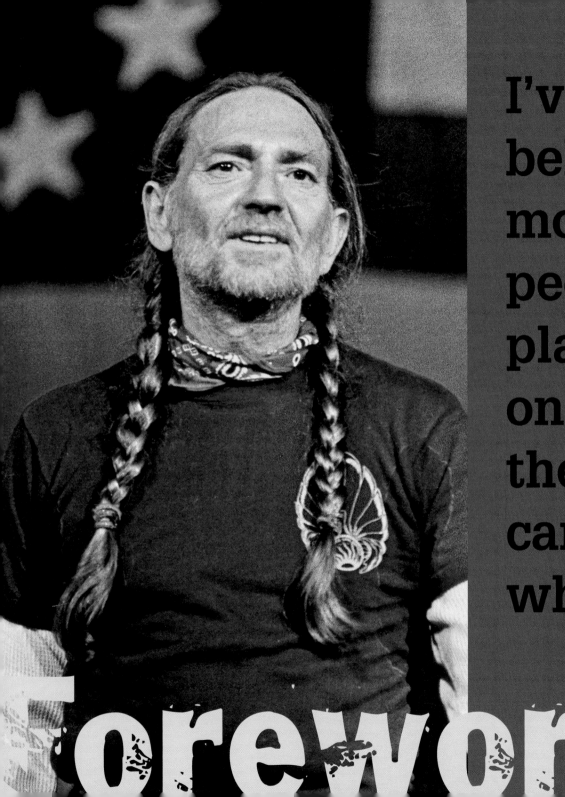

I've always believed that the most important people on the planet are the ones who plant the seeds and care for the soil where they grow.

Foreword

I've always been drawn to family farmers because of my own story and what I've seen with my own eyes. Where I grew up, in the town of Abbott, Texas, my backyard was six miles of beautiful farms and ranches all the way to the town of West. My playground was miles of hay, corn, and cotton fields. It was home to everything from jackrabbits, deer, birds, scorpions, cattle, horses, chickens, and hogs, right down to the small vegetable garden at my back door. I learned the difference between a fresh tomato or a fresh farm egg and the stuff we see in most grocery stores. Working in those fields, I learned the value of hard work; I found out that playing guitar is a hell of a lot easier!

I constantly travel the back roads of America. From New England to the Pacific coast, I listen to farm families tell their stories of both pleasures and struggles in working the land. Few of us know what it's like to drive a tractor through amber waves of grain or to stay up all night for the arrival of baby lambs. Few of us have felt the heartbreaking anguish of being forced to sell the farm and leave the land.

Family farmers are the backbone of the country, the bottom rung on the economic ladder on which all else depends. And when the backbone of our country is broken and the first rung on the ladder is weakened, everything collapses.

I started Farm Aid as a way for you and me to keep farmers on the land. But I want America to ensure that even more young people can start up, own a hundred acres, grow their own food—and yours and mine—and make a good living.

Farm Aid is more than a struggle about farms: It's about the little guy versus the big guy, about the family farm versus the factory farm, and about the community versus the corporation. It's about whether we can produce our food without destroying the soil and water, and whether American family farmers can generate alternative energy for our future.

Farmers and their fields are the fabric that holds our country together. This book is about the connections between farmers and the land, our nation's past and future, rural and urban, producer and eater, old and young.

I'm inviting you to make family farming a part of your own life through the pleasure of eating real family farm food, enjoying Farm Aid music, and loving the land.

Here, in this book—full of testimonials, stories, and photos—you can find your own personal food and farm story that just might change your life. Like the nearly 600,000 people who have purchased a ticket to Farm Aid shows and the thousands of donors who have made a gift, I welcome you to join the Farm Aid family.

I hope that this book will connect you to the soil and water and sunshine, which feed us—body and soul.

Stay strong and positive,

Willie Nelson

WILLIE NELSON
FOUNDER, FARM AID

Preface

Farm Aid's vision is simple: thriving family farms growing quality food for all.

The twentieth anniversary of Farm Aid happily coincides with the emergence of a powerful movement for good food from family farms. This flourishing movement brings Americans home to their roots, to their farmers, to their own kitchen tables, to good health for their bodies.

Thankfully, family farm food can be identified in a variety of ways. Local farmers markets and farm stands are the most obvious, but organic, humanely raised, regionally identified, and family farm–labeled food all advance a good food system that keeps farmers on the land.

Food grown with the most care and close to home, from a family farm, tastes better, is fresher, and satisfies us deeply in ways we might not be able to put into words.

The Farm Aid story is full of hope, a tale of twenty years of making music, fighting for every precious family farm, and shining the spotlight on family farmers as a resource for the nation.

C'mon, take a bite of farm made!

FARM AID
JUNE 2005

Opposite: A field on a California family farm. Inset: Annie Fox, a Vermont
family farmer, with newly harvested chard

Introduction

Eric Schlosser

The United States began as a small, democratic republic of farmers. "Cultivators of the earth are the most valuable citizens," Thomas Jefferson wrote. "They are the most vigorous, the most independent, the most virtuous, and they are tied to their country and wedded to its liberty and interests by the most lasting bonds."

Jefferson believed that so long as Americans maintained their link to rural life, this country would avoid the poverty and corruption that plagued the great nations of Europe. For generations, agriculture was the economic bedrock of the United States, feeding the American people and supplying exports that paid for westward expansion, the building of factories, the construction of railroads. No society in history had ever enjoyed such abundant and inexpensive food. Although the number of American farmers began to decline in the early twentieth century, their hard work played a central role in the defeat of Germany during two world wars and in the triumph over Communism during the Cold War. The United States had enough food not only to feed its allies, but also to supply the Russian people with grain. Our family-owned, independent farms proved themselves far more efficient than the giant collective farms of the Soviet Union. You could hardly find a better symbol of freedom than the American farmer.

Instead of being honored and rewarded for their contribution to America's greatness, family farmers in recent years have been called obsolete and deliberately pushed to the brink of extinction. Over the past two decades, a new form of corporate, industrialized agriculture has gained control. When you calmly and rationally look at America's food system today, there's no shortage of reasons to feel depressed. Everywhere, ranchers and farmers are being driven off the land. Agribusiness companies now wield more power than at any other time.

Supermarkets have more power. Wal-Mart has more power, squeezing producers even harder and paying employees even less than supermarkets do. The same fast food chains sell the same food worldwide. The fast food chains and soda companies aggressively target children in schools. Meatpacking companies abuse their workers, mistreat their livestock, overuse antibiotics and growth hormones, pollute rivers and streams, sell meat tainted with fecal material and harmful bacteria. Farm-raised salmon are often contaminated with pesticide residues, while wild salmon are vanishing from the seas. And then there's the threat of mad cow disease, avian flu, and genetically modified organisms. A clear look at what's happening to food today is bound to ruin your appetite.

Things are bad, all right—but they didn't have to turn out this way. The more time I spend investigating how we produce, market, and distribute our food, the more I realize that none of this was inevitable. Today's food system wasn't the unavoidable result of free market forces, technological change, or "progress." Indeed the free market has had little to do with determining how and why certain foods are now produced. For years the American fast food industry has benefited from government subsidized cheap corn (that becomes cheap animal feed and cheap corn sweeteners), government-funded road construction (so essential for all those drive-throughs), and minimum wage policies that keep labor costs low. Right now, big corporate farmers get billions of dollars from the U.S. government, while little organic farmers get

Opposite: A family farm near Edray, West Virginia
Above: A farmer protesting in Chicago, 1985

just about none. The farm policies chosen by Congress aren't inevitable. But they are predictable. Every year, agribusiness companies and corporate farmers get what they want, family farmers get screwed over, and American consumers pay the bill.

About a dozen corporations now control most of the food that Americans eat. And this unprecedented corporate domination of almost every commodity market is a violation of the free market—not its fulfillment. If America's antitrust laws were enforced today the way they were fifty years ago, during the administration of President Dwight D. Eisenhower, most of America's leading agribusiness companies would be dismantled. Eisenhower was hardly a left-wing activist. He strongly believed in the importance of competition—and during his first year in office he boldly launched an antitrust campaign against the nation's five biggest oil companies. For the past few decades, government policy has favored just the opposite point of view, encouraging centralized power in one industry after another. In 1970 the four largest meatpacking companies in the United States controlled about 21 percent of the beef market. Today the four largest control more than 80 percent. Tyson Foods—the largest producer of both beef and chicken—is now the biggest

Farmer Julia Wiley with her Mariquita Farm produce at the Ferry Plaza farmers market, San Francisco

meatpacking company the world has ever seen. Its market power has huge implications for farmers, ranchers, workers, and consumers. Fate and the free market weren't the guiding forces that brought us to this point. Every step of the way, important choices were made by politicians, corporate executives, and unwitting consumers. Different choices can still be made.

The food we eat has changed more in the last thirty years than in the previous thirty thousand—without most of us realizing it. Today's food looks the same and tastes much the same as it did a generation ago. But too often it's a fundamentally different thing. The fast food that millions of Americans eat every day is much more like an industrial commodity than like anything you could make in your own kitchen. Fast food is some of the most heavily processed food on the planet. It's usually manufactured at an enormous factory, flavored with chemicals made at a different factory, then frozen and shipped to fast food restaurants for reheating. Nobody's ever eaten food quite like this before. If you want to make a strawberry milk shake at home, all you'll need is milk, ice, cream, sugar, strawberries, and a pinch of salt. If you look at the list of ingredients and flavor additives in a typical fast food strawberry shake, you'll find dozens of spooky chemical names that are hard to pronounce. They sound like chemicals you might want in a floor cleaner, not in something you're going to eat. A fast food shake and a homemade shake may look the same. But one's really an illusion, the brilliant creation of modern food science.

How did this happen? How was our food system captured and profoundly changed without most of us even realizing it? The food industry is by far the most important industry—without it, every other industry would disappear—and yet most Americans know more about what's on TV tonight than what's in the food they buy. This is no accident. The agribusiness and fast food giants don't want you to know where their food really comes from or how it's being made. They just want you to buy it. Have you ever seen a fast food ad that shows the New Jersey chemical plants where the flavors of the milk shakes are created? Have you ever seen a fast food ad that shows the huge feedlots—with a hundred thousand cattle crammed together, standing in one another's manure—or the massive slaughterhouses where the hamburgers come from? I don't think so. But I'm sure you've seen lots of fast food ads with smiling, happy, thin people having fun.

During my lifetime, the civil rights movement triumphed in the American South, the Berlin Wall vanished, the Soviet Union collapsed, and apartheid was dismantled in South Africa. Those were epic, monumental changes. So I don't accept that there is no possible alternative to the way we now feed ourselves. I refuse to believe it. Our current system won't last because it can't last. It is not sustainable. This centralized, industrialized agriculture has been in place for just a few decades—and look at the destruction it has already caused. Look at the harm it has inflicted upon farmers, consumers, livestock, and the environment. In the final analysis, our fast, cheap food costs way too much.

How we get our food today isn't the only way to get it. Uniformity and conformity, a blind faith in science, a narrow measure of profit and loss, a demand for total, absolute power—those are the core values of the current food system. We don't need to invent a whole new set of values. We just need to return to some of the old ones.

For more than two hundred years, America's economic strength was largely derived from the unmatched efficiency and productivity of family farms. We must never forget that. Farm Aid supports a food system that is democratic, independent, competitive, and locally based. This isn't an exercise in nostalgia. It's a commitment to a way of life that has endured for generations, that is truly sustainable, and that embodies much of what's best about America. These are values worth fighting for.

Right now, changing our food system is essential—but the change isn't going to happen by itself. People will have to make it happen. The current sense of doom and gloom and futility will have to be replaced by a passionate anger at what's going on and at who's profiting from it. Helping a local farmer is a simple way to help yourself. Every time you buy food, you're supporting whoever produced it. The price of good, healthy food may seem a little higher. But the real price of today's corporate, industrial food is much too high to pay. Championing the right system, instead of the wrong one, doesn't require much sacrifice. There's no need for any violence, hardship, or self-denial.

Green Gulch Farm, Muir Beach, California

What you choose to eat can help change the world, and as the chef Alice Waters likes to point out: This revolution tastes good.

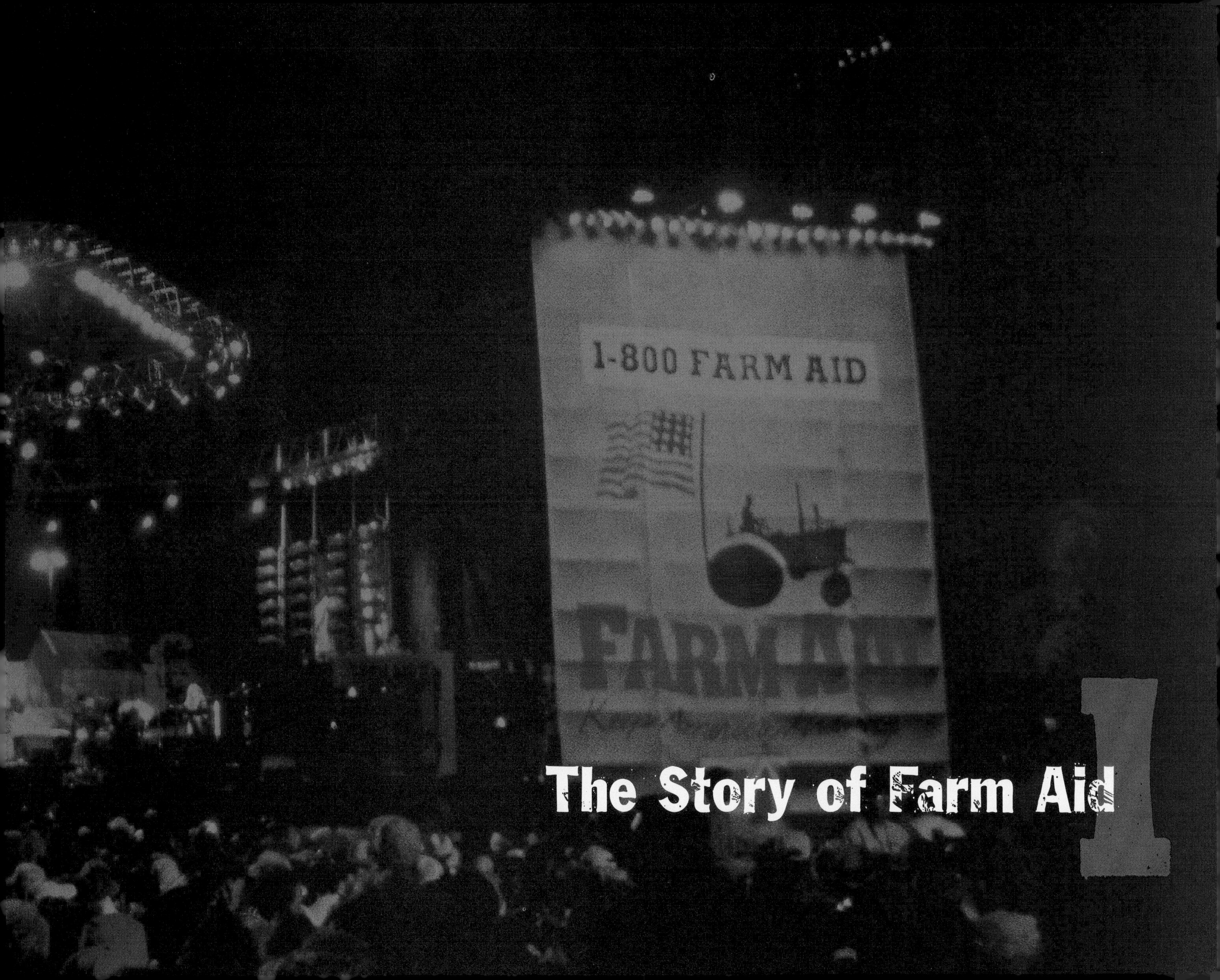

1 The Story of Farm Aid

Making Music/Making Bread: Charity Rock for Social Change

Reebee Garofalo

The year 2005 marks the twentieth anniversary of the phenomenon known as "charity rock"—that string of all-star performances and mega-events that erupted in 1985 with Band Aid, Live Aid, "We Are the World," and, before the year was out, Farm Aid. Beginning with the relatively safe issue of hunger and starvation in Africa—half a world away from the United States—these mega-events quickly took advantage of the cultural space opened up by charity rock to target more politically controversial issues. Little Steven's "Sun City" project and two massive Nelson Mandela tribute concerts focused attention on apartheid in South Africa, and two Amnesty International tours mobilized international pressure and support for prisoners of conscience around the world. By the end of the decade, there was scarcely a social issue that hadn't become the theme for a fund-raising concert or the subject of a popular song or both: the deteriorating environment, homelessness, child abuse, racism, AIDS, industrial plant closings, and U.S. military action in Central America, to name a few. Still, in speaking about his pivotal role in organizing Live Aid, Bob Geldof cautioned, "I would like it to be a movement, but it is not going to be so." The one project that has really fueled a movement is Farm Aid.

Spearheaded by Willie Nelson, following an offhanded comment by Bob Dylan from the Live Aid stage, Farm Aid was launched to draw attention to the plight of the family farm, once the iconic image of rural America. Like the stars associated with other mega-events, early Farm Aid stalwarts were never shy about using their celebrity to approach the seats of power; Willie Nelson, Neil Young, and John Mellencamp went to Washington, D.C., to talk to elected officials even before the first concert. But this early period was also

one of intense listening, at the grass-roots level. Farm Aid did not begin with grand plans for a twenty-year campaign to keep family farmers on the land, challenge the threat of factory farming, and fight for the quality of our food supply. Unlike other projects, which have been organized from the top down, the campaigns that came to define Farm Aid bubbled up from the base—from the very people and groups most affected by the issues.

A cursory look at some of the artists who have performed at Farm Aid concerts—from Alan Jackson to Billy Joel, Garth Brooks to Bon Jovi, Johnny Cash to Sheryl Crow, Loretta Lynn to Los Lobos—suggests that Farm Aid certainly understands the value of star power in the fund-raising effort. Through their efforts and the development work of a tireless staff, Farm Aid has raised more than $27 million in its twenty-year history and has used the funds to support grass-roots organizations and its own program initiatives. Farm Aid has also assembled a much more diverse roster of talent—including everyone from Crosby, Stills and Nash, Tracy Chapman, the Gin Blossoms, Julio Iglesias, and Iggy Pop, to Rick James, Lou Reed, Kid Rock, and Los Lonely Boys—than might be expected for a farm-oriented event. In the process, the organization has exposed its natural constituency to a broader range of genres and performance styles than might otherwise be the case, and it has spread its message far beyond the heartland.

Preceding pages: Farm Aid 1993, Ames, Iowa. Opposite: Willie Nelson, John Mellencamp, and Neil Young greet fans at the opening of Farm Aid 2001, Noblesville, Indiana. Above: Dave Matthews, with Ralph Paige of the Federation of Southern Cooperatives, at the 2002 Farm Aid press conference, Burgettstown, Pennsylvania

"Being a part of Farm Aid is a positive victory in itself because farmers out there who are struggling and think they did something wrong, when Willie takes the stage and talks about family farmers and greets them, they know they're not in it alone. They know it's not their fault—and that is such a positive, uplifting thing. When Farm Aid started, the major cities had food banks, pantries, counseling. They had all these different services. But small-town U.S.A. and rural communities did not have a support network for families who were losing their land. And so Farm Aid has built that support network for the families, as they go through the trials and tribulations of trying to stay on the land. And that's a legacy that will last from now on because Farm Aid started that, and I'm proud to be a part of it."

—CORKY JONES, NEBRASKA FARMER AND ACTIVIST

Neil Young and Willie Nelson at a 1997 Farm Aid rally

This track record, of course, highlights another distinguishing feature of Farm Aid: The organization has held an annual fund-raising event almost every year since its first concert in Champaign, Illinois, in 1985. As with other aspects of Farm Aid, the idea of annual concerts emerged as a response to particular conditions. Farm Aid Executive Director Carolyn Mugar points out that in the beginning, "Willie said many times in interviews, 'We're not having another concert.' " The founders were optimistic that the inequity of family farm foreclosures would be so obvious that "the people would get onboard; certainly Congress would do the right thing," Mugar says. "As it turned out, the farm crisis deepened and every year there needed to be another show. In the absence of a solution, it didn't seem right to stop the work."

Twenty years later, Farm Aid's work is still not done. The organization has grown to a dedicated staff of nine and an impressively active and stable board, who are in it for the duration and committed to addressing farm-related issues, no matter what it takes—and that includes celebrity board members Willie Nelson, Neil Young, John Mellencamp, and, more recently, Dave Matthews. "When Farm Aid was started," observes Mellencamp, "it was a time in America when everybody was feeling very charitable—Hands Across America, Live Aid, this aid, that aid. And twenty years later, we're the only people still doing it." Adds Young, "We'll be back next year. And the year after that. We're not giving up."

Farm Aid has in fact returned year after year, with no end in sight. And where it has chosen to play has been one of the things that has determined the character of the organization and its campaigns. "Willie always said he wanted to play various locations where farmers could go to the concert," according to Mugar. Over the years, this has meant smaller concerts that are more regional in nature. Though all but two concerts have been televised nationally, Farm Aid has moved from a focus on splashy seventy-thousand-seat stadium shows in favor of a more grass-roots approach to building the organization over the long haul. As a result, Farm Aid has produced shows in places like Ames, Iowa; Burgettstown, Pennsylvania; Columbus, Ohio; Columbia, South Carolina; Tinley Park, Illinois; Bristow, Virginia; and Noblesville, Indiana. While not part of a conscious strategy of regionalization, this approach has nonetheless been beneficial to the mission of the organization. In the words of Ted Quaday, Farm Aid's program director, "The fact that the shows move around like that gives us the opportunity

Nelson at a Farm Aid–sponsored hay lift, in which drought-stricken farmers received hay donated by other farmers

to strengthen local food and farm efforts in communities all across the United States."

After twenty years, that infrastructure has matured into a network of grass-roots organizations that is close enough to the ground to speak for the family farmer and, at the same time, strong enough to advance a national agenda. Equally important, Farm Aid staff and board members also are actively involved in developing the network. Willie Nelson "does many things during the year that are not the Farm Aid concert," says Mugar. "He meets with farm groups, he has press conferences (most always turning them over to farmers and advocates), he appears at rallies, he writes letters." Adds Quaday, "He makes the decisions on all of our grants, he signs all of those grant checks." Among other initiatives, Nelson, Young, and Mellencamp joined in the "fight for national organic standards." Farm Aid staff also operate a hotline that came into being when the 800 number that was set up to receive donations from the first concert "got swamped with calls from farmers and all kinds of people with ideas on how to fix the problem," says

"Farm Aid puts family farmers on center stage. We shine a national spotlight on family farmers—for our food, our health, our environment, our country. Farm Aid has always done that."

—CAROLYN MUGAR,
EXECUTIVE DIRECTOR, FARM AID

Mugar. It is through the hotline and regular contact with grantees that the staff stays in year-round contact with the issues and stories that make Farm Aid so compelling and also give its staff the credibility to participate actively in the network-building process. "It's because we maintain contact with all of these groups around the country," says Quaday, "that we understand from farmers what's going on so we can do the right thing."

Perhaps the most important role Farm Aid plays is that of catalyst. "A lot of times the people we bring together haven't always been working together," says Mugar. "When we go to a town, we work a good bit ahead of time with each region and always organize local events around the concert. It really gives people a chance to solidify their connections. Always we have left some-

Family farm advocates banding together at Farm Aid 1995, Louisville, Kentucky

thing better in our wake by coming to the area." There are times when this work fuels efforts that become national campaigns. The staff offers a case in point: "We're working in a network of people who were suddenly saying, 'The genetic engineering issue is becoming a very important issue to us,'" says Quaday. In response, Farm Aid convened two summit meetings at two different Farm Aid concerts to address genetic engineering. In this way, Farm Aid catalyzed the work that ultimately became the Farmer-to-Farmer Campaign on Genetic Engineering in Agriculture.

Over the years, Farm Aid has tried to stay abreast of the changing political landscape of farm country. In the current period, the negative aspects of factory farming and industrial food systems have been accompanied by an increased awareness of the quality of our food supply, as manifested in a growing concern over things like pesticides, genetic engineering, and national standards for organic food. But because the political will to address such issues at the level of policy and regulation seems lacking, there have been attempts to try and harness the purchasing power of consumers to keep family farmers on the land. Farm Aid realizes that such market-based strategies are useful but, in the end, are only a partial solution to the problem. The issues, as Farm Aid sees it, are much more complex and structural in nature, involving entrenched corporate interests, powerful lobbies, and corruptible elected officials. The 2002 Farm Bill, for example, clearly benefits the very largest farms and multinational corporations that produce and trade a handful of commodities, while the majority of farmers receive no government payments at all. To seriously address such problems, adequate resources need to be accompanied by appropriate political will and action.

If there is any one criticism that has been consistently leveled at huge fund-raising concerts, from Live Aid on, it is that they have a tendency to simply throw money at problems that are essentially political. Farm Aid is determined to avoid that pitfall. "That's the tension we're living in right now," says Farm Aid's associate director Glenda Yoder. "How to do education *and* organizing, how to promote a market-based solution *and* achieve a political solution." And if anyone doubts Farm Aid's resolve in rising to that challenge, they need only to listen to one of Neil Young's proclamations on the subject, which he happily reiterated at the 2003 Farm Aid press conference: "We're not big—we know we're small. We're David versus Goliath—there's an army of Goliaths against us. But we're not going away. We are going to keep going."

Neil Young and farm leader and activist Helen Waller at a 1999 rally

"All too often a problem arises, a benefit takes place, and then we walk away thinking, 'Okay, we solved that one.' I believe that sticking with it as Farm Aid has done is unusual and right . . . The problem has not and will not go away. I hold all charitable events and causes that I am asked to do up to Farm Aid as the standard. Farm Aid has managed to pass better than 80 percent of the money they make through to the people who need it. That they have done so is a tribute to the good sense and determination of the board and staff and proof that a few people can make a huge difference."

—DAVID CROSBY, FARM AID ARTIST

Farm Aid's Beginnings:
The Seeds Are Planted

Those of us putting this book together have taken to calling the story of the beginning of Farm Aid the "creation myth." Like the history of all great things, it seems whoever you talk to has a version of the story that's a bit different from the next. Chalk it up to the fact that no one person, not even Willie Nelson, could possibly know every

single thing that happened in those frenzied weeks leading up to what would become the biggest-ever confluence of country and rock & roll in history. We asked a few key players to tell us what they remember about that first concert—because when people tell the stories themselves, you hear all the dirt.

TONY CONWAY, OF BUDDY LEE ATTRACTIONS, WILLIE NELSON'S BOOKING AGENT AT THE TIME AND TALENT COORDINATOR/PROMOTER OF THE FIRST FARM AID: "In mid-August of 1985, Willie and I were in Springfield, Illinois, where I had booked Willie to play at the Illinois State Fair. Out of the blue, Willie said to me, 'I want to do a concert for the American farmers. I want to see if we can do it here in Illinois; I don't care where, just someplace where we can get a sta-

dium.' Willie asked me, 'Do you think you can get a hold of the governor?' I made a few calls and got a callback saying Governor Jim Thompson was on his way to the bus.

"Governor Thompson knocked on the bus door, and Willie welcomed him with a hug. Immediately, Willie said, 'Let me tell you what I've got on my mind . . . I want to do a concert to help save American farms.' Governor Thompson said, 'Great, what can I do to help?' Willie said, 'Well, I need a stadium.' Thompson said, 'I wonder if I could get the University of Illinois Stadium, although they've never done a concert that I know of.' Willie said, 'That'd be great. Let's do it there.'

"Then Willie asked me, 'What's my schedule, Tony?' Willie's schedule was as it is today—jam-packed. But he had one day free, September 22, 1985.

Thompson asked for a phone and made the call right there on the bus. Luckily, the UIC football team was playing an away game on the 22nd. Thompson said to the person on the other end of the phone, 'I want you to hold the stadium for me.' Then he turned to us and said, 'Okay, you've got the stadium.' The governor asked Mike Dubois of the Illinois State Fair to do on-site coordination, so Mike moved to Champaign and lived out of a motel room for the next five weeks.

"We had a few hours left before Willie's gig at the state fair. In those two or three hours, we went to work on Farm Aid. Willie started rattling off names of artists who had to be there, and we just started making phone calls. It continued on like that, sixteen hours a day, every day. We had to get the stage, sound, lights, and the stage crew, and then we had to get the TV deal. It was hard work every day. I give major credit to David Anderson, Willie's tour manager; Elliott Roberts, Neil's manager; Tommy Mottola, John's manager; and Mark Rothbaum, Willie's manager. They poured their heart and soul into this event. At the time, our firm had eighteen or twenty employees, and they were all involved during these four weeks of planning. Instead of our normal day-to-day business, we were not really available for anything aside from Farm Aid. It was a constant stream of activity. We'd call Willie every night and tell him what we'd accomplished. He'd say, 'Did you call Roger Miller? Johnny Cash? Waylon Jennings? George Jones?' By the time we got a stage manager,

we'd already confirmed forty to fifty acts. That was when people started telling us it was impossible. They said, 'There's no way you can do fifty acts on one stage in one day.'

"Arny Granat, from JAM Productions, set out to prove them wrong. He was the production manager and oversaw the staging, the sound, the lights, the set, security, everything. JAM was one of the few national promoters at the time that had done stadium shows. They got the job done, even as everyone said it couldn't happen.

"When we held the press conference to announce the show, things just exploded. Once word got out, we started getting calls from all over the country. People started coming out of the woodwork. It started getting so that we had to turn artists down—we just didn't have room for them on the bill. John Fogerty's people were calling, and I had to say no every time they called. One night, I was talking to my wife, Nancy, and I mentioned, 'This guy's been calling, driving us crazy—John Fogerty.'

" 'John Fogerty?' She said, 'He hasn't performed since the Creedence Clearwater Revival breakup ten or so years ago.' I said, 'Creedence Clearwater Revival, holy shit. *That's* John Fogerty!' I called him back the next day, and I said, 'You're in.'

"One of my other great memories of Farm Aid was setup the night before. There was nobody in the stadium, just a very small crew: the sound

The first Farm Aid, University of Illinois Memorial Stadium, September 22, 1985

Willie Nelson and Governor Jim Thompson enjoy the show.

ways has the same even personality. I saw him just turn the microphone over to the farmer so many times. He never wanted to grandstand—he brought the press, and he turned it right over. It was a great time. It's been a great thing for the farmers. Farm Aid was, without a doubt, the highlight of my twenty-nine years in the entertainment business."

ILLINOIS GOVERNOR JIM THOMPSON: "Willie Nelson played the Illinois State Fair every year I was governor. I brought him to the fair. For each of my campaigns, I would play his albums in our RV. The theme song for all four campaigns was 'On the Road Again.' My assistant press secretary Jim Skilbeck ran the state fair as a staff member and became friends with Willie. One year Jim brought me to the trailer for 'Chili with Willie,' and it became a ritual. Then I started playing golf with Willie in Springfield. He's a pretty good golfer.

"We started talking about the plight of the farmers in American agriculture. He said he had been thinking about a benefit concert. I said, 'Let's do it.' That was the night it started. We decided we'd do it in Champaign, and I was deputized to get permission to hold it in the University of Illinois football stadium. Willie's job was to get all the acts. It was amazing how it all came together in a very short time.

"It was a sensational event. I remember flying over the stadium in a chopper and watching them put in the flooring. And then coming back watching the talent assemble, and then seeing the show . . . Willie took me around and introduced me to all the talent . . . Jon Bon Jovi, Kris Kristofferson. I wasn't a music fan. But since I was a Willie fan, I just did it. He can sing it, and he's an appealing personality. He's got this 'the-rest-of-the-world-will-come-along-with-me' personality. And he can really sing it."

PAUL CORBIN, HEAD OF PROGRAMMING, TNN (THE NASHVILLE NETWORK): "I think it was six weeks but it seemed like two. Six weeks' notice. Willie called me at TNN on a Thursday around noon [through] the switchboard. When they gave me the call, they said, 'Tell us if it's really Willie Nelson.' We were this kind of fledgling little network, hoping that we might make a go of it. We were, like, the sixth cable network on the air. We weren't profitable yet; we were still building toward that, but we really hadn't had the validation of the major artists. We didn't have the big names calling us or working with us except for an occasional show.

guys, Buddy, Arny, and me. Everybody else had gone to bed, but we were doing the final checks before calling it a night. Bob Dylan had requested a sound check. We weren't giving sound checks to anybody because we were still painting the stage at the time—that's how quick everything had to fall into place. But he wanted a sound check. The only time he could sound check was at midnight. He came in a van with Tom Petty. Dylan played with Petty's band for that show. Dylan, Petty, and the Heartbreakers played their whole set to about ten of us. That was a magic moment. And just as they're about to get into their third song, Willie's bus pulled up. He had played a show that night and then drove straight to Champaign. About 1:00 a.m., Willie came walking onstage—the first time he'd seen the stadium, the set, anything. It was pretty emotional for him. He was all smiles and hugging everybody; he just kept looking around, standing on the stage while Dylan and Petty and the band played. These moments are burned in my brain.

"I can't imagine anyone but Willie at the center of anything like the beginning of Farm Aid. I think about the responsibility and the pressure that was on him—he just dealt with it. He doesn't change under pressure—he al-

Opposite: Nelson waving to the first-ever Farm Aid audience

One of the many planning meetings that took place on Willie's bus

"It *was* the real Willie Nelson on the phone and he said, 'We're doing this event to help the farmers.' He said he'd been out golfing with the governor of Illinois and they had planned a little benefit concert. I said, 'Well, when do you want to do that?'

"'Well, we've got a date: September 22nd,' Willie said, 'and we're going to do it in Champaign, Illinois, and we wanted to know if you guys wanted to help us. I'd like you to do the TV part of it.' I said, 'When do you need to know, Willie?' And he said, 'I'm planning on a press conference Saturday,' and this is Thursday.

"I said, 'I'll tell you what, we'll make a decision by noon tomorrow. This is something that we would really like to be part of, particularly because this is for the farmers.' So Willie called on Friday, and I said, 'We would love to do it with you, count us in.' 'Fantastic,' he said.

"Early the next week, I met up with Willie in Detroit. We began to lay out all the pieces: what we were gonna do, what he'd already got other people doing, and who all the players were. Every four or five days, I would fly wherever he was so that we could compare notes, and of course in the meantime we were calling other people, trying to follow the lineup, understand the scope of the project. We were working hand in hand with Willie. Assembling a number of television stations to syndicate the prime-time show was of real interest to us because we had forty million homes, and it would be a shame if we couldn't get wider distribution. It turned out that most of the CBS affiliates dropped their Sunday-night network service and took us on Sunday the 22nd. We had three hundred television stations, and we got four hundred radio stations to pick it up for the full day. It really did wonders for the network. It validated us with the artists, which was a key piece of our reason for doing it, other than the cause, which obviously was important.

"The stadium really started to fill up around 3:00 p.m., and by 5:00 p.m. you could hardly find a place to stand; it stayed like that through to the end. As the concert started to move into prime time, the intensity on the stage was really evident. At dusk, the Beach Boys were doing 'Help Me, Rhonda,' and everybody was jumping to the beat of that song, on their feet, all around the stadium. The people in the press box got very worried, because that whole box was starting to really rock, as if it might collapse with the jumping of those seventy-eight thousand fans.

"It was a real special time. First of its kind in . . . television history. The whole focus of the country was on Champaign, Illinois, for that day and night. I don't think anything's happened that's been bigger since. It was a great uniting force."

ARNY GRANAT, PRODUCER OF THE LIVE FARM AID SHOW, JAM PRODUCTIONS: "When Tony Conway called me to do this event, I said, 'Wow—great idea, great idea, how much time do I have?' 'Oh,' he told me, 'about three weeks.' . . . I'm going, 'Three weeks? This is pretty much impossible!' And then we decided that we would get the people from Live Aid and all these great production people. We had every artist at that time who was huge. It was being televised, a great cause, and I was in charge of it. I said, 'Okay, great.' So we go down to Champaign—I don't think Champaign knew what they were getting into. First of all, we had a great staff, so we did it in the time we did and did it really well. And it's not because of me, it's because my staff was so good. They probably aged about 240 years between all of them. But the bottom line is that it was an amazing thing to be able to put up the show. I mean, if you needed a fire engine, you'd say, 'Give me a fire engine,' and you'd have a fire engine in three minutes. 'Give me a pole bigger than me,' and there'd be a pole over there in two minutes. It was an amazing thing to have that type of ability to have people react like that, to produce and to be a part of the first Farm Aid and to work with the people and the cause. As time went on, I remember that it really bonded me with Willie, who I became lifelong friends with, and Tony Conway; I made a lot of friends from that event who I treasure today. I love the people involved, and I love the cause."

TIM O'CONNOR, NELSON'S PRODUCTION MANAGER AND A COORDINATOR AT FARM AID: "The press conference was a couple of days before we went on sale with the tickets—which sold out really quick. I rode to Champaign with Willie. The press conference went on, and afterward Willie got ready to leave. I started to get on the bus and Willie said, 'No, you're sticking here.' I went, 'What do you mean, I'm sticking here?' Willie said, 'Well, would you help us out on this?' And I said, 'Sure, sounds like fun!'

"One of Willie's great sayings is, 'You can't buy a ticket to this parade.' It's not about money. The way you 'buy' your way into it—if that's the right word—is by the look in your eye. Are you gonna be there—can I count on you?

"I can't speak for the man, but when he looked in those farmers' eyes, I think Willie saw the pain. He understands. He's from Abbott, Texas. He's seen the sodbuster; he understands that basic thing."

JIM MASSEY, FARM ACTIVIST, LAWYER FOR FARMERS LEGAL ACTION GROUP: "In 1985, one of the two watershed experiences of my life happened: I was sitting at my desk in my Minneapolis office and the phone rang, and I picked it up and it was Willie Nelson. I nearly tipped out of my chair, and my voice squeaked. I had been a huge fan of his music and his writing for years and here he is, on the phone. He and Bill Wittliff called me and said they were putting Farm Aid together that weekend—and had I read something in the paper about it?

"We had a really nice talk. They told me what their ideas were, and they asked me if I'd come to Champaign and talk with them and some of the press people about what Farm Aid could raise the money for and how we could distribute it.

"I was booked already on that weekend. I was on the road in Colorado, but I flew out of Denver on a Saturday night, took two red-eyes, and got into Champaign at some ungodly hour. I could barely stand up when I knocked on Willie's bus door Sunday morning. He and I were about the only people at the grounds that early morning, except the crew, who were setting up for the day's festivities. When he opened the bus door, he looked at me with those engaging eyes for the first time. We chatted for a few minutes, and he told me when we'd get back together, and then he said, 'You didn't get your credentials yet?' I said, 'No, where do I go?'

" 'Well, here,' and he took off his pass, which said WILLIE NELSON on it. He put it around my neck and looked at me and kind of winked and said, 'You can do anything with that except go to the mike, they'd probably recognize you.' I was fully engaged at that point with Willie the person—the charismatic personality he is—and began to learn about Willie the loyal friend and committed person."

Willie Nelson and John Mellencamp backstage during the first Farm Aid

"I remember Willie, John, and Neil stepping out onto that stage in Champaign twenty years ago, one by one. The rain started ten minutes before the show, and I remember standing in so much rain and not minding it because it was so very important for us to be there to give and show our support. I remember Jon Bon Jovi carrying his gear in the rain and performing in the rain—because we were in the rain, the farmers were out working in the rain, and he felt it so important that he was, too. To me, this will always symbolize Farm Aid: Regardless of the difficulties or adversities, we must do everything we can, because America's small family farmers desperately need our help and our support—now more than ever. I can't wait for the twentieth anniversary concert—and I'm not bringing an umbrella. If it rains, I will be the first to cheer."

—JIM WEAVER, FARM AID SUPPORTER

DAVID SENTER, FARM ACTIVIST: "The year 1985 had been very busy for me. I was executive director of the American Agriculture Movement, and in March of that year AAM hosted a march on Washington with about five thousand farmers. There were rallies beginning to happen around the farmbelt because of the collapse in farm prices and a whole new round of foreclosures.

"In August I received a call that there was gonna be a meeting in Champaign to discuss having a concert for farmers and that Willie Nelson was the person with the idea. Corky Jones, the president of AAM, and I went to that Illinois meeting with about twenty or thirty farm leaders from around the country.

"Our family farm is about forty miles from Abbott, where Willie grew up. Of course, I knew who Willie was and I liked his music. I thought it was going to be great fun to get to meet him, being a fellow Texan. I knew that having entertainers get involved would take the farm message to the next level and it would reach people who we farmers could not reach. It was pretty exciting.

"After that meeting, I remember sittin' in a restaurant; they had just brought the steak out and set it down on the table, and, boy, I was hungry. Mark Ritchie [president of the Institute for Agriculture and Trade Policy] comes running down and says, 'You got to come with me right now—Neil Young wants to talk to you.' I spent probably an hour with Neil. He was asking very detailed, in-depth questions. I was surprised at the level of questions and the engagement there. Neil came to Washington after the concert, and I went around with him.

"Willie was such a big person, and he was very in tune with what the farmers wanted: 'What do you think? What do you think we should do?' It wasn't anything about 'Here's what I think.' He was like a sponge absorbing what the farmers were saying. That's unique, for someone who is an international icon to still be rooted, to still be *Willie*. *Not* Mr. Nelson. He's Willie to the whole world."

BILL WITTLIFF, FILMMAKER, PHOTOGRAPHER, AND LONGTIME WILLIE NELSON COLLEAGUE: "Jessica Lange had read an article about a family farm that had gone belly-up. Sam Shepard told her about me, because Sam and I did *Raggedy Man*. This was before there was any national attention to the plight of family farmers. We went to Iowa, drove around the back roads, and pulled in on farmers to research for our film *Country* [starring Lange, who coproduced it with Wittliff]. These farmers were really reluctant to talk. It was hell to get them to

Early in the day, September 22nd, 1985

open up. They hadn't talked to their neighbors. There could be two guys sharing the same fence line and both be in trouble and they wouldn't know it. At that time, the government had made them feel like they had violated the land and that's why they were in trouble. It gutted them. They lost their pride.

"There was one guy we were talking to, and the whole time he kept his hand on the telephone, like, if it got too uncomfortable, the telephone was a way out. Jessica being there was really something to them—that a 'celebrity' was interested in their horrors—the fact that a celebrity of Jessica's stature was sitting at their kitchen table. We were talking to one farmer, and he could barely speak. The farmer stirred and shuffled. He looked me in the eye—like family farmers do—and spoke of a recent dark morning on the prairie. He said, 'I got up, walked down to the barn, and made a noose out of baling wire.' He said he was going to hang himself. I asked, 'Why didn't you?' He said, 'Because of my kids.'

"Family farmers have an allegiance to the soil and to the United States. They are the guys who wiggle their toes in the dirt all their lives. That's where they came from and who they were always going to be. In their own minds, it is where God put them. Then all of a sudden, the government says, 'You weren't a good steward of the land.' That was a terrible thing the government did and still does to the family farmer. During the Nixon administration, farmers were told, 'Plant fence post to fence post. We're going to feed the world.' And then because of politics, there was no market. So they told the farmer, 'You weren't a good manager, now pay up.'

"Traditionally the Farmers Home Administration [FmHA] were local guys, so they knew all the local farmers. If somebody came in and had a bad year, they knew they were a good farmer and they knew when they weren't. All of a sudden, here come new guys, trained in agricultural schools, who were accountants; they're not local, they didn't know anybody, it's all numbers. The farmer would come in to talk about a small loan to make a furrowing shed, and then they'd say, 'Don't you need a barn?' Basically selling them money. I wrote a scene right out of the farmer's mouth—that's in *Country*.

"Farm Aid was never a 'thought' thing. It was always a 'felt' thing. That's what made it work. There's a line, 'Whatever you're looking for is looking for you, too.' At that time, when these farmers were looking for help, there was someone looking to help them. Every once in a while these things get in the air and sympathetic souls congregate. One of the most astonishing things is that Hollywood actually made a movie about it. Can you imagine talking to a studio about making a movie about farmers? Outrageous! Even for some of those Hollywood guys, it was in the air.

"In addition to Farm Aid, one place in which *Country* helped was letting farmers know they weren't alone. They started talking to each other, and God knows how many lives that saved once they realized, 'I'm not the only one in trouble.'

"There's a reason they call it the 'heartland,' and it's not because it's in the center of the country. It's the connotations of the word *heart*. That's why Farm Aid worked, and why it attracted people like Carolyn [Mugar], Willie, John Mellencamp, Neil Young. You just name all of them, any of them. The heartland is an inner place."

From the Grass Roots: Carolyn G. Mugar

Glenda Yoder, Associate Director, Farm Aid

"Power concedes nothing without a demand. It never did, and it never will."

—FREDERICK DOUGLASS

A relentless, energetic networker, Carolyn Mugar, Farm Aid's executive director, plumbs a Rolodex that bulges with contacts. On a typical day, attached to her phones, scrolling through e-mail, Carolyn talks with farmers and advocates, responds to artists and their representatives, and handles concert business and organizational decisions. On her bookshelf is *Fast Food Nation;* on her desk are a concert-ticket fragment, newsletters from farm groups, and a handwritten letter from a family farmer. The Farm Aid world can be found in this microcosm on Carolyn's desk.

Before the first Farm Aid concert was staged, Willie Nelson asked Carolyn to come on board as Farm Aid's executive director. The ferocity and impeccable integrity with which Carolyn tackled the issues confirmed Willie's choice, winning the respect of everyone almost instantly.

Most people thought Farm Aid would be a one-time-only event. It wasn't until it became clear that Farm Aid would build a longer-term program that Carolyn moved the spaghetti-sauce-dotted Farm Aid files from her kitchen table into a small office, which was in the hallway of another organization in Cambridge, Massachusetts.

"Farm Aid's first twenty-year impact will be remembered as historic. Few organizations may truthfully claim to spur, lead, and finance a movement touching millions of lives."

—MICHAEL STUMO, ESQ., ORGANIZATION OF COMPETITIVE MARKETS

Guided by her background in union organizing, and the experience of her future husband, John O'Connor, a community organizer, Carolyn's political instincts took her straight to the countryside to gather wisdom directly from the people. A dedicated traveler, Carolyn began driving the highways and country roads, bunking in farmhouses, talking to families out in the barn and around the kitchen table, leaning in to listen quietly to the heartaches. She toured with farm organizers, walked the stubbled fields, and filled up her numbered yellow notebooks with stories of survival. (She is now on notebook #571.) Alert to finding out what would work, she was determined to document and replicate every success story.

Carolyn's expansive spirit demanded that Farm Aid do "everything at once." It would take a wide range of actions to stop the loss of family farms. "Farmers know the solutions. The solutions are on the shelf," she claimed. She found farmers to be clear on the reasons for the failing government policies, and on the new policies that were needed. They had innovative farming techniques that they shared with each other. They knew that they needed to enlist the consumer in order to succeed in changing policy, and realized the necessity of being involved in direct marketing. Carolyn's faith in family farmers and in community organizing became the bedrock of Farm Aid's programs.

Some farmers were suspicious, wondering what this new "aid" effort would mean for the desperate struggles that drained their hopes. Even before the first show, on the Farm Aid Express train from Carroll, Iowa, to Champaign, Illinois, one farmer confronted Carolyn with a question many of them had: "What the hell are you gonna do?"

What Carolyn did was forge a program led by farmers and bent on making change and shifting power. But Farm Aid opened its heartstrings, too, providing for the most basic of human needs: grocery money, the payment of medical bills, and suicide prevention counseling. Carolyn believed in transparent, authentic work that would stand up to scrutiny.

Through the years, Farm Aid has raised funds and spent them promptly on the urgent issues of the day, keeping the Farm Aid bank account on survival mode from year to year. Carolyn believes in a small, efficient staff, hiring mission-oriented people who shared her enthusiasm for hard work and creative strategies. Every staff member has a dual role, one for the ongoing work of the organization, as well as a concert-planning role. An array of advisors are often called upon.

Embodying the enormous pleasure of working with a passion, Carolyn has created a can-do mood of joy and generosity. The celebration of family farm food is a rallying point, in the office and beyond. These days, the Farm Aid staff routinely gathers around the kitchen-cum-conference table to make decisions—fueled by family farm, organic, and local food—showing how the connection between eaters and farmers can be a delicious choice. Led by Carolyn, the Farm Aid staff will continue to work with an ear to the ground and an eye to the future. 🚜

Backstage during Farm Aid 2004, Seattle: Neil Young, John Mellencamp, Carolyn Mugar, Dave Matthews, and Willie Nelson (from left)

"Neil and Willie and John Mellencamp and now Dave Matthews, they do a great job with all the talent, but Farm Aid wouldn't be there without Carolyn Mugar. She's been there all along."

—PAUL ENGLISH, WILLIE NELSON DRUMMER AND FARM AID TREASURER

FARMS NOT FACTORIES!
FARMS NOT FACTORIES
STOP FACTORY FARMS

The Farm Aid Mission

Ted Quaday

With an artist's sudden clarity, Willie Nelson came to the idea of staging a benefit concert for family farmers. He'd seen inspiration strike dozens of times in his career as a singer and songwriter. His own creativity had been applied to numerous hit songs, and, in the summer of 1985, Willie's creative personality took an unexpected turn. Why not put on

a huge concert to raise money for family farmers? Other benefits were raising millions. Surely the giving people of the United States would come to the aid of farm families in a time of crisis. Willie was correct about the generosity of the American public.

Willie's agrarian background in Texas gave him special understanding of the hardscrabble life of the family farmer. During his early struggles as a country music songwriter in Nashville, and through his years of touring as a headlining performer, Willie Nelson stayed close to his roots. Today, he dedicates more than half of each year to touring with his road band. He crisscrosses the country, playing date after date in small towns and big cities. In that way, he's stayed close to everyday people. He regularly meets with fans, and talks with truckers, farmers, and ranchers in truck stops and cafes across the nation. He meets, too, with national leaders, presidents, and congressional representatives. Over the years, he's gained tremendous insight and understanding about national and world events and their impact on people. Through those conversations, he came to realize early on that family farmers were in crisis and that the good times of the 1970s had given way to low crop prices, falling land values, high interest rates, mountains of debt, and, for many family farmers, no way out.

While the headlines trumpeting the farm crisis faded long ago, it is significant to note the depth of the crisis as it evolved. Joel Dyer did just that in his 1997 book *Harvest of Rage,* in which he noted that "rural America has lost between seven hundred thousand and one million small-to-medium-sized family farms since 1980.

"At the peak of the crisis in 1986-1987," Dyer continued, "nearly one million people were forced from their land in a single twelve-month period. Other years before and since have been much the same, with 500,000 forced

from the land here, 600,000 there." Today, there are roughly 565,000 small-to midsize family farm operations in the country, and United States Department of Agriculture (USDA) figures indicate that farmers are still leaving the land at the rate of 330 per week.

By 1985, when the first Farm Aid concert was staged, the immediate crisis in farm country had been building for at least four years. Many, including Willie, understood that the problems faced by family farmers extended back even further. Generations of American family farmers have struggled to make a living on the land. Some of those challenges can be blamed on weather, others on economic cycles. Still others can be traced back to farm policies that drive family farmers off their land and prevent them from continuing to farm.

For people living in farm country, caught up in the day-to-day struggles of economic survival in rural America, evidence of the crisis came early. As farm prices fell and land values dropped, it became harder for farmers to get the credit they needed to put new crops in the ground. Federal fiscal policy at the time didn't help matters either. To control double-digit inflation, the Reagan administration tightened the money supply, driving the cost of borrowing through the roof. That hurt farmers because most rely on annual operating loans to keep their farms alive. Suddenly, if they could get a loan at all, their cost of production was significantly higher because of the higher cost of borrowing money. Those who were unable to get loans couldn't plant, and their income dried up. The resulting economic squeeze drove thousands of farmers off their land and hundreds to the brink of destruction and beyond.

In his 1990 book *Bitter Harvest,* Jim Corcoran commented on the despair brought on by tough economic conditions and bad policy. By 1983, the situation had reached crisis proportions throughout farm country. "It seemed

Opposite: Willie Nelson works for Farm Aid offstage as well as on.

19

that no matter how hard the farmers worked, or prayed, or fought, the hard times on the farm wouldn't go away," said Corcoran. "A deep sense of hopelessness and failure settled over the heartland. The fabric of the rural community started to unravel. Crisis hotlines were deluged with desperate calls as more and more farmers unleashed their anger and frustrations on their spouses and children, sought refuge and solace in alcohol and drugs, and tried to escape through divorce, suicide, and murder. Many incidents passed without notice, and casualties to anger, frustration, and lost hope were mourned quietly only by family members and a few friends. But as the crisis deepened in the 1980s, a few incidents were so sensational that they grabbed attention throughout the region and, in some cases, the country."

Violence erupted all across the heartland. In Oklahoma, Minnesota, North Dakota, South Dakota, Iowa, and elsewhere, despondent farmers, convinced they were about to lose everything, raised weapons—often intent on killing themselves but sometimes killing bankers, local law enforcement officers, federal marshals, and even their own family members.

For social service agencies, local churches, food banks, and other groups working in rural areas on issues like housing, the environment, and land use, the rising number of calls and contacts from farmers caught in financial crisis roared over them like a river in a spring flood. Crisis hotlines and other crisis-intervention services sprang up in response. In addition, the farmers began talking more seriously about getting together to challenge the economic and political structure that seemed bent on writing their epitaph.

Reverend David Ostendorf was working on rural issues in Iowa in the early 1980s, and he remembers that in 1981, a group of farmers calling itself the Iowa Farm Unity Coalition began forming around economic issues on the family farm. Groups from Minnesota, Wisconsin, Nebraska, and elsewhere were also involved, and in 1982, a national Farm Crisis Day was organized with activities in a dozen states throughout the upper Midwest and the South. While successful, the day's activities pointed to one key thing: More work was needed. Ostendorf sees his efforts at that time as work toward creating the conditions for a new social movement in the heartland.

Organizing activities had been underway at the local, regional, and state levels in Iowa and other states, and, as 1984 neared its end, in Ostendorf's view, two economic factors were pressing the farm movement into overdrive. First, the general economic crisis had intensified and grown more widespread. Second, family farmers who had taken out loans received their loan due notices in the mail from bankers and from what was then known as the Farmers Home Administration (FmHA)—now known as the Farm Services Administration (FSA)—in late December and early January of each year. Ostendorf says he remembers January 2, 1985, as the day the family farm movement really arrived.

"Fires had been lit in so many places that our phones were ringing nonstop on that day, and it was clear to me that this was no longer a matter of a few farmers here and there with some financial problems. It had encompassed the breadth of American agriculture. So on the heels of that day, it was absolute nonstop organizing of the movement through the late spring and early summer."

To acknowledge the shift in focus toward building the family farm movement, Ostendorf and others he was working with in Iowa moved to form an independent organization, which they called PrairieFire Rural

"When I think of Farm Aid, I think of *action*. I think of a grassroots movement going in a positive direction. I think of guts, decency, and compassion. Farm Aid has helped our family farm directly because of the immediate attention it placed on our farm. Kim and I have been strong advocates for healthy, sustainable farming practices for a long time. The Farm Aid concert, with the educational messages to consumers, added legitimacy to what we believe in. It was an affirmation."

—ANN AND KIM SEELEY,
PENNSYLVANIA DAIRY FARMERS

Opposite: Mellencamp and Nelson traveled to Washington, D.C., to testify about the farm crisis before a congressional committee in 1985.

"Since 1986 until today, Farm Aid, through grants to the Louisiana Interchurch Conference, has provided me with the means and support to provide 'hands on' assistance to family farmers in financial trouble and emotional turmoil. When new farm legislation was passed, Farm Aid sponsored workshops for farm advocates that included legal assistance from Farmers Legal Action Group, Inc. and the support of the National Family Farm Coalition. These workshops educated farm advocates about the various changes in the laws that affected family farm agriculture. As a farm advocate, I was able to use this knowledge when I assisted many farmers throughout the years."

—BETTY PUCKETT, FARM ADVOCATE

Family farmers protest at a local USDA office, Chillicothe, Missouri, 1986.

Action. PrairieFire became a hub in the farm activist movement that grew out of the crisis.

It was into this cauldron of discontent, despair, and fierce determination to make positive change for family farmers that Farm Aid plunged on September 22, 1985, with its first massive fund-raising concert, in Champaign, Illinois. What emerged was, for family farmers and those who work with them, a miracle of compassion, concern, and for most who have been touched by Farm Aid and its commitment to family farmers, a real reason for hope.

Given the critical needs in farm country at the time of the first concert, Willie and all those associated with the fund-raising effort decided that the money raised should begin flowing immediately to those in need—and within hours of the concert's end, it was.

Farm Aid quickly focused on some primary concerns. Because of the desperate nature of the crisis, a variety of emergency assistance was provided. Sometimes that meant a means to buy food or to cover other household expenses. Other times it meant making sure there were experts on farm credit issues available to help farmers in crisis. Sometimes it meant seeing to it that people with a background in suicide prevention were available to step in when the emotional stress associated with economic hardship became too great. Offering support to hotlines and other types of emergency assistance became central to Farm Aid's work.

In addition, there was an early commitment to bringing family farmers together so they could begin working and speaking with a strong voice about the need to make changes in farm policy aimed at helping farmers achieve a fair measure of prosperity. "Farm Aid gave to the emergency aid agencies and to the workers who were already out there trying to change the situation," Carolyn Mugar explains. "I knew right away that we had to be sure to give money to the groups thinking structurally about the problems—organizers working to gain strength and build a solid base of people on the ground, solving problems and creating options."

The National Council of Churches became a Farm Aid partner to channel emergency grants deep into the countryside. Farm Aid provided a small team of legal advisors a grant that helped launch the Farmers Legal Action Group (FLAG) in St. Paul, Minnesota. Farm Aid supported the Federation of Southern

Cooperatives, based in Georgia and rooted in the African-American struggle for civil rights, to secure the rights of black farmers. Initial funding was provided by Farm Aid for the National Family Farm Coalition, known at the time as the National Save the Family Farm Coalition, to bring about policy changes at the state and federal levels.

Farm Aid's mission reflects the wishes and vision of its founder, Willie Nelson. Farm Aid has assembled the voices of prominent artists to awaken the public to one of the most pressing concerns of our time: ensuring that our family farms remain economically viable so that local communities remain strong and so that each of us can be assured of fresh, healthful food for our families. As Nelson has said many times over the years, "If you eat, you have a stake in what happens on our family farms."

Concern over access to fresh and healthful food has guided Farm Aid toward support of programs to train farmers in environmentally sound production methods, and to help them build local markets for the food they raise. Groups working to link farmers with direct marketing opportunities are getting support, as are groups like the National Campaign for Sustainable Agriculture, which is fighting hard to ensure meaningful standards for organic growers and the public. Even farmer-owned, income-creating ideas in the alternative energy arena are gaining support, including biodiesel and electricity-generating wind turbines.

What it comes down to is this: Farm Aid listens to people and connects them with information and the help they need. At the same time, it raises a collective voice of hope and is fully engaged with family farmers in creating a new vision of American agriculture capable of sustaining farmers on their land, raising food, fiber, families, and now even fuel, in a way that strengthens not only the hearth but the heartland, and the nation as a whole.

"Farm Aid is in the vanguard as the forum for exposing wrongheaded U.S. farm and trade policy. Willie Nelson and the Farm Aid leadership were right on target in the 1980s. I was agency director of the Nebraska Wheat Board then, and we were on the same page with Farm Aid. We challenged the 'free trade' farm and trade policy agenda. We were right! Agribusiness-driven farm and trade policy has now led the United States over the slippery economic slope that Farm Aid warned against. Farm Aid is still on target today. There is still important work to do."

—DAN MCGUIRE, CEO, AMERICAN CORN GROWERS FOUNDATION

Mona Lee Brock: Angel on the Other End of the Line

Dave Hoekstra

A cloudy afternoon on the Oklahoma plains can appear hopeless. The sky is low and there is no end in sight. Several years ago on such a day Mona Lee Brock received a telephone call from a farmer. Since 1985, Brock, a former farmer herself, had been a crisis counselor in Oklahoma City for one of many rural advocacy groups supported by Farm Aid. Brock later operated a twenty-four-hour crisis and suicide hotline out of her home in Madill, Oklahoma.

The caller, who was in his early forties, had been commander of a SWIFT boat in Vietnam. In a voice as soothing as a ripple in a country lake, Brock says, "He had a wheat farm about ninety miles from Oklahoma City. I listened to him. His farm was in a trust, so that could not be taken out. But all his cattle were taken from him. He had terrible problems.

"He was as suicidal as suicide could be," Brock says. She cut a deal with the farmer. "I told him, 'If you made some good German potato soup, would you promise to have some when I get there? Then while you're getting dressed, I will eat some of your potato soup and I will take you to the VA hospital.' " There was a long silence.

The caller whispered, "Would you do that?"

Brock answered, "I will. But have that soup made because I will not have a chance to eat lunch."

Brock, a former elementary school teacher and children's diagnostic counselor, pays attention to details. Brock inquired which door she should knock at when she arrived at the farm. The caller told Brock to enter through the kitchen door. "I knocked on the door," she says in measured tones. "I banged on the door. Then I started calling

names. I thought, 'I'm too late.' I opened the living room door. And there he sat.

"He was on his knees with a rifle and ammunition all around him. His gaze was just fixed. You talk about praying? I was praying hard. I said, 'Do you have that potato soup made?' " The farmer got up and escorted Brock into his kitchen. After a couple of spoons of the awful-tasting soup, Brock told the farmer to pack a bag for a trip to the VA hospital. "He grabbed hold of my skirt as if I was going to run away," she says. "We got into the car and he held on to that skirt all the way to the VA hospital." Once they arrived at the hospital, doctors and a psychiatrist treated the farmer. He had no money for medication, so Brock purchased it for him. "I took him home about 2 a.m. Later, he was given appropriate medical treatment, and we helped him work out his farm problems. This did save his farm as well as, possibly, his life."

Willie Nelson says of Brock, "This gal has been there. She was taking those calls day and night, 24/7, of people losing their farms. She heard gunshots over the phone more than once. She is a great lady. I love her. She's really good to Farm Aid

and mostly the farmers." Carolyn Mugar adds, "Mona Lee Brock has been the angel on the other end of the line, the person who Farm Aid has always relied on for the most desperate farmers. She has experienced firsthand the pain of losing the farm and the terrible consequence of that loss. She is also a brilliant financial strategist, offering farmers her wealth of experience in credit counseling and debt restructuring. She listens and swings into action."

Mona Lee Brock entered this world in 1932 about five miles south of Madill (pop. 7,000). Mona Lee and her husband, who everyone knew as F.M. Jr., farmed cotton, corn, beans, and wheat in Madill until 1964. In recent years they owned 240 acres of land and leased 1,000 acres in Lincoln County, three hours north of Madill. "F.M. Jr. raised a lot of cattle," she says. "He was an excellent cattleman. His parents were farmers. So were theirs. So were mine."

During the late 1970s and early 1980s, Brock taught school during the day, keeping the same hours as her two sons. After work, says Brock, "I would get on one tractor and my husband would get on the other, and we'd just do the chores. The boys would work. We spent our lives like that. In 1985, we had a $35,000 indebtedness [after four years of crop failures]. We lost our farm. The lender would not accept payments." Their family farm went under on July 1, 1985.

F. M. Jr., at fifty-six, suffered a fatal heart attack in September 1985. Brock believes he died of a broken heart. Not long after his death, Brock received a call from farm advocate Dr. Max Glenn, asking her to be an agricultural hotline counselor for the

Oklahoma Conference of Churches in Oklahoma City. Farm Aid had given the group a $25,000 seed grant to establish the hotline.

"I am a licensed mental health professional as well as a retired educator," Brock says. "I was heartbroken and, like all other farmers, so depressed over the loss of the farm. I went into Oklahoma City, and I stayed to help for two days."

The forty-eight-hour visit turned into a twenty-year commitment to counseling distressed farmers. When Brock left the Conference in 1994, Farm Aid asked her to stay on as an independent counselor for the state of Oklahoma. For a while, she still made the two-and-a-half hour drive one way to Oklahoma City from Madill. "I'd leave home early Monday morning and get to work by 6 a.m.," she recalls.

"I set those hours because I knew some farmers would be up and calling before they went to the fields or whatever. And when I walked in, the red light would be flashing on the phone. I would work until 10:00 at night. And my body would be exhausted within itself. There were families my age with grown children. Farm people divorcing, who would never ever consider doing such a thing under a different circumstance. I got mental health services for people who were suicidal. The Oklahoma State Department of Mental Health loaned us Dr. Glen Wallace, their very best clinical psychologist. He was so instrumental in helping. A lot of times I would call him and say, 'Here's the farmer's name and telephone number, go north, go east.' "

Other times they were too late. Brock once walked into a home to find a farmer who had just blown his head off with a shotgun. Brock says that pressure from lenders brought down many family farmers. "The lender would say, 'I'm going to take you under,' " she recalls. "They'd continue, 'If you go across the street and get a few more $100,000 life insurance policies and make us the benefactors of each one, come back and I might talk to you about financing the operation for another year.' Then when the farmer came back in with the policy, it would be nothing for the lender to say, 'You're worth more dead to your family than alive.' "

Brock's farming background and patience helped her on the front line with her callers. "It would be something like this . . . 'Do you have family? How old are your children?' Anything to get their mind off of the act of taking his or her life. I'd tell them we have temporary assistance and Farm Aid funds. If they couldn't buy groceries, I'd tell them we had funds available. There is sunshine tomorrow. There is always a rainbow at the end. Then they would ask, 'How do you know? You have never been there.' But I had been there. I told them that my husband passed away from a sudden heart attack three months after we were put off of our farm. I told them stories of taking farmers who had been evicted by federal marshals into my house. I tried to do anything to get their mind off of taking their life." Brock had a favorite saying she would tell callers: "You can't change yesterday, you don't have a guarantee for tomorrow, you have to make do with what you got today."

According to figures from the federal Centers for Disease Control and Prevention published during 2005 in *The American Journal of Public Health*, suicides in America (1989–1999) are highest in rural areas and most suicides are committed using guns. In cases where guns are used, the suicide rate in rural counties is higher than the homicide rate in urban counties.

When Brock began answering crisis center phones in 1985, she averaged forty-eight phone calls a day from distressed farmers. Dr. Glenn says, "At one time we were processing over one thousand calls a month, and Mona Lee can document about five hundred lives saved. The hotline was one of the most successful in the country."

"It did drop off over time," Brock says. "It got down to the point that I had 160 a month in 2003. But there is so much work to be done."

In June 2004, doctors told Brock to retire from her advocacy work to rest her ailing heart. Today, she stays up-to-date with Farm Aid and the farm movement and still networks with Oklahoma farmers. "Willie Nelson has done a great job," she says. "He is a caring person. His eyes are so compassionate, and he does what he says. One time, in the early nineties, I stayed late at work and a lady with four little children called from northern Oklahoma. We had no funds left to send them. I thought, 'Lord, tell me what direction to go.' But even churches and food banks were depleted. Suddenly, the phone rang and it was Willie. I told him my problem. And he overnighted me a $5,000 personal check. We put that in the fund, and I sent the money out for groceries."

Brock is a devout member of the First Baptist Church in Madill. The power of prayer often helped Brock through her crisis calls. The core of her spirituality is shaped by an abundant faith. It is a belief that delivers light into the darkest moments, and for this Farm Aid is forever grateful.

When Farm Aid arrived on the scene in 1985, the country's economic and farm policy meltdown had been wreaking havoc in farm country. Family farmers were almost without hope. Sometimes—and it began happening more and more often as the farm crisis deepened—they turned, in desperation and anguish, to emergency hotlines that had sprung up in farm country in response to the crisis.

In Iowa, Reverend David Ostendorf was among a group of activists who founded PrairieFire Rural Action. In 1981, Ostendorf and his associates created a hotline and started working to link farmers in their community with attorneys and others who could help with financial issues. "It wasn't too long into the experience that we began developing our own expertise," says Ostendorf. "We began to have our own internal capacity to help farmers. They'd call us, and we'd link them up with their neighbors. The hotline put us in direct communication with people all over the country, and eventually we used the hotline as an organizing tool as well as a way to offer emergency services."

One link went back to Ostendorf's home region in southern Illinois, where a small grassroots organization called Illinois South was working on land use issues involving the coal industry and farmland preservation. Illinois South organizer Susan Denzer says Ostendorf sent his associates "down and gave us a kitchen table crash course in handling complaints from farmers about the USDA's Farmers Home Administration [FmHA]." At Illinois South the hotline wasn't so much implemented as it was demanded by the high volume of family farmer calls that deluged the small organization in late 1983.

"Farmers were getting word that the FmHA was no longer going to offer them credit," Denzer explains. "They were being cut off, and they were frightened."

Acquiring the expertise to effectively handle technical financial issues was not easy in the early days of the crisis. Back then, family farmers were often on their own, and they learned the ins and outs of federal rules and regulations by going head-to-head with FmHA in their home counties. Indiana farmer Susan Bright was among those who learned to fight back after her family was caught in the economic squeeze. As word circulated in her community that she was challenging unfair credit policies, other farmers began calling her for advice, and eventually she was running a crisis hotline out of her home, dedicating her own time and money to the cause.

"I wanted to help people," says Bright. "We were struggling ourselves and had three small children, and it was very difficult. I spent so much time on the phone, and I had no job, but I had a lot of desperate people on the line. Some of them wanted to commit suicide. It was stressful, yes, but I'm not sorry for one minute that I did it."

Bright remembers getting a call from Farm Aid Executive Director Carolyn Mugar, who told her that she would be receiving a grant from Farm Aid. "There wasn't any question about its value, because I wasn't going to be able to keep going, spending several hundred dollars a month for phones and postage and copies. I was sitting there one evening close to Christmas, and finances were very tight, and Carolyn called with the news. When I told my husband the hotline had been funded, one of my daughters said, 'Mommy, does this mean we're going to have Christmas after all?' And it was, 'Yeah, we're going to have Christmas.' And you know it was a better Christmas than even she knew, because this money meant we could reach so many more people."

Susan Denzer says she was skeptical when she first heard that there would be a special concert to draw attention to the farm crisis and to raise money. After the concert, when she was contacted by Carolyn Mugar, she had a major change of attitude: "Farm Aid kind of came out of nowhere. It was like a gift from heaven that no one could believe. We'd been working hard for a year and a half, and we were all tired. I was very cynical at the beginning. I couldn't believe it could be as pure of motive as it was. We were all asking, 'What's the catch?' But it was just phenomenal, and it has just stayed that way."

At PrairieFire, Ostendorf viewed the cash infusion provided by Farm Aid as an important part of feeding the growing family farm movement. PrairieFire's first grant of some $50,000 was used to continue supporting its hotline, its crisis intervention services, and its general work to bring farm families together. But Ostendorf saw added value in Nelson's contribution: "Farm Aid definitely added fuel to the whole effort, and from a cultural point of view, Farm Aid speaking out about the crisis in farm country legitimized the grievances and the petitions of the people. The reality is that when Willie Nelson and the other performers at Farm Aid got up and talked about the crisis in American agriculture and the countryside, people listened. It added a great deal of legitimacy to the work. I don't think anybody could ever say enough about the positive power of Willie Nelson and all the other artists involved in Farm Aid. It has been absolutely, incredibly great."

In addition to the hotline intervention many groups were offering, Farm Aid, from the beginning, was intent on providing emergency assistance to farmers in crisis. To make this happen, Willie Nelson turned to the National Council of Churches (NCC).

Mary Ellen Lloyd served as the NCC's administrator of Farm Aid contributions. She's particularly proud of the fact that "all the Farm Aid funds went to farm families. With no overhead charged, not even for distribution." The money went to farm families in $100 and $200 increments, and Lloyd says it meant a lot to the recipients. "It was the emotional response of knowing that people cared. People were losing century-old farms that had been in their families for generations. The banks were closing in, and farmers felt there was no way out. To have anybody showing any kind of support or donating food meant so much. Sometimes just the knowledge that someone cared to help was enough." It still is.

Farm Aid itself has operated a crisis hotline from the first days of its existence. Originally intended as a line to receive cash pledges during the first concert in Champaign, 1-800-FARM AID began receiving calls almost immediately from family farmers seeking help, and the line has served a dual purpose ever since. "Farmers called in with many kinds of questions," says Mugar. "You know, 'How do you get help?' 'Where's the money going?' 'How do you get money?' We were besieged with farmers' calls and letters."

The late Jody Fischer, Willie Nelson's assistant, played a key role in handling hotline calls in the early days. Jody set the tone for compassionate listening as she fielded hundreds of calls from farmers who sought support. Consistently respectful and resourceful, she spent hours building the connections between farmers and local rural service groups. The Farm Aid hotline was born from that fierce advocacy.

Tens of thousands of phone calls, letters (such as those reprinted at right), and, more recently, e-mails from farmers in crisis have been handled through the hotline and emergency services offered at Farm Aid. All members of the Farm Aid staff answer hotline calls. Additional support services are now provided to family farmers who have questions about growing organically or more sustainably. Farm Aid continues working with the broad state-based advocates network it helped to build, and picks up 1-800-FARM AID every day.

"Mother and I have tried to raise cattle and horses, but in the past few years the market for both has gotten so poor we are getting further and further in debt. The bank foreclosed on our mortgage, and the farm will go up for public auction in November. My mother is eighty-three, and this has been her home all her life. I don't want her to lose it, but at this point there is nothing I can do."

—AURORA, MINNESOTA, SEPTEMBER 24, 1985

"My daddy raises cotton and soybeans on about five hundred acres. Presently, we are in a precarious situation with the FmHA. Yes, my daddy is a good farmer, and he is in the process of becoming another victim. He did not create inflation, the embargo, and now deflation—the squeeze—which will probably be his undoing. He has farmed for over forty years, and now what? To me, it's a very real American tragedy. I am angry and totally frustrated in my efforts on his behalf; God help what my daddy must feel and think."

—NEW ORLEANS, LOUISIANA, JULY 11, 1986

"I am writing this letter to you hoping that you can help me resolve a problem I have concerning the Farmers Home Administration. I know that you deal with farmers' and ex-farmers' problems on a daily basis. What I need to know is where I can find a lawyer or legal society to consult with on this matter. Without going into lengthy detail, I feel I was unfairly treated by the Farmers Home Administration and as a result had to give up my farming business to them. Any help in locating legal advice in this matter would be greatly appreciated."

—LAKE CITY, PENNSYLVANIA, AUGUST 28, 1990

"It really made our day when we received your letter informing us that you had sent $100 to our electric company on our behalf. It will be a big change for us as we scale down from full-time farming to part-time farming and off-farm income."

—VILLAND, MINNESOTA, MARCH 16, 1993

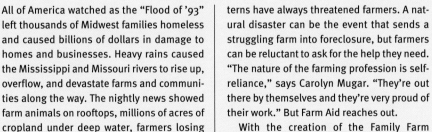

Farm Aid Program Family Farm Disaster Fund

All of America watched as the "Flood of '93" left thousands of Midwest families homeless and caused billions of dollars in damage to homes and businesses. Heavy rains caused the Mississippi and Missouri rivers to rise up, overflow, and devastate farms and communities along the way. The nightly news showed farm animals on rooftops, millions of acres of cropland under deep water, farmers losing everything.

Destructive, unpredictable weather patterns have always threatened farmers. A natural disaster can be the event that sends a struggling farm into foreclosure, but farmers can be reluctant to ask for the help they need. "The nature of the farming profession is self-reliance," says Carolyn Mugar. "They're out there by themselves and they're very proud of their work." But Farm Aid reaches out.

With the creation of the Family Farm Disaster Fund, Farm Aid was among the first agencies to respond to the 1993 disaster.

Since then, the Fund has been activated in response to other severe weather disasters, such as the Drought of '96 and the Blizzard of '97. The fund helps farm families survive weather-related disasters in several ways: by providing short-term relief in the form of emergency assistance for food and family living expenses; by supporting emergency hotlines, which provide legal, financial, and emotional counseling; by providing one-on-one legal and financial advocacy to farmers in danger of losing their farms.

Each time the Family Farm Disaster Fund is activated and Farm Aid puts out the call for help, Americans respond generously with donations and assistance. "It's too bad, you know, that bad things have to happen to bring people together—but in all your life, you see that when people really need to get together, they do," says Willie Nelson.

American Family Farmer Tom Trantham

Instead of whispering to horses, Tom Trantham listens to cows. He's been listening and watching them ever since the day they broke out of their pasture and changed his life. It was April 1989 and the Trantham dairy was going broke fast. Even though his Holsteins were winning South Carolina production awards, they couldn't produce enough milk to pay their feed bill, which gobbled up to 65 percent of Tom's gross income.

"Financial advisors told me to get out of the business," recalls Tom. "They said there was no way for me to make it. Those were dark days; I'd wake up and think maybe the place had burned down or all the cows had died in the night and I'd be free."

Then one day, the cows pushed through the confinement feeding area into a seven-acre field full of lush April growth—rye grass, a little clover, and fescue. At the next milk pickup, there was a two-pound average increase of milk per cow.

Thinking maybe the cows were trying to tell him something, Tom opened all the gates on his farm and began experimenting with grazing. On the free-range pastures, the cows produced about five pounds more milk each day and began leaving some of their grain uneaten. Tom had glimpsed the dairy farmer's dream of more milk on less money and was determined not to lose it.

The new grazing system took years to get off the ground. And in 1994, a bad drought nearly did in Tom and other farmers in the region. Tom needed help, and Farm Aid was there. Farm Aid mobilized a farmer-to-farmer emergency hay lift, bringing donated hay to starving cows. That was the boost that gave Tom a few months to get back on his feet and get the grazing program up and running. Farm Aid helped him survive until he could thrive. "Without Farm Aid," says Tom, "I wouldn't have made it. I believe the farmers of today have the responsibility of leaving things in better shape for the next

generation of farmers," he adds. "What I've learned would go to waste if it stopped with me. I hope to pass along not only my land but my philosophy to my grandchildren."

Part of that philosophy is caring for the land he depends on. Tom hasn't used commercial fertilizer on his fields in sixteen years. Allowing the manure to be spread by the herd as they rotate through paddocks has caused his soil to test high in fertility without purchased inputs. A soil tester told Tom his soil was of the highest quality with no deficiencies, something he had never seen in his thirty years in the business.

Milk processing and direct marketing are the latest frontiers for Tom and his wife, Linda. They made that decision in the summer of 2000 when a letter from the milk co-op informing them that milk prices would stay flat for the next year arrived on the same day they heard that consumers would be paying nine cents a gallon more

at the store. Tom said, "Let's go look at some processing equipment."

Happy Cow Milk is now available right on the Trantham farm. Six days a week, customers can buy whole milk, buttermilk, and chocolate milk, as well as Florida juices and Wisconsin cheese, from a drive-through window and an on-farm store. The store is the crowning achievement for Tom as a dairyman. "I think the time is right for this," he says. "More consumers are learning about the nutritional differences in milk from grazed cows as compared to cows in confinement. . . For twenty-five years, I have produced milk of superior quality and had it pumped, transported, and mixed with other milk on the way to the customer. Now I finally have the experience of watching people stand on my property, drink a glass of milk, and say, 'Tom, this is the best milk I've ever tasted,' *and* they pay me a fair price for it."

—SKY DEMURO

Opposite: Dairyman Tony Azevedo, owner of a family farm in California.
Above: Farmers helping farmers with a Farm Aid–sponsored hay lift

America's Voice: Willie Nelson

Dave Hoekstra

Willie Nelson's bus sits in the shadow of an emerald fence at Stanley Coveleski Stadium, across the street from a forgotten train station in downtown South Bend, Indiana. Nelson is on a tour of minor-league baseball parks with Bob Dylan. Throughout the late summer of 2004, Nelson's Honeysuckle Rose III bus crisscrosses with Dylan's through the heartland. They play towns like Des Moines, Iowa; Peoria, Illinois; and Oklahoma City. Many acts ignore these places, so the gypsy troubadours seem larger than life. Dylan and Nelson are characters who live on the outskirts of every small town. People talk about them. They sing about Bloody Mary mornings, watchtowers, and nightlife. They should be riding horses instead of buses. On this tour, Dylan and Nelson sing a ballad together that they cowrote in 1993. It is called "Heartland" and they harmonize: "There's a home place under fire tonight in the heartland/And the bankers are taking my home and my land from me/There's a big achin' hole in my chest now where my heart was/And a hole in the sky where God used to be."

Nelson began his American journey when he was three years old and was paid three dollars a day to pick cotton in the fields of Abbott, Texas, his hometown south of Dallas. He went on to become a door-to-door bible salesman, traveling vacuum cleaner salesman, plumber's assistant, disc jockey, songwriter, gospel singer, outlaw, activist, and a damn good golfer. In 1960, Nelson left Pasadena, Texas, and drove his 1951 Buick in a serious fever to land in Nashville for the first time. "Hard work is nothing I have shied away from," he has said. "I picked cotton, pulled corn, baled hay. But my desire to escape manual labor can't be overstated."

On a warm summer day in 1978, Nelson and then Illinois governor "Big" Jim Thompson were kicking back in Nelson's bus eating chili and drinking beer. Nelson had just made his first appearance at the Illinois State Fair off of Old Route 66 in Springfield. Nelson loves chili, and the Thompson camp had cooked up a photo op called "Chili With Willie." Nelson returned to the

Illinois State Fair in 1980, and this time the photo op was on the golf course. Nelson (who has a handicap of 9) and Thompson continued to develop their friendship. Thompson invited Nelson to stay at the governor's mansion in Springfield. You know they hit it off: Thompson was able to get Nelson off his bus for a night.

When Nelson began planning Farm Aid, Thompson was the first nonartist he turned to. Thompson secured the University of Illinois Memorial Stadium, in Champaign, for Farm Aid. Located at the state's flagship agricultural school in the corn and soybean fields of central Illinois, it holds seventy-eight thousand people. "The glue was still wet on the new Astroturf for the stadium," Nelson's longtime tour manager David Anderson recalls. "The athletic director wasn't too pleased with the idea, but what could he say? The governor said, 'Do it.'"

Nelson adds, "These guys in the heartland know the problem. You don't have to explain to them that agriculture is in trouble. So they are the first to be there to set up, to ask, 'What can I do to sell tickets, to buy tickets?' And the entertainers are the same way. A lot of the entertainers knew about it before the politicians, because they hear from the people every night."

Nelson keeps a hand in farming today. He lives about twenty miles outside of Austin, in Luck. He likes to say, "You're either in or out of Luck." He continues, "We've got some small spots of acreage that we're growing organic. But I have more horses than anything. I also have an electric windmill and solar power for the garden, the wells, and the town there." Featuring a faux church and a feed store, Luck was built as a movie set for his 1986 film *Red*

Opposite: Willie Nelson at Farm Aid 1985, Champaign, Illinois. Above: Nelson in costume as the Red Headed Stranger for the 1987 movie by that name, filmed in his Western town Luck; accompanying him is his daughter Lana Nelson.

"Why have I played Farm Aid? Because Willie asked, period. Willie is Gandhi-like, and if Willie decided that it was his cross to bear, the least I could do was hold one end of it for him. Or help lift somewhere. I respect and admire him enormously for doing Farm Aid. In the midst of all his own problems at times, he was still doing it. It's as much a testament and tribute to Willie Nelson as it is to anything, and to his belief that each of us can make a difference if we're willing to try."

—DWIGHT YOAKAM, FARM AID ARTIST

The Buschkoetter family of Nebraska and Terry Spence of Minnesota greet Nelson backstage at Farm Aid.

Headed Stranger. Nelson also provides solar power for the swimming pool at the golf course near Luck, and there's a biodiesel tank and pump that fills the bus tank before Willie goes back on the road.

Farm Aid board member Dave Matthews was empowered by Nelson the first time he heard Patsy Cline sing Nelson's "Crazy." Matthews says, "Thank goodness, fashion goes in circles, because out of all of us, Willie is the hippest. I hate to say that I'm going to come stone last, but as far as cool is concerned, Willie's got me hook, line, and sinker. His popularity is growing, and people are not only listening to his music and being inspired by his life, but [they] also listen to what he says, because in this country he's the [Nelson] Mandela sort for the farmer's movement. Every time I talk to him he blows me away."

Nelson always stands tall for the little guy who still gets a kick out of minor-league baseball, chili with beef, and pedal steel guitar. Farm Aid Executive Director Carolyn Mugar adds, "Willie's commitment is unwavering. He's the definition of the real deal. What's cool is that the [three 1985 founders] come to Farm Aid from real different places. Regardless of where they come from, these artists are brilliant communicators."

Nelson says he talks to Mugar once a week. "I get a lot of faxes and e-mails from the Farm Aid folks, too," he says. He's referring to the nine staff members who work out of a small office in Somerville, Massachusetts. Willie is proud of the low overhead of the organization: He never wanted to create a bureaucracy, and Farm Aid will never be one. Nelson is sitting in his own tiny office near the front of the bus. "Trigger," his tattered acoustic guitar covered in autographs from friends and neighbors, rests nearby. "I'm still the guy who signs the checks," he says.

Nelson often delivers his message with a musical journey. While on tour, he frequently meets with farmers and press. In the late 1990s, Nelson met with farmers fighting factory farms and the corporate consolidation of agriculture. Meetings and press briefings were held on Nelson's bus near Columbus, Ohio, to challenge factory egg producers who were polluting and driving family farmers out of business. In Montana, Farm Aid and Nelson linked up with Northern Plains Resource Council and the Western Organization of Resource Councils to hold briefings on livestock issues in Missoula and Red Lodge. In 1997 Nelson said, "We don't have that many family farms left. Farm Aid was organized to make people aware of the situation, and after all this time if someone doesn't know about the situation, they must be on the moon. It's so important because, as we know, when the small farmers go out of business, the businesses in the town go out with the schools and the hospital, and there's another town dried up."

Nelson's wife, Annie, has seen her home state of California lose many of its family farms: "I watched Southern California go from paradise and clean oceans to a place where you can actually see the air become dense," she says. "It was sad. All the farming went away. It was all Portuguese dairy farms when I lived there, on the southern end of L.A. County." Annie's father, Gregory D'Angelo, was a mason who also was a laborer at McDonnell-Douglas. He died in the spring of 2005. "He could grow anything," she recalls. "We didn't have a lot of money, and often that's how we ate—from fishing and the food he grew. Since then I've embraced the whole idea of organic."

Several years ago, Willie received a black belt in tae kwon do, a martial art that specializes in balance. With his seventieth birthday in the rearview mirror, Nelson still zigzags across America for roughly 180 sold-out shows a year. "I talk to truckers, drivers, people in motels," he says. "Usually the roadies and the truckers can tell you more what is going on than anybody. I call into XM Radio every week [Bill Mack's Open Road Truckers channel]. We talk to the truckers, and they call in. We talk about biodiesel, music, and whatever else they want."

A couple of years ago, Annie Nelson wanted to purchase a biodiesel car for their home in Maui. "I said, 'What in the hell is that?'" he recalls. "She told me it was a car that runs on vegetable oil. So she bought a [diesel] Volkswagen, and sure enough it ran like a clock on vegetable oil. So I had to have one. I bought a diesel [2005] Mercedes, and I've never had anything in it but vegetable oil. And it smells good! The tailpipe smells like french fries. They recycle it from the grease at the restaurants in Maui. Right now, there's almost five hundred vehicles on the island of Maui that run off vegetable oil."

Nelson's and Neil Young's six tour buses now run on biodiesel made from soybeans and other crops; all of Toby Keith's nine tour buses are using biodiesel; and singer-songwriter Jack Johnson's 2005 tour runs on biodiesel. "There are so many ways we can use farmers to grow our fuel rather than fight wars over it," Nelson says. Nelson is in a limited-liability biodiesel partnership

Nelson in the studio with longtime band mates, sister Bobbie Nelson and Paul English, 1971

"Willie Nelson was the first guy I ever played in a band with, and he'll be the last one I ever play with."

—DRUMMER PAUL ENGLISH

"HEARTLAND"

Bob Dylan and Willie Nelson

There's a home place under fire tonight in the heartland
And the bankers are taking my home and my land from me
There's a big achin' hole in my chest now where my heart was
And a hole in the sky where God used to be
There's a home place under fire tonight in the heartland
There's a well where the water's so bitter nobody can drink
Ain't no way to get high and my mouth is so dry that I can't speak
Don't they know that I'm dyin'—why's nobody cryin' for me
My American dream fell apart at the seams
You tell me what it means, you tell me what it means

There's a home place under fire tonight in a heartland
And bankers are taking the homes and the land away
There's a young boy closin' his eyes tonight in a heartland
Who will wake up a man with some land and a loan he can't pay
His American dream fell apart at the seams
You tell me what it means, you tell me what it means
My American dream . . .

There's a home place under fire tonight in the heartland
(repeated three times)

Farm Aid Program
Exploring Alternative Fuels

Farmers producing energy is nothing new. Just two generations ago, farmers fed 50 percent of their production to livestock on the farm to "power" the "machinery" to plant and harvest. Another 25 percent went to horses and mules for transportation in the cities and towns.

Today, as oil prices soar and tensions increase over diminishing oil supplies, renewable energy produced by America's family farms is increasing our energy self-reliance. Biofuels and renewable energies (biodiesel, wind, and others) produced on America's family farms represent a hopeful way to help family farmers stay on their land.

New farm and energy policies will be needed to ensure that family farmers—and not giant energy corporations—reap the benefits of growing energy for America. If so, biodiesel, wind, and other "renewables" can provide family farmers economic opportunities that can help them stay on their land and add to the number of America's farm families, all while increasing our energy self-reliance.

Nelson fuels one of his tour buses with biodiesel, while Young looks on, Farm Aid 2004.

Nelson, 2001

"WHAT WOULD WILLIE DO?"

Bruce Robison

I was lost in trouble and strife, I heard a voice and it
    changed my life
And now it's a brand new day, and I ain't afraid to say

You're not alone when you're down and out
And I think you know who I'm talking about

When I don't know how I'll get through
I ask myself what would Willie do . . .

with Carl's Corner truck stop, on I-35 north of Hillsboro and south of Dallas, Texas. Since 1984, the truck stop has been owned by Willie's pal Carl Cornelius. "I think I've won that truck stop two or three times in poker games, and I always try to lose it back," Nelson says. "This time I decided it would come in handy. So we have a biodiesel pump there where we're pumping out 'BioWillie.' The other day we had a bunch of school buses out there, and we filled them up with BioWillie. It's a great idea for the farmers, which is the reason I'm doing it." According to the Environmental Protection Agency, every year in Texas, one school bus emits the pollution equivalent to 114 cars' exhaust. Biodiesel burns cleaner, lessens our dependence on oil, and provides another market for farmers.

Willie's hazel eyes later intensify in the dim light of the bus. He points out, "Farm Aid hasn't solved the problem yet. We've made some people aware of the problem. We've been able to collect a few dollars and pass it out to people who really need it. Other than that, the problem has compounded. But there's hope. We need to get farmers back on the land, and get young farmers started on the land. We need to pay farmers a fair price and give them no-interest loans for several years, say. We need to encourage organic growing. If we could take a million farms a year and do that for five years in a row, getting farmers to grow organic food, supported by the government and the people—that would be a huge turnaround. That is one of my dreams. And it is not impossible."

Nelson gets up, crouches over, and wanders toward the back of the bus. Soon it will be time for him to walk out of the emerald shadow and sing his songs. Headlines and silver trains may have forgotten places like South Bend, but it is these small towns that Willie Nelson holds close. Every beat of his heart sounds for the American family farmer.

"If America had one voice, it
would be Willie Nelson's."

—EMMYLOU HARRIS, FARM AID ARTIST

"Farm Aid is a wonderful cause. I have performed twice at Farm Aid. I think the reason for Willie's success and continuance with Farm Aid is his dedication to the farmers of America and the fact that artists in all genres of music love and respect Willie, so they are more than willing to go and give their time when he calls."

—GEORGE JONES, FARM AID ARTIST

Farm Aid Backstage Mark Rothbaum

"I've been Willie Nelson's manager since 1973. We put on big Fourth of July picnics for many years. All the management and crews would work together, so I was familiar with that kind of concert. There were never any difficulties like upstaging and bickering among artists. It was pretty smooth, and this got transferred to Farm Aid concerts.

"Every year, the lineups come from a combination of everything. The acts want to support the Farm Aid cause. These musicians and their crews that make up the touring bands that play music in America are fortunate enough to get out and see the farmlands and see the people and meet them. They drive and drive on a tour bus and stop at truck stops and meet farmers. If you play Fargo, North Dakota, and Duluth, Minnesota, and Minneapolis and St. Cloud, you're going to meet these people. You bring

them music, and they love it, and they want your autograph, and they're good people. They're hardworking people. They bring us good crops. Musicians who play Farm Aid just want to give back to the people who give to them, who support their music, and support their ability to do what they love to do—to play music. The musicians, in turn, want to support their ability to farm.

"This bunch of pickers, this bunch of musicians, are going to remain a thorn in the side of agribusiness and the politicians. When you sit and listen to Neil, Willie, John, and Dave, you realize how much they really know about this stuff. It's impressive. I talk to Willie and he's just like a walking encyclopedia. I'm around Willie enough to see farmers and people come up, shake his hand and really give it a pump, and say so much with so few words, like, 'Thank you.' They know.

"Farm Aid is Willie's legacy. When you think about the gift of stardom, it's like, What do you do, really do, with it? Do you give it back? You could make this a better world in some ways. And these fellas mixing it up like they do every year and getting together onstage at Farm Aid—it's almost like a religious service. When I go to Farm Aid concerts, it does my heart good to see Willie and John and Dave and Neil together and whoever else shows up. It just gives me a sense that the music is on the right track. You have to give something back. You're not entitled to just make your money and that's it.

"But for Farm Aid to work, it isn't just Willie Nelson. It's Glenda [Yoder] and it's Carolyn [Mugar], and it's David Anderson [Willie's tour manager] and it's [Willie's production manager] Poodie, and it's Mickey [Raphael] and

it's [Willie's wife] Annie and it's me and it's Paul English. It's all these people. It's the travel agents, it's the booking agents. And don't think for a second that each and every one of us don't take the same pride out of a day like Farm Aid that Willie does. We all share in the glory of the day and the righteousness of it, and I guarantee you that if anybody wrote a résumé, Farm Aid would be right at the top.

"The Farm Aid office does an incredible job. Carolyn Mugar is right up there with the great people I've met in my life. She has just been so kind and considerate to Willie through the years since they first met. She has the same concerns for his well-being that I do. She knows everybody and brings out the best in others. I don't know if people know just how remarkable she is. There wouldn't be a Farm Aid if it weren't for her."

The Farm Aid Vibe

Glenda Yoder, Associate Director, Farm Aid

Like a gospel service that fires up the faithful, Farm Aid concerts are an annual old-home-day get-together. The concertgoers, the workers, and the artists who perform all focus on one thing: a day of music for the cause of family farmers. For food and farm activists, a Farm Aid concert is like coming in off the road—a little weary, seeking kindred souls for rejuvenation, letting the music restore hope.

The fact that every artist donates his or her performance and travel expenses sets the stage as a powerful invitation to everyone: Give all that you can, and the reward is a trip to a musical heaven!

Farm Aid "day" actually begins sometime in the night, when Willie's and Neil's buses roll into the backstage area, often from a concert the night before. The security guards, primed to welcome the bus drivers, open the backstage parking gates. Daylight marks the arrival of the catering crew, the first of the production crew, and maybe a few stagehands. More artist buses ease into their parking places.

THE PRESS CONFERENCE AND THE FANS

Part pep rally, part teach-in, the Farm Aid press conference launches and energizes the day. Seated on platforms before hundreds of journalists and family farmers, the artists and farmers pull their mikes close and let loose. Their words, straight from the heart, challenge the nation's leaders to change the course of events. Americans are urged to take action, to give, to seek out family farm food, to bring agriculture into their lives. Later, journalists will base themselves in the press tent to meet with farmers, artists, and activists throughout the day.

The first concertgoers bunch up at the gates as they open, usually around noon. Out in the parking lot, they drop off canned goods they have brought for local food banks. The fans holding lawn tickets are eager to get in early with their blankets and chairs to claim a prime spot. The crowd continues to build until early evening, and, as the headliners take the stage, people are on their feet. It's always a long show.

In seventeen concerts, it has rained only twice during the shows, in Champaign (1985) and in Seattle (2004). Sunny, brilliant days have graced most of the performances, but as any farmer knows, you have no control over the weather.

Many Farm Aid fans are "Farmheads" who take pride in following the shows around the country, swapping stories of musical highlights and favorite bands. Wearing old Farm Aid T-shirts, they stock up on new ones. There's a palpable feeling that this concert is different from others. Jame Boastik, from Champaign, has been to *every* Farm Aid show: "Farm Aid is second to none in helping the farmers in this great nation of ours." Edith Arp has also never missed a show: "Living on a family farm that my grandfather purchased, where five generations of my family have resided, makes the Farm Aid chant, 'Family farms—yes! Factory farms—no!' have a great deal of meaning to me," Edith says.

Lee Ann Musselwhite, a frequent and loyal concertgoer, claims, "Farm Aid is like a buffet for the senses . . . I am stimulated on levels beyond my love of music. After tasting the food and samples from the various family farm–friendly vendors, and learning the roots of the real message . . . one can't help but come back year after year."

Mark Tilsen, a faithful volunteer, put forward another powerful memory: "At the conclusion of Farm Aid IV, in Ames, Iowa, Willie joined Neil Young onstage for the first live performance of 'The Farm Aid Song.' As the cold Iowa wind blew, the crowd erupted to this incredible musical moment. The performance was so powerful that it left everyone in awe. Later that night, on the ride home, my son turned to me and said, 'Dad, now I have lived long enough to see everything.' He was nine years old at the time."

Thanks to special presales, fan clubs of the four board members always

Top: Neil Young, Carolyn Mugar, and Young's longtime manager, Elliott Roberts, backstage at Farm Aid, Columbus, Ohio, 2003. Bottom: Matthews, Young, and Mellencamp at the 2003 Farm Aid press conference

cluster together in their own sections, enjoying their favorite artist appearing onstage in unusual collaborations.

Volunteers at the donation booth dispense information about Farm Aid and its goals and collect a remarkable amount of money from concertgoers eager to join the mission. Each year Farm Aid provides the means for people to register to vote, a service more important than ever.

BACKSTAGE AND VOLUNTEERS

A mingling of farmers, sponsors, activists, volunteers, artists, and their friends and families fill the backstage, greeting each other with hugs and tales to fill in a year. The sheer number of people behind the scenes often astonishes the venue staff—they've never seen anything quite like it. But the serious purpose and the enormous goodwill of the day create an orderly flow. People pursue their duties with every expectation that they can make this concert the most memorable ever. It's a remarkable goal; many people work almost nonstop for days on end.

The volunteers perform the hardest—and sometimes the most thrilling— jobs. The walkie-talkie crackles: "Somebody threw up on the donation booth!" "We need someone to interview Dave Matthews for our Farm Aid online blog!" In 2004, Farm Aid asked volunteer Esther Bloch to answer the phone in Farm Aid's backstage office trailer. The 1-800-FARM AID number, answered every day at the Farm Aid office, had been forwarded to the backstage so that no farmer calls would be missed. Esther recalls the assignment: "I expected the calls to be about tickets and the concert. But I spoke to more than a few farmers who were calling for help. Their crops had been destroyed due to recent tornadoes, and these farmers were desperate for help. Their livelihood was in jeopardy. These were emotional conversations. I learned firsthand how farmers rely on Farm Aid for guidance and assistance and how powerful Farm Aid can be."

Members of the Teamsters Union volunteer as drivers before, after, and during the show to shuttle artists and staff from airports, hotels, and the venue. Sometimes they can grab only a few winks backstage after the show before taking an artist to the airport at 3:00 a.m. Their work is rewarded, though. One year John Mellencamp and his mother joined the Teamsters backstage for a game of euchre. One lucky driver was serenaded by Emmylou Harris as he drove her to the venue. The generosity of the Teamsters has extended throughout the year as well. Teamsters have donated trucks and drivers to help Farm Aid bring hay to farmers in time of drought.

THE PRODUCTION CREW

Until 1997, Farm Aid was a stadium show. It took almost a week to build a stage, cover a field, hoist tents, place trailers, and load in. The last seven years Farm Aid has been staged in amphitheaters, with a set stage, fixed seats, and an expansive lawn. While simplifying production, the "sheds" also offer amenities like dressing rooms and offices. Still, there aren't enough dressing rooms to go around, and artists gamely vacate the rooms for the next batch of performers. Tour buses pack in tightly; the loading dock is a labyrinth of boxes and instruments.

At the end of the day, as the bills come in, the invoices always reflect deep discounts, as well as donations of labor, materials, radios, and trucking. For example, Bandit Lites, Stage Call, and ShowCo, lighting, trucking, and sound vendors, respectively, have been among the most generous. The road crews of the four major artists pitch in to help all day.

Since the first concert, David Anderson, Farm Aid board member and Willie Nelson's tour manager, has played a crucial role, from producer, to advisor, to liaison with bands and crew. David has created a "founders compound" backstage, a little corner formed by Willie's and Neil's buses to block passage so that the founders can walk easily to the stage to sit in with bands and to the interview areas to talk to the press. By facilitating Willie's densely packed schedule on show day, David keeps the production on track minute by minute. You can always spot David clearing the way for a Willie entrance and waiting patiently while Willie greets his friends.

RON STERN, FARM AID'S PRODUCER: Ron worked on the first Farm Aid show as an employee of JAM, the Chicago-based promoter that took charge of production. Ron had pioneered producing large-scale stadium events, like the Amnesty International tours. He innovated outdoor stage construction and designed backstage areas in amphitheaters. Having retired from touring in 1995, Ron now runs the 4,300-seat Rosemont Theatre, near Chicago. These days, Ron returns to the road only once a year—for the Farm Aid show.

"When I first started with Farm Aid, I looked at it as an honor to be involved in such a large and complicated event," Ron says. "I was proud to be asked to do it. The first years, I looked at the event purely from the produc-

Left: Farm Aid concert producer Ron Stern. Right: Concert production coordinator Lyle Centola

tion aspect. I had always lived in big cities like Chicago, Los Angeles, or Detroit. I really knew nothing about farming. As the years went by, I was fascinated by the commitment of time and money by the artists. The dedication of the Farm Aid staff and the many local, hardworking family farm organizations intrigued me. I started paying more attention to farm issues, and I started to understand how important Farm Aid is to the American people—all of us! I am proud to be involved with Farm Aid, and I believe our show is unique in the industry. We don't supply limousines—we've even had farmers provide transportation in donated vehicles. The backstage is a combination of workers, press, artists, Farm Aid staff, and others all there for a common cause. I've never seen this anywhere else!"

Producers like Ron depend on the latest technology to run a tight schedule. "In 1985 we were using a Radio Shack Tandy computer to write our schedule," according to Ron. "The big technology innovation that year was something new to me called a fax machine. We installed a phone line at the stage and at the mix area in the audience and sent our changes in staging diagrams back and forth. Today, we have T1 lines for press, and we broadcast the show on our Web site. But the backstage vibe has stayed the same—a bunch of people working hard for a good cause."

LYLE CENTOLA, PRODUCTION COORDINATOR: Lyle went to his first Farm Aid concert in 1987 and returned in 1996 as a member of the staging crew. From there, he began to help manage the stage and later became coproduction

Farm Aid Vibe

Bonnie Raitt surrounded by the Fabulous Thunderbirds, 1986

Matthew McConaughey, 2002

John Doe and friend, 1985

David Allan Coe and Willie Nelson wait for a piece of cake from B.B. King, celebrating his sixtieth birthday, 1985

Farm Aid, 1985

Texas Tornados: Doug Sahm, Flaco Jimenez, Freddy Fender, and Augie Meyers, 1992

Dave Matthews, Neil Young, and John Mellencamp, 2001

Loretta Lynn and Merle Haggard, 1985

Emmylou Harris, 1985

Hootie and the Blowfish and Dave Matthews Band join Willie on his bus, 1995

Farm Aid, 1985

Dennis Hopper and Steve Earle, 1992

Tanya Tucker, Willie Nelson, and Hoyt Axton, 1985

Carole King, 1985

Lyle Lovett with the New Maroons: Don Was, Jonelle Mosser, Ringo Starr, Mark Goldenberg, Benmont Tench, 1993

Farmer Corky Jones, Neil Young, and Marty Stuart, 1997

Nelson and Tipper Gore, 2000

Kris Kristofferson and Deana Carter, 1994

Johnny Paycheck, 1985

The Blasters' Dave and Phil Alvin, 1985

Willie and Neil, 2001

Young and Nelson jam at Farm Aid 2002, Burgettstown, Pennsylvania

Kid Rock: "I'm here to learn a little bit about this today. To observe some of the greatest guys to make music ever, and help this wonderful cause out. . . . And, rock the *#$%!@ house."

Leo Gerard, president of the Steelworkers Union: "Hey, that guy sounds like a steelworker."

John Hansen, president of the Nebraska Farmers Union: "No, that guy's a dairy farmer!"

—FARM AID PRESS CONFERENCE, 2002

manager with Ron. Lyle has worked for many performers, including Neil Young, Josh Groban, Bruce Springsteen, Janet Jackson, Tina Turner, and Ringo Starr. Lyle is responsible for logistical routing of the dozens of bands and the vendor selections of lights, sound, video, power, and trucking, as well as hiring the crew that will work the show, doing the staging and the catering. With scrupulous attention to all the details, he does the settlement accounting and spreadsheets at the end of the night.

A family man from Louisiana, Lyle said he appreciates "the Farm Aid yearly event that has grown into such a family get-together. A family gathering is always good, but such a worthwhile cause makes it even better!"

Together, Ron and Lyle ensure the set changes go as quickly as possible, as the gear from each artist is pushed away on rolling risers and a new ensemble appears. They keep everyone on task to stick to the schedule so the show will run on time with TV production. They negotiate the necessary compromises as every band settles into doing things "the Farm Aid way."

RICH MACDONALD, SITE COORDINATOR: A Boston native, Rich began with Farm Aid as a volunteer. As producer of Boston's renowned Fourth of July Pops concert, attended by a half-million people and televised live, Rich is highly qualified to deal with all kinds of spatial details: mapping the compound, placing trailers, "dropping" tents, and solving the problems of electricity, phone lines, and computers. In 2000, when Tipper Gore's attendance brought with it Secret Service protocol, it was Rich who had the expertise to redirect the necessary flow of people and equipment. Rich's Boston accent on the walkie-talkie inspires a lot of joking, but the Farm Aid crew enjoys the diversity. Like the farmers who attend the show, the production team represents the far-flung places from which they come.

STEVE MACDONALD, SECURITY AND CREDENTIALS: A Boston firefighter, and Rich's brother, Steve has volunteered every year since 1987. He works with building security to ensure a safe backstage environment. With a briefcase full of backstage passes, Steve is a sought-after character. He can be just elusive enough to handle the tough job of allocating that popular laminate.

KELLY SHAUNESSY AND VICKI KYSAR: Two essential members of Farm Aid's production team are "graduates" of the Farm Aid office, in Somerville, Massachusetts. Each of them worked as office manager, and now they return each year to handle ground transportation and artist hospitality logistics, and assist in production. Both Kelly and Vicki have enormous reserves of energy, and they bring many years of experience to Farm Aid; they know how the organization works and what it asks of people.

STEVEN DEPAUL: A Springsteen road veteran, Steven helped produce shows from 1987 to 1997. He liked the community of road crews, he says: "Farm Aid concerts were always a place where the unexpected meeting of old friends could take place backstage, in a food tent, a dressing room corridor, or in a circle of buses. Members of the Farm Aid production team had worked together in different capacities before, and the communication was so easy, it felt like we had worked together for twenty straight years."

RIGHTEOUS T-SHIRTS

As the garment business over the years began to mirror the food business, sweatshop T-shirts from overseas became the norm at many concerts. Not at Farm Aid. Thanks to a politically active screen printer named Rick Roth and his union shop, Mirror Image, Farm Aid sells quality, often organic cotton T-shirts made in the U.S.A.

"My support of Farm Aid is personal as well as political," says Roth. "My grandparents' dairy farm went bankrupt and was sold at auction. My grandparents' home is now office condos, and my grandfather's garden a parking lot. This loss devastated my uncles and cousins, and I never want to see that happen to anyone else.

"I'm proud to work on Farm Aid T-shirts. We get good designs and good prints, and as a result, the merchandise sales at concerts outperform industry standards. Farm Aid is extremely well-organized, and all the staff and volunteers work effectively with such passion."

"Having been a farm activist for the past forty-five years, I would be really pessimistic about the whole future of family farming if it were not for Farm Aid. Farm Aid, to me, has really saved family farming over the past twenty years. If it hadn't been there, there would have been no support for some of the farm groups that are doing some good things. That's important—for the groups to work in unison and not separately. Every year, Farm Aid brings lots of diverse people together. Frankly, I don't go to Farm Aid concerts for the music; I come to schmooze with colleagues who I haven't seen for months. I've been to the past twelve or so concerts. For me, one of the best was in Ames, Iowa, in 1993. The crowd just went crazy. Not only for the music, but because most of those kids had an uncle or their parents or somebody who was still farming, and they knew what the situation was."

—A.V. KREBS, FARM ACTIVIST, AUTHOR

Musician David Amram, farmer Corky Jones, and farm activist David Senter (from left), all of whom faithfully attend Farm Aid every year

SPONSORS

Farm Aid welcomes sponsors who support family farmers. More and more organic and family farm food companies value their association with Farm Aid. As the organic businesses have grown, Farm Aid is seen as a valuable partner to increase the demand for and supply of family farm food.

Steve Demos, CEO of Silk Soymilk, backed Farm Aid as presenting sponsor in 2003 and 2004. At the 2003 press conference, prior to handing a $300,000 check to Willie Nelson onstage, Demos said, "The organic family farmer is the absolute backbone of our business, so to all of the independent farmers farming the twenty-five thousand acres that supply us, this is our gift back to you."

George Siemon, CEO of Organic Valley Family of Farms, says, "Farm Aid is a beacon of hope for all of us who work to keep America's family farmers on the land, build a strong system of family farmer–supported agriculture, and protect the environment that we will one day hand down to our children."

Travis Forgues, one of the nearly seven hundred farmers in the Organic Valley co-op, is a dairy farmer from Alburg, Vermont. He has found that ". . . nothing is more humbling than to stand in the midst of thousands of people listening to the music of Willie Nelson, John Mellencamp, Neil Young, and Dave Matthews. . . . Months later, I'll be out milking, and memories from the concert will come back to me. I just feel so grateful for Farm Aid. The concert stays with me all year!"

FAMILY FARM FOOD

Beginning in 1997, Farm Aid worked to source the food for backstage catering almost exclusively from local family farms and organic food companies. A logistical challenge sometimes met with resistance, the effort has been galvanized by Sonya Kugler and her partner Ed Kugler. After eight years of helping with the food at Farm Aid, Sonya reflected backstage in 2004, "This is a wonderful outreach piece, part of the education that Farm Aid does, venue by venue. But this is how you make change—one small step at a time!"

Concertgoers, too, are treated to family farm food vendors. Sponsors provide samples of organic snacks, dairy, juices, and soy milk.

FARMER EVENTS AND PROMOTIONAL ACTIVITIES

From a congressional subcommittee meeting, to a presidential candidates forum, to a town hall meeting with Secretary of Agriculture Dan Glickman, to conferences on genetically engineered crops, farmer events always accompany the Farm Aid show. Because so many farmers and leaders from around the country come to the concert event, it's a natural time for many farm organizations to schedule meetings.

Lance Jones, general manager of the Post-Gazette Pavilion, in Burgettstown, Pennsylvania, describes how the promotional activities of Farm Aid helped to make the 2002 concert there a huge success: "We felt a strong affinity with the Farm Aid team from the first meeting; they came prepared, they came with enthusiasm, and they came as willing to learn from us as we were from them. When a big tour comes to town, there's usually a huge buzz factor—and we had the buzz begin within our own ranks, with the first internal announcement of the show! There was an immediate sense of pride in hosting such a unique musical event, one that had as its driving force a core of four socially conscious and multitalented musicians.

"Some major tours stage one big media event to garner press and generate excitement; some just rely on their stature to propel sales. Farm Aid's route

"I think one of the more amazing things that people never really understand is that Farm Aid is the only organization that doesn't pay the way for everything. Unlike other charities where the press and celebrities get a free ride, at Farm Aid, artists pay their own way. If they haven't talked their band and crew into working for free, artists have to pay them, and they have to pay to get them all there. It's just unheard of. If members of the press come to Farm Aid, they buy a ticket. I think they're kind of shocked initially, but then they really admire the fact that this stand was taken. That's one area that kind of tells you the heart involved in Farm Aid. It's a testament to the organization and feelings that people have for Willie and the idea of the farm struggle."

—EVELYN SHRIVER, FARM AID BOARD MEMBER

A variety of the artful logos that have been designed over the years for Farm Aid concerts

seemed almost organic, from the initial selection of rural Burgettstown—the first Pennsylvania location to host the event—through the 'slow build' of community awareness and activism in rounding up public and media support. The venue's management and marketing team worked hand in hand with the Farm Aid staff in laying the base for a huge on-sale day. It paid off with a sellout.

"Beyond the community impact, the event generated for the venue a whole new wave of positive press and a high profile. We found ourselves, shortly after the on-sale, inundated with requests for directions to the facility, a sure sign that because of Farm Aid, we were bringing into our midst a huge number of first-time users. The ability to host brand-new concert fans in such an emotionally rich and positive setting was an unparalleled opportunity for us."

A TELEVISION SHOW FOR AMERICA

Willie Nelson always said that the purpose of Farm Aid was to raise awareness as well as money. The television shows made the concert a national event, inviting all of America to participate. The first Farm Aid concert was televised live on TNN (The Nashville Network) for twelve hours, with additional prime-time syndication on other networks, so that the show reached 100 percent saturation of the country. It was a monumental logistical challenge and a musical first. VH1 picked up the show the next year, but TNN returned to telecast the concerts from 1987 through 1997, except for the 1994 New Orleans show, which was filmed by the House of Blues (but never shown in the United States). For the next five years the concert was broad-

cast by CMT: Country Music Television. In 2003, Farm Aid aired on PBS as a Thanksgiving special. Over the years, these broadcasts have included the most talented music-television producers in the country: Dick Clark Productions, KLRU–Austin City Limits, High Five Productions, Automatic Productions, and Soundstage. In the mid-1990s, Farm Aid began Web casting the show as well, thanks to David Anderson, who saw the future of music on the Web.

Inspired by "Farm Aid Moments," pretaped segments filmed at family farms, and the power of the artistic passion exhibited by the performers, thousands of TV viewers have made donations by calling Farm Aid's 900 and 800 lines, or by logging onto the Farm Aid Web page. "Moments" documentary filmmakers have included Sharon Pelton, Kennedy Wheatley, and Cob Carlson.

Susan Steiner is another independent filmmaker who created many of the "Moments": "I had the privilege of going out into the heartland and meeting farm families who were willing to tell their story so Farm Aid could share it with America," says Steiner. "While it may not have been easy for them, generous farmers let us into their lives to share their heartbreak and their dreams. They did so to let the rest of America see with their own eyes what was happening in farm country. I felt honored to be the one to capture their stories."

Year after year, Westwood One Radio has made a multitrack sound recording and created radio shows on their syndicated network.

CONCERT RELEASES

In 2000, Farm Aid created and released its first music product, a double CD issued by Best Buy's Redline label. Producer Mike Wanchic, of John Mellencamp's band, culled through hundreds of tapes, discovering past performance gems. Having been to every show, Mike had vivid memories of great musical moments. He restored the old, deteriorating recordings by baking them and then transferred the tracks to digital. Later, DVDs of the 2001 and 2003 shows were also released. The artists, publishers, and record labels all donated the tracks for these products.

Farm Aid has been documented on CD (left) and DVD.

Farm Aid Backstage Mudslide

At every Farm Aid concert, there's a valuable player backstage parking buses, carrying guitars, or giving directions. His skin is tan from years in the sun, giving him the look of a farmer meets 1970s surfer. The Farm Aid family knows him as Mudslide. Ask Willie Nelson about Bob Dylan or Django Reinhardt and he answers in tones as mellow as a Hawaiian sunset. Mudslide? "Mudslide is a story all by himself," Nelson says with ebullience. "He has shown up at almost every Farm Aid and a lot of my own concerts. He hangs out in Maui a lot [with Nelson and his family]. He's a great gardener and worker. He'll do anything. He'll wash your car or pop up your bicycle. He can also play, sing, and write pretty good." He's also hard to track down.

I finally found Mudslide slipping in between Nelson's and Neil Young's tour buses at the 2004 Farm Aid. "Lincoln, Nebraska [September 1987], was my first Farm Aid," Mudslide said, standing in a cool mist. "I've been at almost every one since. I missed Kentucky because I had a centipede bite. My foot was about eight inches in diameter. I couldn't walk." You might guess that Mudslide, 54, is the kind of guy who doesn't like to wear shoes.

In 1987, Mudslide was playing music and living in Maui. He sings and writes what he calls "rippie music: half redneck, half hippie." That June Mudslide was helping build a stage for a Willie Nelson concert on the island. Nelson met Mudslide at the gig and invited the stagehand to a Fourth of July concert he was hosting at the legendary Carl's Corner truck stop, south of Dallas. Nelson had moved his annual Fourth of July picnic from outside Austin to his friend Carl Cornelius's truck stop as a benefit for the American trucker. "I ended up in the back of a police car at Carl's Corner," Mudslide said. "The Greyhound bus dropped me off at the truck stop, and the cops picked me up. Nobody believed that I was there to work with Willie.

"I can't say enough about Willie," Mudslide continued. "The band is a family. Everybody—the crew, the whole enchilada. They've tolerated me the last eighteen years now. At Farm Aid concerts, I do whatever it takes: I'll park buses, run around and get ice, shuttle artists back and forth. I try to be useful and stay out of the way. That's the trick—stay out of the way."

In 2004 Nelson asked Mudslide to plant a family garden at his home in Maui. Nelson wanted it to be organic and to include okra and mustard greens. But Mudslide had a hell of a time finding organic seeds in Hawaii (because they can't import seeds from the continental states). "I didn't give it a second thought when I asked him to do it [organic]," Nelson said. "In Maui, I figured they had everything."

Even Mudslide.

—DAVE HOEKSTRA

Bottom left: Farm Aid photographers Ebet Roberts and Paul Natkin, 2003. Center: Willie Nelson and longtime colleague Evelyn Shriver, a Farm Aid board member. Right: Carolyn Mugar, Paul English, and Glenda Yoder, backstage at Farm Aid, 2004

Finding Love at Farm Aid

As a result of the intensive teamwork and camaraderie involved behind the scenes at Farm Aid concerts, many deep personal relationships develop among those involved. And in some cases, a Farm Aid show has been the location of a chance meeting that turns into the love of a lifetime: Several marriages have resulted from couples who've come together with Farm Aid as a musical backdrop. In fact, in 1995, two longtime musical participants at Farm Aid, John Mellencamp bassist Toby Myers and Willie Nelson harmonica player Mickey Raphael, celebrated Farm Aid's tenth anniversary in a very special way: Toby and his wife, Roberta, got married onstage at Farm Aid. And Mickey met his wife-to-be Heidi backstage; after a whirlwind romance, the two married. Another musician also fell in love with his soul mate at Farm Aid, in 1999: Supersuckers vocalist/guitarist Eddie Spaghetti and his wife, Jessika. Here are their stories.

TOBY MYERS: "My wife, Roberta, was introduced to me by John's wife, Elaine; they were roommates in New York when they were first modeling. I had been dating Roberta for about three years, and we were taking the bus from southern Indiana to Louisville to do Farm Aid, and John started telling stories about when he eloped as a teenager. The first time he got married, he went across the border from Indiana to Kentucky, because I think he only had to be sixteen to get married down there, and you had to be eighteen in Indiana. At any rate, John started badgering me and Roberta saying, 'You've been going with this girl for three years, you know you're

Roberta and Toby tie the knot at Farm Aid, 1995

going to get married, so why don't you do it tonight?' And the more he badgered me, the more I started thinking, 'Well, gosh, why not?' John likes to make the joke that I just got married at Farm Aid so I could get out of playing 'Pink Houses' [the song the group usually encored with]. Harry Sandler, who was managing John at the time, said, 'You actually have your choice of denominations here.' But he introduced us to [Reverend] Enid Watson [who was a Farm Aid volunteer], and we really liked her.

"During our set, John made a cryptic announcement, saying, 'We're going to do something a little different at the end of this set tonight.' We had written our vows and made some aluminum foil rings. We needed a judge, too, so the state troopers blasted out of the stadium and went and got a judge. It was about 8:00 at night, and he was not at all happy about coming down there, but once he got down there and saw the crowd, he lightened up a little bit. He was a really big, imposing dude. When he said to the audience, 'Can I get a witness?' the roar of

forty-five thousand people yelling, 'Yes!' was awesome."

Roberta and Toby had a son, Cash, in 1999, and after eighteen years with Mellencamp, Myers left the band so he could "stay home and be a dad" in Indiana. Toby and Roberta will celebrate their tenth wedding anniversary when Farm Aid celebrates its twentieth.

"I officiated at the wedding onstage in front of forty-five thousand Farm Aid fans and under the stars of our maker. I gained a new appreciation for the pressures on performing artists to create and sustain the energy of a performance. Now I am known as the Minister to the Stars, though the real stars are the family farmers!"

—REVEREND ENID WATSON

HEIDI RAPHAEL: "It was October 1, 1995, and I was at Farm Aid in Louisville at the stadium. I happened to be working [as a record label consultant] in Louisville that week and stayed for the weekend to go to Farm Aid. Mickey and I started talking, and he seemed really nice. At this point, I had no idea who he was. Neil Young was onstage playing acoustic by himself, and then Mickey said to me, 'Don't go anywhere, I'll be right back. I'd like to talk to you.' He started to walk onstage, and I remember whispering to him, 'Where are you going? You can't cut across the stage,' and he walked onstage and pulled this harmonica out of his pocket, and that's when I realized he was a musician."

Mickey Raphael onstage, 2004

MICKEY RAPHAEL: "I had noticed Heidi that day off and on. At the eleventh hour, with a couple more acts to play, I was still waiting to go on. Heidi and I were talking some light little chitchat. I said, 'Can you wait a minute? I'll be back in a minute.' I went out and played with Neil, then came back, and she was kind of astonished. We hung out and exchanged numbers, and I kept in touch with her."

HEIDI: "And we have been together ten years now. We got married about four years later. We go every year to Farm Aid and celebrate. That's where we met and we consider that our anniversary. Farm Aid is great because it's all about family. It's kind of a family reunion."

The future Mr. and Mrs. Spaghetti, Farm Aid 1999

"Farm Aid holds such a special place in my heart and in my wife Jessika's heart. We fell in love at Farm Aid. I hear a song title!"

—EDDIE SPAGHETTI, FARM AID ARTIST

"Farm Aid became a powerful voice for family farms, a part of America too easily forgotten and overlooked in an economy often solely driven by the ruthless dictates of faceless economic forces. I am proud of the small contributions I was able to make to keeping that voice alive, to making sure the thousands of family farmers keep alive the core values from which our culture grew, and stay on the land to protect it and continue their enduring contribution to our economy. Farm Aid's story truly is an American story and one in which we can all take pride."

—DAN GLICKMAN, FORMER U.S. SECRETARY OF AGRICULTURE

"This struggle is for all of us . . . So many hard-working decent men and women and their children are being spit out of the economy, and we're losing a whole generation of producers. And this will be bad for family farmers, bad for our rural communities, bad for the United States of America. I want people in our country to know that what is happening to family farmers is not inevitable . . . It is the result of failed economic policies."

—PAUL WELLSTONE, U.S. SENATOR, MINNESOTA

Farm Aid 1990, Indianapolis

Two Decades of Farm Aid Concerts

Dave Hoekstra

Walking a long line between tradition and tomorrow, the American farmer shares a path with the American musician. With measured steps, the family farmer and popular artist have made Farm Aid a national treasure. With its hybrid of musical idioms, Farm Aid concerts have blazed a trail by intermingling artists from all over the musical map. During

a period when radio fragmented music into strictly country, rock, jazz, rap, and other narrowly formatted stations, Farm Aid stepped up to the plate and nurtured the connection between diverse cultural and musical forces. That is America. Not only has there been a spectrum of sounds at Farm Aid, performers have ranged from newcomers seeking their first hit to pioneers who have helped invent rock & roll and country music.

The first Farm Aid, subtitled "A Concert for America," took place on a rainy September 22, 1985, at the University of Illinois Memorial Stadium in Champaign, Illinois, only four weeks after the idea was hatched—one of the greatest logistical achievements in live music history. With fifty-four acts appearing before a crowd of approximately seventy-eight thousand people, the first Farm Aid was the biggest combined country and rock concert in history. Tickets were just $17.50.

Of all the concerts for causes that began in the mid-1980s, Farm Aid is the only one that still has the commitment of its original founders, Willie Nelson, Neil Young, and John Mellencamp. Nelson asked Dave Matthews to join the board in 2001. "Farm Aid is unique," said social critic Reebee Garofalo. "I don't know of any other benefit festival that has become annualized and has lasted for twenty years—anywhere. That's remarkable."

Some of Farm Aid's greatest moments occur when artists who otherwise do not have a chance to work together meet onstage. During the twelve hours of the first Farm Aid, Bob Dylan and Tom Petty and the Heartbreakers performed together, covering Dylan's "Maggie's Farm" with Nelson as sideman— a role Nelson would relish over the next twenty years. Rickie Lee Jones and

Bonnie Raitt duetted on John Prine's "Angel From Montgomery." And in a historic performance, Eddie Van Halen and Sammy Hagar, who would later be chosen to replace David Lee Roth as Van Halen's lead singer, rocked out onstage together for the first time.

Joni Mitchell, who was raised in a Canadian wheat-farming community, sang her ballad "Dog Eat Dog." The Nitty Gritty Dirt Band backed John Denver, and Glen Campbell helped out Willie Nelson, Waylon Jennings, and Johnny Cash (three-quarters of the Highwaymen) on "Highwayman." An unknown band was almost bumped from the lineup, but at the last minute was given a slot in the early morning hours of the show. That band was Bon Jovi, who would return to the next Farm Aid as superstars. John Fogerty's performance was his first as a solo act since departing Creedence Clearwater Revival thirteen years earlier. Fogerty sang "The Old Man Down the Road," "Zanz Kant Danz," and the Steve Cropper–Eddie Floyd soul chestnut "Knock on Wood." Like many artists drawn to Farm Aid, Fogerty hails from generations of farmers.

The test of time has given Farm Aid credibility, but the first Farm Aid was met with some skepticism. David Anderson, Nelson's tour manager since 1974, recalls, "The amount of press we got on that first one was phenomenal. The press corps at Farm Aid was nine hundred strong. But the tone was at times very hostile. People were very unsure because the farmers had been screwed over long before we got there. They thought this was just another scam to come in and take money. They grilled Willie at every corner. It was a learning curve for all of us."

Opposite: John Mellencamp and band onstage, Farm Aid 2003, Columbus, Ohio
Above: Wilie Nelson at the first Farm Aid in Champaign, Illinois, 1985

Bob Dylan, 1985

Sammy Hagar and Eddie Van Halen, 1985

Half of the Highwaymen: Johnny Cash and Waylon Jennings, 1985

Jon Bon Jovi, 1985

Covering the story, a Chicago television station dispatched a financial analyst to talk money with Nelson. After the TV man left the Honeysuckle Rose bus, Nelson smiled and said, "I was in the Future Farmers of America and I raised a few cows. One year I went broke raising hogs. I bought some wiener pigs at twenty-four cents a pound and fed 'em for six months and wound up selling them for seventeen cents a pound. You could say I learned a little bit about the farm industry."

Still, some farmers were not impressed. In a Main Street café in Elkhart, Illinois [pop. 450 in 1985], farmers talked about it over breakfast. American farmers are a proud and stubborn group. They didn't like the perception that they needed to be bailed out, and they had distrust for the government. Other farmers were glad for the attention Farm Aid was bringing to the problem. They knew the concert wouldn't solve it, but damn if the media coverage didn't hurt. Outside the diner, one Elkhart farmer stood proudly by his 1974 pickup. "You've never seen anything so rusted in your life," he promised. "This," he said while gently patting the truck, "is what I'm going to drive to the concert."

Another concert highlight was Carole King, who sang "Sweet Seasons" and "You've Got a Friend." King had spent the previous eight years living on a working Idaho ranch. In the spring of 1985, she spoke before the House Task Force on Agriculture. King said, in part, "We don't need any more MX missiles—we can't eat MX missiles. If things must be built, let it be things that will benefit our world and its people, starting from the ground up." B.B. King sang "Every Day I Have the Blues," and celebrated his sixtieth birthday with a cake shaped like Lucille, his beloved guitar. Randy Newman duetted with Billy Joel (who grew up next to a potato farm in Hicksville, New York) on the blues classic "Stagger Lee." Lou Reed sang "Walk on the Wild Side" and a country-fried version of "I Love You, Suzanne."

Los Angeles Times critic Robert Hilburn wrote, "The concert reunited country and rock in a way we haven't seen since the fifties, when Elvis Presley, Johnny Cash, Roy Orbison, and Jerry Lee Lewis pioneered rockabilly." But aside from the great music, "the main point of Farm Aid," Governor Jim Thompson said, "is to bring the plight of the American farmer to the attention of the nation." Farm Aid did that—it brought sunshine on a rainy day, raising millions and getting people to talk about what to do to help the family farmer.

" 'Farm Aid is really nice,' Petty said. 'You never see a show with country acts and rock acts, but there's not all that much difference between the two. The thing that interests me is how easily the audience accepts it. I'm thrilled to be here . . . I got to meet Loretta Lynn.'

"Bob Dylan nodded. 'Yeah, I agree with that,' Dylan said. 'Music shouldn't be put into [categories]. I've always loved people like Johnny Cash and Waylon Jennings.'

"Then he paused and smiled as he looked at Petty. 'The only thing I want to know,' Dylan said, 'is why I didn't get a chance to meet Loretta Lynn, too.' "

—*LOS ANGELES TIMES*, SEPTEMBER 29, 1985

A historic performance, Farm Aid 1985: Heartbreaker guitarist Mike Campbell, Heartbreaker drummer Stan Lynch, Willie Nelson, Tom Petty, Heartbreaker bassist Howie Epstein, and Bob Dylan (from left)

Julio Iglesias and Willie Nelson, 1986, Austin, Texas

TEXAS TWO-STEP

Farm Aid stayed close to the heartland throughout the late 1980s. Farm Aid II was held on July 4, 1986, near Austin, in Manor Downs, Texas, as one of Willie's annual Fourth of July Picnics. The concert featured 112 individual acts or groups that performed on one stage, the largest roster of any Farm Aid show. The talent pool ran as deep as the heart of Texas, from the Playboy Girls of Rock n' Roll to Rick James, from Stevie Ray Vaughan and Double Trouble, to Emmylou Harris. Los Lobos made its only Farm Aid appearance, and Roger "King of the Road" Miller made his last Farm Aid appearance. War performed "The Cisco Kid" and "Why Can't We Be Friends," followed by Jerry Jeff Walker dealing his classic "Mr. Bojangles." Roger McGuinn covered Bob Dylan's "Mr. Tambourine Man," while Dylan returned to the Farm Aid stage via satellite, a relatively new concept at the time, to sing "Rainy Day Women #12 & 35." The Grateful Dead also played a set by satellite.

Hot off of recording their duet "To All the Girls I've Loved Before," Julio Iglesias wanted to perform with Willie Nelson in Austin, but Iglesias was appearing in Las Vegas at the time. To make the show, Iglesias chartered a

Farm Aid Backstage ✹ John Conlee

When he's not singing country music, John Conlee rolls up his sleeves on farms he runs in Kentucky and Tennessee. He wears a heart on each of those sleeves. Conlee was one of the very first to volunteer when plans for the original Farm Aid concert were announced. Conlee, who had Urban Cowboy hits like "Rose Colored Glasses" and "Backside of Thirty," appeared at nine consecutive Farm Aids—from the first one in 1985 to Farm Aid '96.

Even today, Conlee remains a proud farmer. He operates his family's farm in Versailles, Kentucky, and runs a newer seventy-five-acre farm outside of Nashville. "I'm still hands-on," Conlee said. "I've done it all my life. And I'm still running the farm I was raised on. I'm at least fourth generation, and I'm sure it goes back further than that. Growing up in Kentucky, we had hogs, chicken, tobacco, cattle, and hay. We're pretty much down to cattle and hay now. The tobacco program is in its dying stages.

"When the farm crisis reared its head in the spring of 1985, I kept noticing it was buried deep inside the third section of the newspa-

per," Conlee said. "No headlines, no attention. So I organized [and headlined] a concert in Omaha, Nebraska, along with the help of the National Farmers Organization [founded in 1955]. That was in June 1985. Shortly after that, Willie announced the first Farm Aid. I promptly called him and said, 'I would love to be a part of whatever you're doing.' He said, 'Come onboard.' It was that simple." Conlee has a bushel full of fond Farm Aid memories. At the first Farm Aid, he sang a country-blues version of Harlan Howard's "Busted" (popularized by Ray Charles) and his own smash "Rose Colored Glasses."

A member of the Grand Ole Opry since 1981, Conlee lives on his Tennessee farm with his wife, Gale. They have three grown children, Rebecca, Jessica, and John. In the fall of 2004, John, then eighteen, joined the United States Marines. Will the Conlee family farm move on to the next generation? Conlee took a long pause and answered, "It's my hope that we keep the land and it will be handed down. But who knows?"

—DAVE HOEKSTRA

Lou Reed, 1990, Indianapolis

"I love rock & rollers. We're all here [at Farm Aid] for the same reason—for the farmers. We all have to eat. And we all have the same roots. Even city people have ancestors who had their hands in the dirt. And as musicians, country and rock aren't that far apart, really. We all come from the same place."

—JUNE CARTER CASH, FARM AID ARTIST

private jet, flew out of Vegas after his appearance the night before Farm Aid, performed the next afternoon in Austin, and immediately jetted back to Vegas in time to go onstage at Harrah's that same night. "I've never asked Julio to do anything where he said, 'no,'" Nelson said. "He really wanted to do that show. I didn't know for sure if he was coming. It was a surprise when he showed up."

In what was to become something of a Farm Aid "against all odds" tradition, the Austin concert moved sites three times in two weeks, with the final shift occurring only forty-eight hours before show time. Three miles of road had to be built overnight to get the crowd and production crews to Manor Downs.

NEBRASKA

In its third year, Farm Aid still had the ability to reach people long after most celebrity benefit efforts would have fizzled. Farm Aid III sold out within two days. The concert was held on September 19, 1987, before seventy thousand people at Memorial Stadium in Lincoln, Nebraska. Dennis Hopper, who was raised on a Kansas farm, was a host. Farm Aid is known for giving a number of acts their first shot at playing before a huge crowd, and Farm Aid III was the first major venue appearance by Lyle Lovett. Lovett still lives in Klein, Texas,

Lyle Lovett, 1993, Ames, Iowa

the small farming community named for his great-great-grandfather. Lovett had been a member of Future Farmers of America (FFA) while in high school, and he proudly wore his FFA jacket that day (and again when he returned in 1993).

John Mellencamp's band helped ignite "Sweet Jane" for Lou Reed. Willie Nelson told the crowd that America was losing two hundred farms a day: "We've been working hard, but there's still work to do."

PICK HIT IN INDIANA

Farm Aid rolled into the 1990s with one of the most provocative concerts to date. Many Farm Aid regulars pick Farm Aid IV, held April 7, 1990, at the Hoosier Dome in Indianapolis, as one of their favorites. Farm Aid IV was the quickest sellout, moving forty-five thousand tickets in less than two hours. The lineup included Jackson Browne, Soviet rock band Gorky Park, Steve Earle, and Hoosier native John Hiatt. Dwight Yoakam tackled Merle Haggard's "Mama's Hungry Eyes," and Neil Young performed a rare set with Crosby, Stills and Nash. Iggy Pop sang "I Wanna Be Your Dog" backed by Was (Not Was), and John Carter Cash took on "Redneck Love."

Guns n' Roses made its final live performance with its original lineup. The band covered the U.K. Subs punk hit "Down on the Farm." It certainly marked the only time Guns n' Roses appeared on TNN: The Nashville Network, which televised the concert. Garth Brooks, who opened the concert at 10:00 a.m., and Alan Jackson were newcomers on the bill. Father of Bluegrass Bill Monroe led the crowd on a sing-along of "Blue Moon of Kentucky," and Taj Mahal played "She Caught the Katy" with eighty-year-old Indianapolis mandolin legend Yank Rachell. Mellencamp's band lit a fire under Joe Ely singing "Settle for Love."

Elton John was a surprise guest at Farm Aid IV. A few days before the show, Mellencamp had run into Elton John at the bedside vigil of eighteen-year-old Indianapolis AIDS victim Ryan White and extended an invitation to Elton John to play at Farm Aid. While visiting backstage with Bonnie Raitt and waiting for his surprise walk-on, John learned that Ryan had suddenly taken a turn for the worse. He asked Farm Aid staff to secure a golf cart to rush him out of the arena so he could return to the hospital. As he was leaving the stadium, John changed his mind about canceling his appearance, stopped, and asked if there was a piano onstage. Farm Aid concert producer Ron Stern delayed the next act (the Kentucky Headhunters), and John immediately took

John Fogerty, 1997, Tinley Park, Illinois

Kris Kristofferson, Bonnie Raitt, and Jackson Browne, 1990, Indianapolis

Little Joe Hernandez, 1990

Farm Aid Backstage ♦ John Doe of X

"Around 1985, we'd been touring the United States and the Midwest for five or six years, and we could see a definite change in the attitude and the morale of the Midwest. It was depressed—you get a feeling for that.

"The first Farm Aid was overwhelming—how many people were there—and it was like being let loose in the coolest clubhouse ever. The very first thing I remember was us parking behind David Allan Coe's bus, which got there after driving all night. [Coe] stepped off his bus, with his huge long hair, big fringe jacket, and he said, 'I haven't even thought about a guitar this early in the morning.' And Hoyt Axton's bus was next to us, and then in the artist compound, there was Randy Newman over here and Bob Dylan over there and Tom Petty over here. We got to go on Johnny

Cash and June Carter's bus, and Johnny Paycheck was there looking totally crazy. I was taking one look at Johnny Paycheck and thinking, 'I wouldn't mess with him on a bet.' It was raining as we played, so the rain was completely soaking us, and we were standing onstage thinking, 'There's about a million-gazillion volts at our feet and we're soaking wet . . . *hmmm*.' It was definitely the largest crowd we ever played for. It's sort of like doing the red carpet, where there's a hyper-reality to everything. Your heart is just pounding out of your chest because you've just met Johnny Cash, and then you're going to go onstage, and there's nearly eighty-thousand people. For us, it was just an overwhelming experience."

Axl Rose of Guns n' Roses, 1990

to the stage for a tender solo piano version of "Candle in the Wind," with slightly changed lyrics dedicated to White. It seemed as if the entire audience held lighters high in the dark arena. White died hours after John's performance.

Nelson himself received a devastating blow on Christmas Eve 1991 that would have knocked out a lesser man. Nelson's son William Hugh Nelson Jr. (cowriter of his father's "Put Me on a Train Back to Texas") hanged himself at home. He was thirty-three. "I doubled up on work," Nelson said in measured tones. "Farm Aid. Shows. Right after that I had six months in Branson booked. I could have canceled, but I went on." But Nelson didn't record again until the end of 1992. His coming-out album was 1993's *Across the Borderline,* which featured "Heartland," the searching Nelson-Bob Dylan ballad about the American family farm. "A long time ago, Bob and I talked about writing a whole album together," said Nelson. "That never happened. But 'Heartland' was all his idea. He went into the studio, cut the track, and hummed a melody. Then he sent me the tape and said, 'Write the lyrics.' "

RETURN TO TEXAS

By the mid-1990s, Farm Aid had become part of the American fabric. Farm Aid V took place on March 14, 1992, near Dallas in Irving, Texas. Paul Simon and Nelson performed a set together that included the Simon hit "Graceland," which Simon later produced on Nelson's *Across the Borderline.* Tracy Chapman performed with Living Colour guitarist Vernon Reid. The always smiling Doug Sahm and his Texas Tornados thrilled the crowd with "Who Were You Thinking Of?" before Tornado Freddy Fender nailed his solo hit ballad "Wasted Days and Wasted Nights." The supergroup theme continued later in the show when the Highwaymen (Willie Nelson, Johnny Cash, Waylon Jennings, and Kris Kristofferson) harmonized on the Jimmy Webb ballad "Highwayman," and Little Village (Ry Cooder, John Hiatt, Jim Keltner, and Nick Lowe) sang their wacky "Solar Sex Panel."

IOWA FLOODLANDS

A little over a year later, on April 24, 1993, Farm Aid VI went to Ames, Iowa, when the great floods of '93 were on the minds of all Americans. Heavy rains caused the Mississippi and Missouri rivers to rise up and overflow, swallowing entire towns. A few days after Farm Aid VI, the stadium itself would be flooded, but luckily the water held off for the concert.

Cool weather in Ames didn't prevent presidential brother Roger Clinton from showing up early to sing "Keep the Faith" and then keep company backstage throughout the rest of the day. Clinton remains the first and only relative of a serving president to perform at Farm Aid. Roseanne Barr and Tom Arnold hosted large segments of the show, even performing an entire set, which included "The Ballad of John and Yoko" and the theme song from *Green Acres*. Willie Nelson could barely stop laughing at the memory of their appearance. "Yes, that was a bizarre set," Nelson said. "It was another one of those appearances that I didn't know was going to happen. But I'm glad it did. Something like that could never be planned." Equally odd was Russian comic Yakov Smirnoff onstage introducing Western-swing stars Asleep at the Wheel. Neil Young debuted "The Farm Aid Song" with Willie Nelson, and John Conlee delivered a scorching cover of the Percy Mayfield hit "Please Send Me Someone to Love." In the stable of forgotten supergroups sits the New Maroons (Don Was Band with Ringo Starr, the first Beatle to perform at Farm Aid, and Nashville singer Jonelle Mosser), who tackled the Dan Penn classic "Dark End of the Street."

BIG TIME IN BIG EASY

For the first time in its history, Farm Aid headed to the Deep South in 1994. The Louisiana Superdome, in New Orleans, was the September 18th, host for Farm Aid VII. Astronaut Buzz Aldrin commemorated the twenty-fifth anniversary of the first moon walk at the show. John Mellencamp had performed at every previous Farm Aid, but was absent in New Orleans due to illness. Nelson dedicated the concert to Mellencamp, who missed the Farm Aid debut of country singer Deana Carter and the return of tattooed outlaw David Allan Coe (who appeared at the first Farm Aid). New Orleans jazz cats Pete Fountain and Al Hirt helped kick off the show with "When the Saints Go Marching In" and "Pin Root Blues," respectively. The first family of New Orleans funk and soul graced the stage when the Neville Brothers sang "Hey Pocky Way"/"I Walk on Guilded Splinters" and "Yellow Moon." The Gin Blossoms followed with "Allison Road" and "Hey, Jealousy." Kristofferson filled Mellencamp's headline slot with "Me and Bobby McGee" and a rugged version of "Why Me?" Farm Aid and Comic Relief collaborated to bring comedians Paula Poundstone and Paul Rodriguez to the stage to entertain the crowd between sets.

Aaron Neville of the Neville Brothers, 1994, New Orleans

Lee Ann Womack, 2002, Burgettstown, Pennsylvania

Little Village: Nick Lowe, Jim Keltner, John Hiatt, and Ry Cooder (from left), 1992, Irving, Texas

Kid Rock, 2002, Burgettstown, Pennsylvania

John Trudell, 1993, Ames, Iowa

The concert's compelling subtext centered on Nebraska farmer Ernest Krikava. The sixty-year-old farmer was sentenced to prison for illegally selling $35,000 worth of his hogs during his family's bankruptcy proceedings, to prevent the hogs from dying of starvation. The family had no food, their hogs were starving, and the bank refused to release funds to operate the farm. Tragically, Ernest's wife died of an illness because she could not afford to go to a doctor. Krikava was later pardoned by President Clinton, due in part to the advocacy work of Nelson and Farm Aid. "You can't just let them [hogs] die," Nelson told *The Tennessean* a month before the concert. "You're in the pig business and even though you're raising them for food, you love them. I've raised cattle, and even though you know eventually someday they're going to be steaks for somebody, you still care for those cattle, at least till they become steaks. You can't let them starve to death, and for those bankers to put that man in that position, to me, that's a criminal action." Krikava's son Kevin was Nelson's guest at the New Orleans concert.

All the production costs for the concert were covered through the efforts of New Orleans' Jackson Parish sheriff Harry Lee. As a payback, Lee got to sing "To All the Girls I've Loved Before" with Nelson.

TENTH ANNIVERSARY IN KENTUCKY

Farm Aid commemorated its tenth anniversary on a sunny October 1, 1995, at Cardinal Stadium, in Louisville, Kentucky. The historic concert symbolized a shift for Farm Aid: Previous shows jammed as many acts as possible into a long day's journey into night. At Louisville, fewer acts played longer sets, a format Farm Aid still follows today.

More than forty-seven thousand fans saw full sets from Hootie and the Blowfish, the Supersuckers, and the Dave Matthews Band, who made their Farm Aid debut with a charging cover of Bob Dylan's "All Along the Watchtower." The buzz that year was around Matthews, who would later become a Farm Aid board member, and his band from Charlottesville, Virginia. Before the concert, Hootie's Darius Rucker said, "It's amazing for us to play our little four-minute pop songs ahead of Willie Nelson, Neil Young, and John Mellencamp." Nelson joined Eddie Spaghetti and the Seattle-based Supersuckers punk band for a breathless version of "Bloody Mary Morning." The crowd was really congenial: Fans made permanent friends across the aisles, all while groovin' on the baseball field turned concert stadium.

Willie Nelson onstage with the Supersuckers, 1995, Louisville, Kentucky

"Every year, the Farm Aid concerts are like a big celebration. Musically, since 1985, there have been some great moments: When Elton John came out and played unannounced, it was really special. And all the stuff Neil Young does has always been brilliant, whether it's with Crazy Horse or by himself, which is when I get to play with him. John Fogerty was incredible. Ringo [Starr] came one year and we put a band together and played with Lyle Lovett. And what's cool is that people are coming to Farm Aid for the music, and then they're being educated about the family farmer once they get there."

—MICKEY RAPHAEL, FARM AID ARTIST

Farm Aid Backstage Dave Alvin

Americana singer-songwriter Dave Alvin has the distinction of being the only artist to perform as a member of three different bands at three different Farm Aids. Alvin appeared at the first Farm Aid, in 1985, with the Blasters. Alvin played with X at Farm Aid II, held in 1986 in Austin. He perfected the trifecta in 1987 by performing with the Allnighters in Lincoln.

Alvin has vivid memories of the first Farm Aid. The Blasters were at the top of their game, the toast of the L.A. cow-punk scene. John Mellencamp was such a fan in early 1985 that he wrote and produced the pop-soul ballad "Colored Lights" for the band. During a midafternoon set in Champaign, the Blasters followed George Jones and ripped through "Marie, Marie," "Common Man," and the anthem "American Music." "The lineup for that Farm Aid was stunning," said Alvin. "I was a big fan of John Conlee. I just dug his whole

thing. Lou Reed *and* John Conlee? *Wow!* X was there, too. That first show was intense because I don't think that kind of lineup had ever been put together where you had that variety of acts. I'd stand backstage looking around and, 'There goes B.B. King.' And, 'There goes Merle Haggard.' Or 'There goes Neil Young.' It was close as I ever got to Monterey or Woodstock and that kind of feeling. And it meant a lot to be invited because it meant that maybe we didn't suck."

Alvin said the vibe was more relaxed at the third Farm Aid, in Lincoln. True to their name, the Allnighters (with Alvin's longtime compatriot Greg Leisz on lap and steel guitar) flew in the night before the show. "We stayed at the Corn Husker or some hotel where you saw the

plains," Alvin said. "I was in my room at 2:00 a.m. and I opened my curtains. You could see the line of cars coming across these black plains. It was stunning."

Alvin is from Downey, California, a small town of avocado and orange groves in the southeast corner of Los Angeles County that turned suburban in the late 1950s.

Alvin's father, Cass, was an organizer for steelworkers' unions in the western states. Alvin does not pretend to be an expert on farm issues, but he does feel a personal connection to his homeland. He said, "To me, the problem in the southern San Joaquin Valley around Bakersfield is all the corporate farming. The smaller family farms are in the central and northern part of the valley. You drive on the back roads of the southern San

Joaquin and it's miles of farmland, miles of one crop, and you know it's corporate."

While coming of age, Alvin, now fifty, was enthralled with the fertile musical landscape of the southern San Joaquin Valley. "As [the Bakersfield Sound architect] Buck Owens told me, the West Coast thing was about dancing, whereas the Nashville stuff was not about dancing. His take was that in the East, you had to dance with an appropriate space between you, but once you got to California or Arizona, a lot of those mores were gone, and you could do the buckle polishing or you could do the rock & roll dancing." Alvin added, "You can easily translate the independence of the family farm into a metaphor for rock & rollers and their independence."

—DAVE HOEKSTRA

SOUTH CAROLINA HOEDOWN

After the tenth anniversary show, Farm Aid concerts were referred to by year. Farm Aid '96 was held on October 12, in Columbia, South Carolina, with a decidedly country spin, featuring Tim McGraw, Robert Earl Keen, Martina McBride, the return of the Texas Tornados, and ringers like Jewel and Son Volt, the latter of whom contributed a moving version of "Tear Stained Eye." Hurricane Bertha had battered much of the Carolinas, while a drought covered the Great Plains. Before the concert, Farm Aid coordinated a farmer-to-farmer haylift, where farmers from the Carolinas sent hay to drought-stricken families in Oklahoma and Texas. David Crosby sat in on harmonies with Hootie and the Blowfish for their hit "Hold My Hand." Crosby returned around midnight to sing harmony and play acoustic guitar with his old pal Neil Young on a heartfelt version of "Helpless." In Farm Aid fashion, a unique amalgam of musical styles occurred when Neil joined the Beach Boys onstage, singing the chorus "And we'll have fun, fun, fun/Now that Daddy took the T-bird away."

Willie Nelson and his band set a Farm Aid "Night Life" record by taking the stage around 1:30 a.m. and singing until 2:30 in the morning. The long night was caused by a late concert start due to the collapse of the soundstage just as the concert was set to begin. No one was injured, and no one was worse for the delay, although the late hour showed in some drooping eyelids. Certainly, nothing can stop Willie Nelson.

ILLINOIS INTERLUDE

The 1997 concert got off to a rocky start. Due to poor ticket sales, the show booked for Texas Stadium in Dallas had to be relocated. Chicago's JAM Productions and Arny Granat welcomed the show to Tinley Park on October 4, reopening their closed-for-the-season amphitheater. In less than two weeks, Farm Aid '97 sold thirty thousand tickets. Every major act that had been booked re-routed to Chicago to support family farmers.

The last-minute fans were rewarded with first-rate sets. Beck played bluegrass versions of "Ramshackle" and "Jackass" from his album *Odelay*. Nelson introduced the singer as "Mr. Beck," before joining him for a sprightly cover of "Peach Pickin' Time in Georgia." John Fogerty rocked through his Creedence Clearwater hits: "Born on the Bayou," "Green River," "Fortunate Son," "Proud Mary," "Travelin' Band," and his cover of Dale Hawkins's "Suzie Q."

Willie Nelson and "Mr. Beck," 1997, Tinley Park, Illinois

Martina McBride, 2001, Noblesville, Indiana

Barenaked Ladies, 1999, Bristow, Virginia

"THE FARM AID RAP" BY BARENAKED LADIES

Farm Aid 1999

It's good to be here right now on the stage
We're going to talk about the farms with y'all
We're going to do what we can
We're going to have a big ball

Everybody out there wanna see your fist in the air
(C'mon, raise 'em, folks)
Everyone knows that eggs have yolks
And the eggs, they come from chickens on the farm
We don't want the farmers to lose their left arm

CHORUS
You eat your food with a fork and a knife
We're here to preserve a very special way of life

The Dave Matthews Band jammed through "Ants Marching," and the Allman Brothers meshed their "Blue Sky" with the Grateful Dead's "Franklin's Tower." Billy Ray Cyrus jumped in the fray with his hit "Achy Breaky Heart," and Nelson joined Cyrus for "Stop Pickin' on Willie," a song about Nelson's tax troubles.

Neil Young dedicated his "Mother Earth" to the Neuse River in North Carolina, explaining that the waterway and the state's residents were plagued with toxic waste from a factory hog farm. Young's all-acoustic set appropriately included Nelson joining in on the Stephen Stills–Young hit "Long May You Run." As an inspired Nelson walked off the stage, he called Farm Aid '97 "the best one yet."

Farm Aid '97 was so successful, it returned to Tinley Park for Farm Aid '98. Fans braved brisk twenty-five-mile-per-hour winds to hear Nelson collaborate with Beach Boy Brian Wilson on "The Warmth of the Sun" and hipster hempster Woody Harrelson sing "Jailhouse Rock" with Hootie and the Blowfish. A new country artist named Toby Keith joined Brian Wilson and Matt Jardine (son of Beach Boy Al Jardine) for backing harmonies on the Beach Boys hit "Do It Again," and Nelson's longtime guitarist Jody Payne sang Merle Haggard's "Workin' Man Blues" with *Late Show* bandleader Paul Shaffer on keyboards. Chicago-based Wilco performed an eight-song set that included "James Alley Blues," "She's a Jar," and "New Madrid" with the lineup of vocalist-acoustic guitarist Jeff Tweedy, Jay Bennett on lead guitar, John Stirratt on bass, LeRoy Bach on piano, and Ken Coomer on drums.

The jam band Phish made its Farm Aid debut. Phish had been active in its home base of Vermont, helping to stave off expansion of a factory egg farm. Neil Young joined Phish onstage for a twenty-minutes-plus version of "Down by the River." In his evening slot, Nelson broke tradition from a greatest-hits set to play some songs from his new album *Teatro* with Daniel Lanois, including "I Never Cared for You" and "Darkness on the Face of the Earth." Their cresting version of Lanois's "The Maker" stunned the crowd.

KNOCKING ON THE CAPITOL'S DOOR

With a Farm Bill pending, the artists wanted to take their message to the policymakers, so Farm Aids 1999 and 2000 took place in Bristow, Virginia, in the shadow of Washington, D.C. At Farm Aid '99, on September 12, Willie Nelson said, "Having this event so close to Washington will help bring our message from the countryside right to the Congressmen on Capitol Hill."

Susan Tedeschi and Trisha Yearwood made their Farm Aid debuts at the September 1999 concert. Barenaked Ladies did their "Farm Aid Rap." Progressive blues singer Keb' Mo' showed up, as did Steve Earle and the Dukes, who ripped through the rural American anthem "The Rain Came Down," as well as "Hard Core Troubadour" and "Copperhead Road."

The success of the 1999 concert set the stage for an encore visit in 2000. On September 17, 2000, music history took place at Farm Aid when Tipper Gore, wife of Vice President Al Gore, sat in on congas with Nelson for "Whiskey River." It was Gore's third live musical appearance since high school, when she performed in an all-girl band called the Wildcats. Into politics even back then, Gore, with the Wildcats, had written a song called "Barry's Boys," about 1964 Republican presidential candidate Barry Goldwater. "I must be getting more normal," Arlo Guthrie quipped to backstage reporters. "Thirty years ago, they wouldn't let me within five miles of the vice president's wife, and now she walks right past me." Other notable Farm Aid 2000 performers included the North Mississippi Allstars, Travis Tritt, Alan Jackson, and, once again, Barenaked Ladies. Crosby, Stills, Nash and Young tore into a greatest-hits set that included "Marrakesh Express" and "Our House."

Trey Anastasio of Phish and Neil Young, 1998, Tinley Park, Illinois

RETURN TO INDIANA

The most heartrending Farm Aid concert since the 1990 Indianapolis show was Farm Aid 2001, held September 29, in Noblesville, Indiana, outside of Indianapolis. The concert took place eighteen days after the terrorist attacks of 9/11. Many people feared Farm Aid would be called off. The artists wouldn't think of it. In fact, Farm Aid felt compelled to offer "A Concert for America," holding up family farmers as a resource for the nation. "Farmers are always among the first to reach down, to dig deep to do whatever they can, to help a neighbor in need," Nelson said. "When a farmer becomes ill, the community mobilizes to help the harvest. When a barn burns down, neighbors gather to raise a new one. American farmers know how to respond to adversity and devastation. They know how to maintain enough hope to plant seeds in the ground and keep going."

Arlo Guthrie helped begin the day's proceedings with a tender, stripped-down version of his father's "This Land Is Your Land." His empathetic choir included John Mellencamp, Dave Matthews, Neil Young, and Martina McBride. Susan Tedeschi contributed saucy guest vocals to Willie Nelson's

Wilco, 1998: Jay Bennett, LeRoy Bach, Jeff Tweedy, John Stirratt (from left)

"Crazy." Young later performed a relentless eight-minute version of "Rockin' in the Free World," Mellencamp offered a passionate take on "Peaceful World," and McBride sang "Love's the Only House." McBride grew up on a Kansas wheat farm, and Farm Aid 2001 was her fourth Farm Aid appearance. Before closing with "Independence Day," she told the sold-out crowd of twenty-five thousand, "With everything that's been going on in this country, I feel for the first time in my life what it really means to be an American. I'm proud of the way we're standing together and helping each other through this incredibly difficult time, and I'm proud of you for coming out today and helping our farmers, because they are the heart of America." The lawn beyond the seats was a waving sea of red, white, and blue. The day was full of healing.

One tall figure stood offstage. Wearing a creased blue denim shirt accented by gray hair and a tired face, he could have passed for a farmer. He was on his first day off since September 11. He was Harold Schaitberger, president of the International Association of Fire Fighters (IAFF), which had lost hundreds of its members in the 9/11 attacks. Farm Aid invited Schaitberger so the nation could honor all those who died, and some concert funds helped restore the farmers market destroyed at the World Trade Center. Farm Aid remained grounded in the spirit of hope and resilience it had nurtured since 1985.

DOWN HOME IN PENNSYLVANIA

Farm Aid came to Pennsylvania for the first time on September 21, 2002, when the concert was held in rural Burgettstown, outside of Pittsburgh. Pennsylvania is known for its commitment to sustainable agriculture, and since 1989, when the Pennsylvania Farmland Preservation Program was created, the state has protected more than 1,958 farms, totaling nearly 240,000 acres. That's more farms and more acres preserved than any other state in America. The Pennsylvania concert sold out within forty-eight hours of going on sale. The extraordinary show included Latin showmen Los Lonely Boys (two years before they broke big), roots rockers the Drive-by Truckers, and rising country stars Keith Urban and Lee Ann Womack. Blues artist Kenny Wayne Shepherd performed with Double Trouble (which had been Stevie Ray Vaughan's band), and country hitmaker Toby Keith did "Angry American (Red, White and Blue)." Kid Rock won over the Keystone State with "Cowboy" and "Bawitdaba," and Americana artist Gillian Welch joined John Mellencamp at the microphone.

Opposite: Los Lonely Boys' Henry, JoJo, and Ringo Garza (from left), 2003. Above: Sheryl Crow, 2003, Columbus, Ohio

Emmylou Harris, 2003, Columbus, Ohio

OHIO

On September 7, 2003, Farm Aid landed in suburban Columbus, Ohio. More than twenty thousand fans filled the sold-out Germain Amphitheater to hear Brooks & Dunn kick ass through "How Long Gone" and "Only in America." Sheryl Crow made her Farm Aid debut singing "Steve McQueen." Los Lonely Boys returned, as did Harris (for the first time since 1986), who sang a moving solo version of Townes Van Zandt's "Pancho and Lefty" and collaborated on some songs with Daniel Lanois.

SEATTLE SERENADE

For the first time in its history, Farm Aid headed west on September 18, 2004, when the event took place at the White River Amphitheater on the Muckleshoot Indian Reservation near Auburn, Washington, outside of Seattle. Dave Matthews, a Seattle resident, served as unofficial host. "Seattle is a perfect example of how a city might embrace the philosophy of healthy food, from the farm to the table," Matthews said. Playing solo acoustic, Matthews sang "Gravedigger" and an equally chilling cover of Bob Dylan and Jacques Levy's "Oh, Sister." Lucinda Williams made her Farm Aid debut with a country-shaded set that included "Drunken Angel." Her honky-tonk version of "Joy" included Steve Earle on guitar and Nelson band mate Mickey Raphael on harmonica.

Jerry Lee Lewis also graced the Farm Aid stage for the first time, tearing through his classics "Whole Lotta Shakin' Goin' On" and "Great Balls of Fire," as well as a stark version of Hank Williams's "You Win Again." Lewis's appearance made a whole lotta sense: Lewis and his father were farmers who sold thirty dozen eggs to raise the money to get to Memphis to meet Sam Phillips at Sun Records, where Lewis made his first recordings and found fame. It was the first time many of the younger audience members had ever heard of—not to mention had enough luck to actually hear—the legendary showman.

There are still more songs to be sung, and no doubt Farm Aid's heirloom artists—along with a new crop of dedicated performers—will rise to the challenge. 🚜

Steve Earle, bassist Taras Prodaniuk, and Lucinda Williams (from left), 2004, outside Seattle, Washington

Farm Aid Live!

Dwight Yoakam, 1993

Jewel, 1996

John Mellencamp and Gillian Welch, 2002

Daniel Lanois, 2003

Shelby Lynne, 1996

Dave Matthews, 1997

Jackson Browne, 1990

Keb'Mo', 1999

Keith Urban, 2002

Trick Pony's Heidi Newfield and Nelson, 2003

Elton John, 1990

Drive-by Truckers, 2002

Wisdom Indian dancer and Neil Young, 2003

Pat Green, 2000

Sheryl Crow, 2003

Andy York, John Mellencamp, and Mike Wanchic, 2003

Joni Mitchell, 1985

Jeff Tweedy of Wilco, 1998

Don Henley, 1990

Toby Keith, 2002

Taj Mahal, 1990

Young and Nelson, 1997

A Fond Farewell:
A Tribute to Late Farm Aid Artists

Dave Hoekstra

Farm Aid audiences have been fortunate to witness once-in-a-lifetime performances from some of the legends of rock, country, R&B, folk, and pop. Sadly, some of the greats have passed on since appearing at Farm Aid, including Rick James (who was in the 1960s band the Mynah Birds with Neil Young), Townes Van Zandt, June Carter Cash, Johnny Cash, Waylon Jennings, Roger Miller, Roy Orbison, Bill Monroe, blues mandolin player Yank Rachell, Doug Sahm, John Denver, Jerry Garcia (who appeared via satellite with Grateful Dead), Carl Perkins, Dottie West, Toy Caldwell, Eddie Rabbitt, Mickey Newbury, and Stevie Ray Vaughan. I was honored to meet and interview some of these artists during the past two decades; my remembrances of some of the late great follow.

Johnny Cash and June Carter Cash, 1985

JOHNNY CASH AND JUNE CARTER CASH

Like a tree in autumn, Johnny Cash cast a colorful tone over the early evening hours of the first Farm Aid. Cash was in good spirits because the Highwaymen were together again, making their second public appearance since Willie's Fourth of July picnic in Texas. The Farm Aid version of the Highwaymen featured Cash, Willie Nelson, Waylon Jennings, and Glen Campbell, the latter of whom was filling in for Kris Kristofferson, who left the show early to fly to Hawaii. Cash was in a playful mood, even though he didn't commit to the event until three days before the concert because his father was ill. Cash opened his solo set with a robust version of "Folsom Prison Blues" before he and June Carter Cash led the crowd in a parody of "Old MacDonald" that became a pointed attack of bank foreclosures on farms. Cash received a standing ovation. He was as real as manual labor.

Cash was born in a three-room railroad shack in Kingsland, Arkansas. His father, Ray Cash, was a farmer who, when unable to live off the land, worked on the railroad, picked cotton, and chopped wood. Under a New Deal program, the Cash family moved to a more fertile northeastern Arkansas farm in 1935, where Cash began work as a child on his dad's twenty-acre cotton farm. The family had cleared the land themselves. By the time he was fourteen, Johnny Cash was making $2.50 a day as a water boy for work gangs along the Tyronza River. He ate fatback and turnip greens between his shifts.

"The hard work on the farm is not anything I've ever missed," Cash said in an engaging 1987 talk at his stone-and-timber home in Hendersonville, Tennessee. "After I got in the business and life got to be on such a fast pace, I wrote songs about the farm life as I knew it. Songs like 'Pickin' Time,' 'Flesh and Blood,' and 'Five Feet High and Rising' were my way of reflecting on the quieter and more peaceful times. I was thinking about the country, the creeks, and the hills, and I think the country and farm influences come out pretty good in my songs. A lot of those things I sang and wrote about, I was seeing it through my daddy's eyes." Cash coughed and closed his eyes.

The room was quiet. Cash trailed off down a distant track and returned, "Like when we had to leave our farm when we were flooded out, and we had to get on a train to go to the hills. The railroad tracks were covered with water. Those experiences lasted, and I wrote songs about them later. I know what I'm talking about when I sing about hard work, but it's been a long time since I've had to work like that manually, of course."

Cash only appeared at one more Farm Aid, in April 1993, in Ames, Iowa. He reprised "Folsom Prison Blues" and joined the Highwaymen (this time with Kristofferson) for Jennings's "I've Always Been Crazy" and a tender version of Guy Clark's "Desperados Waiting for a Train."

Cash died of complications from diabetes in September 2003, just four months after his wife June passed away following heart surgery. At a November 2003 memorial tribute at the Ryman Auditorium in Nashville, John Mellencamp, Nelson, Kristofferson, and others bid adieu to their friend. With voice cracking, Kristofferson said, "He was a dark, dangerous force of nature, prowling like a panther." Wherever there is a family farm, you are sure to hear a song from Johnny Cash.

CARL PERKINS

The pastiche of musical influences that defines Farm Aid was a perfect setting for Carl Perkins. The rock & roll pioneer appeared at one Farm Aid, the 1990 concert held before forty-five thousand people at the Hoosier Dome in Indianapolis. Perkins found himself singing "Matchbox" and "Blue Suede Shoes"

Carl Perkins, 1990

sandwiched between Elton John and Lou Reed.

During the mid-1950s, Perkins was a key player in blending country, rhythm & blues, and primitive rock & roll to create rockabilly music. He was raised in the only white share-cropping family on a plantation near Jackson, Tennessee. His first guitar was made from a cigar box and a broomstick. After World War II, his family relocated to Bemis, Tennessee, where his uncles labored in cotton mills. "I grew up working with black people in the fields," he said in 1989. "In the afternoons, the hot sun would beam down and they'd start singing. I loved the rhythms they sang and old gospel, too. When I started playing, I mixed that black rhythm with the country songs I heard on the radio."

In 1987, Perkins said, "My kind of blues is [country] kicked up into overdrive. If you slow down the guitar break on 'Blue Suede Shoes,' you hear old Muddy Waters. It's just speeded-up blues. It's a white man's lyric set to a black man's music." Perkins wrote and recorded "Blue Suede Shoes" in 1956 for Sun Records in Memphis. His version sold two million copies

before Elvis Presley made it an even bigger hit. Perkins said in a 1985 interview that his biggest thrill was getting a gold record for "Blue Suede Shoes": "After all those days in the cotton fields, the dreams came true on a gold record on a piece of wood."

During the 1960s, Perkins was befriended by the Beatles, who popularized his songs "Matchbox," "Honey Don't," and "Everybody's Trying to Be My Baby." Between 1965 and 1975, Perkins worked as the road guitarist for Johnny Cash, who also featured him doing a couple of solo songs during the show. In 1969, Perkins wrote "Daddy Sang Bass," which became a hit for Cash.

A year after his Farm Aid appearance, Perkins was diagnosed with throat cancer. He often termed his subsequent comeback from cancer as "a miracle." Perkins died in January 1998 from complications related to a series of strokes. His funeral in Jackson drew the likes of Jerry Lee Lewis, Sun Records founder Sam Phillips, and Memphis soul legend Rufus Thomas. George Harrison led a small choir that included Wynonna Judd and Ricky Skaggs in a rousing gospel-tinged version of Perkins's "Your True Love." Carl Perkins truly maintained a farmer's spirit. With a lifetime of lofty successes, he always kept his shoes close to the ground.

ROY ORBISON

You couldn't tell for sure where Roy Orbison was looking when he sang his 1961 hit "Crying" at the first Farm Aid. He wore his trademark black Ray-Bans, even though it had been raining all day. But you could hear a cool September breeze roll across the seventy-eight thousand fans who had filled Memorial Stadium. The audience was spellbound by Orbison's three-octave range. Orbison also

rocked out with "I Got a Woman" and "Oh, Pretty Woman," leaving a tough act for blues legend B.B. King to follow.

Orbison always found the sunlight in a song. A humble native of Vernon, Texas, Orbison grew up in Wink, where he learned guitar from his father, who worked in the oil fields. Orbison picked cotton to pay for his first guitar. He claimed "You Are My Sunshine" as the first song he learned. The first Farm Aid concert set the template for Orbison's role in the Traveling Wilburys; future Wilburys Bob Dylan and Tom Petty were also on the bill. The idea for the Wilburys was

formalized early in 1988 when Orbison was working on the *Mystery Girl* album sessions with other Wilburys George Harrison and Jeff Lynne.

Sadly, Orbison died of a heart attack in December 1988 while visiting his mother in Hendersonville, Tennessee. He was fifty-two. The Traveling Wilburys had recorded one album. (Future endeavors were dedicated to "Lefty Wilbury.")

Orbison knew he wanted to play guitar as early as six years old because the chords resonated in the open Texas fields. "The soldier boys would come by—usually they were

Roy Orbison photographed shortly before his death in 1988

uncles and cousins of mine—and they always wound up playing music at night," Orbison said. "The atmosphere was supercharged because all the boys were going off to one theater of war or the other [through nearby Fort Worth], and they didn't know if they'd ever be back. So they ate, drank, and made merry. I was very aware of the situation. You didn't just sing a song just for the hell of it. You really sang a song because those were the times." By his late teens, Orbison was touring Texas with his own band, the Wink Westerners.

Orbison's sense of conviction made him accessible to younger artists, as well as peer groups. Linda Ronstadt had a hit with Orbison's rustic "Blue Bayou," and Creedence Clearwater Revival updated Orbison's "Ooby Dooby." Bruce Springsteen name-checked Orbison in "Thunder Road." Farm Aid was fortunate that Orbison chose its path in 1985. Roy Orbison really sang his songs, because he knew those were the times.

WAYLON JENNINGS

Original Outlaw Waylon Jennings appeared at three Farm Aids, twice as a member of the Highwaymen. At the first Farm Aid, he strolled onstage in his creased black cowboy hat, silver belt, and black boots to play hard lead guitar for Johnny Cash.

When Jennings arrived in Nashville in 1966, he moved in with Cash, who had just separated from his first wife. As Cash launched into "Folsom Prison Blues," he dealt a joker's smile and looked at Jennings as if the old dog had just moved in again. Jennings also played a short solo set that day, which included his evocative take on the J.J. Cale ballad "Clyde."

Willie Nelson said, "Waylon was always there for us, he would be one of the first peo-

Waylon Jennings, 1985

ple we would call." In 1978, Waylon and Willie had a major crossover hit with "Mamas Don't Let Your Babies Grow Up to Be Cowboys." Before the first Farm Aid, Jennings told reporters, "Farmers need to know that someone cares about them. I need to be there."

Jennings was born in the black-dirt back roads of Littlefield, Texas. His father was a farm laborer. In his 1996 autobiography (written with Lenny Kaye), *Waylon,* Jennings wrote, "We grew cotton and maize on the patch of land we worked. When Daddy got back from a day in the fields, he had to milk about twenty head of cattle. On hog-killing day, we'd get out the ice cream freezer and break open watermelons. Yellow meat watermelons. They'd weigh fifty or sixty pounds, and nothing tasted closer to heaven."

On the side, Jennings's father was also a truck driver and played guitar in a regional band. The Jennings family often didn't have enough money to make ends meet. Their

home had a dirt floor. Jennings left school in tenth grade (it wasn't until 1990 that he got his General Educational Development certificate). Coming from that poverty, Jennings later became concerned about hunger and the food for the world's future. In 1990, he became a spokesman for Feed the Children.

Jennings's last Farm Aid stand, which he played with the Highwaymen, was on April 24, 1993, in Ames. In his last years, Jennings was fond of talking about the genesis of his gospel ballad "I Do Believe," which appeared on 1995's *The Road Goes On Forever,* the final Highwaymen album. Jennings was on a tour bus in the middle of the night with author-preacher Will Campbell when Campbell quizzed him about spirituality. The song came out of those sessions down the highway. Jennings would always sing the song in his declarative tones that shook the earth: "In my own way, I'm a believer/But not in voices I can't hear/I believe in a loving father/One I never have to fear/That I should live life at its fullest/Just as long as I am here." Jennings died of complications from diabetes on February 13, 2002, at his home in Arizona. He was sixty-four. His full spirit will be around as long as Farm Aid rolls down America's highways.

BILL MONROE

While growing up on a farm in Rosine, Kentucky, Bill Monroe was so shy he used to hide behind a barn. But the Father of Bluegrass commanded the stage when he made his only Farm Aid appearance in April 1990 at Farm Aid IV. Fronting an acoustic quartet, Monroe hit all the high notes of Jimmie Rodgers's "Mule Skinner Blues (Blue Yodel #8)." Monroe had performed a rakish version of the tune during his 1939 debut at

Bill Monroe, 1990

the Grand Ole Opry. Monroe grew up the youngest of eight children. His crossed left eye, which embarrassed him, caused him to seek refuge when strangers visited the farm. He loved baseball but was unable to play because of his eye—until it was surgically corrected many years later. The Monroes had a musical household. His mother played accordion, fiddle, and harmonica; her brother Pendleton Vandiver (immortalized in Monroe's "Uncle Pen") played fiddle, and his brothers played guitar and fiddle. A $3 mandolin was the only instrument left for Monroe. He learned how to play it from Hubert Stringfield, a farmhand on the 360-acre Monroe homestead.

The audience at the Indianapolis Farm Aid was very fortunate to witness a performance by the man who invented bluegrass music. And Farm Aid IV was a Hoosier homecoming for Monroe. In 1932, Monroe and his brothers Birch and Charlie lived in East Chicago,

John Denver, 1985

Indiana, and performed as the Monroe Brothers. During the day, Bill Monroe loaded and washed barrels at the Sinclair Oil Refinery in East Chicago. On the weekends, the brothers would appear on Gary, Indiana, radio stations, or, when not working, listen to oldtimey Kentucky music on the popular WLS Barn Dance radio show.

Monroe died at age eighty-four in September 1996 at a hospice center outside Nashville. He had suffered a stroke earlier in the year that left him unable to speak. Six months after he died, Monroe was inducted into the Rock and Roll Hall of Fame.

JOHN DENVER

A galaxy of stars graced the stage at the first Farm Aid, but few performers went over as big as John Denver. Fronting the Nitty Gritty Dirt Band, the cherub-faced singer had seventy-eight thousand people on their feet singing along to his hit "Thank God I'm a Country Boy." In a segue that could only happen at Farm Aid, Sammy Hagar followed with "There's Only One Way to Rock."

"I first became in touch with the earth and aware of the seasons on the small family farm that my father was raised on," Denver said before the concert. "That's where the land— Mother Earth—started to mean something to me. There, I discovered a true sense of peace."

Denver was a true Farm Aid favorite. At 1987's Farm Aid III, in Lincoln, Nebraska, he sang the ballad "Let Us Begin (What Are We Making Weapons For?)." In 1985, Denver had been invited by the Soviet Union of Composers to perform in its country, and "Let Us Begin" emerged from that rare visit. At 1990's Farm Aid IV, in Indianapolis, Denver led another sing-along, with "Rocky Mountain High." According to Willie Nelson, "John always volunteered. We ran into each other in Vegas or Reno. We were jogging together when he said he would be interested in doing the first Farm Aid."

Born Henry John Deutschendorf Jr. in Roswell, New Mexico, Denver devoted much of his life to social change. He was asked to serve as a member of the Presidential Commission on World and Domestic Hunger and was one of the five founders of The Hunger Project. He founded Plant-It 2020, an environmental foundation that urges people all over the world to plant as many indigenous trees as possible. Nearly one million indigenous trees have been planted since the foundation was started in 1992.

Denver was killed in an October 12, 1997, plane crash when his small aircraft plunged into Monterey Bay, near Salinas, California. He was fifty-three.

DOUG SAHM

Douglas Wayne Sahm was a cowboy at heart. Wearing his black cowboy hat, dark shades, and permanent smile, Sahm led his posse of Texas Tornados (Freddy Fender, Flaco Jimenez, Augie Meyers) to Irving, Texas, for Farm Aid V and to Columbia, South Carolina, for Farm Aid

Doug Sahm, 1992

81

'96. The band's '96 Farm Aid swan song was memorable, as the Tornados stormed through "Who Were You Thinking Of," "Little Bit Is Better Than Nada" (their left-field dance hit), and the polka-based "(Hey Baby) Qué Pasó."

Sahm was born in San Antonio, Texas, and was playing steel guitar by the age of six. He would get duded up in a cowboy suit and sit in with Webb Pierce, Hank Thompson, and other outfits who came through town. During his preteen years, Sahm absorbed the rhythm & blues of Hank Ballard and Bobby "Blue" Bland, who sang at the Eastwood Country Club, across the plowed fields from his house. Willie Nelson knew Sahm through all his musical "lifetimes": Sahm's 1960s pop group the Sir Douglas Quintet; Doug Sahm and Band (the 1973 ensemble that included cameos from Bob Dylan and Dr. John); and the Tornados. Sahm was in the studio band on Nelson's 1972 album *Shotgun Willie,* and the Tornados and Willie performed together at President Bill Clinton's 1992 inauguration. Sahm was a creative free spirit who found a natural setting within the eclectic Farm Aid lineups. He once said, "I'm a part of Willie Nelson's world and at the same time I'm a part of the Grateful Dead's world. I don't ever stay in one bag."

At fifty-eight, Sahm died of a heart attack on November 18, 1999, while vacationing in Taos, New Mexico. If there's one thing Sahm loved more than music and baseball, it was the open spaces that symbolize the dreams of American family farmers. He saw possibilities reaching across plowed fields and marigold meadows. "I'm more comfortable on the road," he said. "I get in the car and drive in the desert under a full moon . . . and I'm cruising into the great beyond. I'm the happiest cat in the world."

STEVIE RAY VAUGHAN

Stevie Ray Vaughan performed at Farm Aid II in 1986 in Texas with a set including an up-tempo version of Willie Dixon's "You'll Be Mine," along with Vaughan's first hit, 1983's "Love Struck Baby." It was to be Vaughan's only Farm Aid appearance, but the independent Lone Star spirit of that Fourth of July show remains a Farm Aid template.

A Dallas native, Vaughan moved to Austin in 1970 at the age of sixteen to pursue a music career. The music scene in Austin was wide open due to the presence of the Armadillo World Headquarters, a nightclub located in an old National Guard armory building. There, artists took the stage devoid of any musical boundaries. Vaughan played the Armadillo, and so did Willie Nelson, who was the ambassador of Austin music during the 1970s. The club booked Frank Zappa and Bruce Springsteen but also Waylon Jennings and Commander Cody. The Armadillo bridged the gap between Texas rock & rollers and traditional country music fans—just as Farm Aid would do. The Armadillo's mix-it-up became the model for the popular PBS program *Austin City Limits.* Willie Nelson did the pilot for *Austin City Limits* in 1974, and since then, the show has featured Vaughan, Dave Matthews, Steve Earle, Nanci Griffith, Roy Orbison, Lucinda Williams, and B.B. King—all of whom have appeared at Farm Aid.

In spirit, Farm Aid '86 was an Armadillo redux. The diverse performances included the late Rick James singing "Super Freak," Judy Collins's tender version of Ian Tyson's "Someday Soon," War playing its hit "Low Rider," and Armadillo regular Jerry Jeff Walker singing "Mr. Bojangles."

On August 26, 1990, Vaughan and Double Trouble appeared with Buddy Guy, Eric Clapton, and others at the Alpine Valley Music Theatre in East Troy, Wisconsin. The show's final encore was a twenty-minute version of "Sweet Home Chicago." After the encore, Vaughan and three members of Clapton's entourage boarded a helicopter for Chicago. Just after midnight on August 27, 1990, Vaughan, the pilot, and Clapton's group were all killed when the helicopter crashed into a ski slope, blanketed by fog. Vaughan was thirty-five. He's been gone for fifteen years now, but Vaughan's freewheeling Texas style will always be a part of the Farm Aid motif.

ROGER MILLER

Anyone traveling Old Route 66 through Oklahoma will run into the friendly legacy of Roger Miller. The prolific singer/songwriter and Farm Aid comrade was from Erick, Oklahoma (pop. 1,053), about thirty miles east of Amarillo, Texas. Route 66 cuts through downtown Erick at what is now the intersection of Roger Miller and Sheb Wooley Boulevards. Entertainer Wooley married Miller's cousin. The town was that small.

Miller was born in 1936 in Fort Worth, Texas. His father died at the age of twenty-six from spinal meningitis when Roger was a year old. He was sent to Erick to live with an uncle. Miller grew up in the cotton fields and worked on the land. Wooley, of "The Purple People Eater" fame, once said, "It's a good thing that he made it in the music business 'cause he would have starved to death as a farmer."

Miller went on to write some of the most unique songs in country music history, like "King of the Road," "Dang Me," "Chug-a-Lug," and "The Last Word in Lonesome Is Me." His appointed, witty style is the proto-type for contemporary masters like John Prine and Pat McLaughlin. In 1995, Merle Haggard said, "I was closer to Roger Miller more than anyone else in this business. I met him at the Blackboard [nightclub] in Bakersfield, California, in 1962. He walked in and sang 'Summertime.' I was playing bass in a band. It was about five days and five nights before we said goodbye."

Miller appeared at the first and second Farm Aids. He called the first Farm Aid his emergence from a "fallow period," after having spent time away from the music business, in Santa Fe, New Mexico, with his wife, Mary, and their son, Dean. At the second Farm Aid, in Austin, he went outside the box to cover George and Ira Gershwin's "Summertime" and "Big River" from his Tony-winning Broadway musical. Miller's rural conviction was firmly rooted. Erick is a farm community where people grow peanuts, cotton, and wheat.

In 1981, Miller's old Nashville running buddy Willie Nelson asked Miller if he wanted to record a duet album. Miller said, "Well, Will, you've done a duet with about everyone."

Nelson replied, "I know, but we're down to the M's." Miller agreed, and they sang a song Miller wrote about his Oklahoma roots. It was called "Old Friends," and Ray Price sat in on the session. Miller and Nelson also sang "Old Friends" together at the first Farm Aid. "I'm a farm boy from Oklahoma," Miller said before the concert. "We musicians don't have all the answers to the farm problem. We're just trying to bring attention to it."

Miller died of throat cancer on October 25, 1992. His son, Dean Miller, performed at Farm Aids '97 and '98. 🚜

Farming in
American History
and Culture

The Legacy of Our Land

Mark Ritchie

North America has always enjoyed an abundance of food. For tens of thousands of years, people have hunted, fished, gathered, harvested crops, and raised animals to feed, clothe, transport, and care for themselves and their families. Blessed with rain, sun, rich soils, and abundant native plants and animals, this continent has largely been spared from the ravages of famine that so many others have suffered.

In the 1400s and 1500s, early explorers of North America described in exquisite detail the continent's beauty and bounty, and the skill of its indigenous people in making use of its natural resources. In the 1600s and 1700s, when Europeans moved from exploration to full-scale colonization, the issue of control over this plentiful land sometimes caused bloody conflicts between indigenous people and the newcomers.

Most Europeans brought with them a belief system centered on the principle of private ownership of property. Indeed, the new immigrants saw the prospect of owning a small parcel of land in this bountiful "new world" as a ticket to freedom and a path to fulfilling life's basic needs.

For most indigenous people, however, their life experience and cultural history led them to believe that careful tending of the natural resources—"the commons"—and collective attention to the provision of food, shelter and clothing were key to their freedom and well-being.

From the earliest settlements of European immigrants on the Atlantic Coast through the westward expansion to the Pacific, American economic and agricultural development, based on the principle of private ownership of

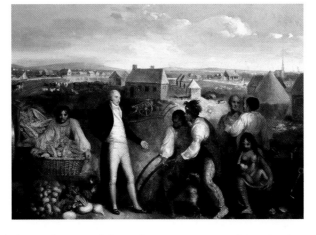

land, went hand in hand with the massive appropriation of lands inhabited by indigenous people. The forced removal of the indigenous from their ancestral lands often brought death and destruction through disease, poverty, and violent conflicts.

At the same time that indigenous people were removed to open the land for agriculture, Africans were enslaved to provide forced labor for the plantation system that dominated the South. When slavery came to an end in the 1860s, newly freed slaves demanded forty acres and a mule—their own land and the ability to turn the land into the food, fuel, and clothing they needed to survive. To them, the link between the land and freedom was clear.

As a nation, we still struggle to overcome these contradictions of our founding, finding ways to combine the best from all traditions and cultures.

As stewards of the land, indigenous people and family farmers with ancestors from Europe, Africa, Asia, and Latin America inherit the duty to care for the land and the natural resources that are the commons. They embody the nation's founding ideal that both the protection of the commons and the widespread ownership of small parcels of land by many individual owners are the best ways to nurture productivity and democracy. 🚜

Opposite: A Dorothea Lange photograph for the Farm Security Administration of a Utah farm family in the orchard during peach harvest time, 1938. Above: "Benjamin Hawkins and the Creek Indians," unidentified artist, circa 1805; oil on canvas, 35⅞ x 49⅞ inches; Greenville County Museum of Art, Greenville, South Carolina, gift of the Museum Association, Inc. Overleaf: A family farm, Wetzel County, West Virginia

"Cultivators of the Earth are the most valuable citizens. They are the most vigorous, the most independent, the most virtuous, and they are tied to their country and wedded to its liberty and interests by the most lasting bands."

—THOMAS JEFFERSON

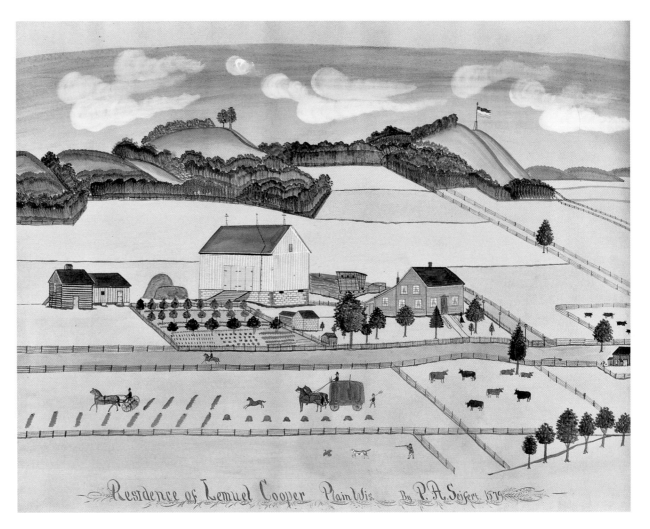

Right: "The Residence of Lemuel Cooper," Paul A. Seifert (1840–1921), Plain, Sauk County, Wisconsin, 1879; watercolor, oil, tempura, ink, and pencil on paper, 21⅞ x 28 inches; Collection American Folk Art Museum, New York. Opposite: "Sarah Ann Garges Appliqué Bedcover," Sarah Ann Garges (c. 1834–c. 1887), Doylestown, Bucks County, Pennsylvania, 1853; cotton, silk, wool, and wool embroidery, with muslin backing, 98 x 98 inches; Collection American Folk Art Museum, New York.

Residence of Lemuel Cooper Plain Wis. By P. A. Seifert 1879

"The glory of the farmer is that, in the division of labors, it is his part to create. All trade rests at last on his primitive activity. He stands close to Nature; he obtains from the earth the bread and the meat. The food which was not, he causes to be."

—RALPH WALDO EMERSON

"Let us never forget that the cultivation of the earth is the most important labor of man. When tillage begins, other arts follow. The farmers, therefore, are the founders of civilization."

—DANIEL WEBSTER

"GIVE ME THE SPLENDID SILENT SUN"
[excerpt]
Walt Whitman

Give me the splendid silent sun
with all his beams full-dazzling,
Give me juicy autumnal fruit ripe and red from the orchard,
Give me a field where the unmow'd grass grows,
Give me an arbor, give me the trellis'd grape,
Give me fresh corn and wheat, give me serene-moving
   animals teaching content . . .

   —FROM *LEAVES OF GRASS*

Farm Aid Backstage  Merle Haggard

The American spirit of Merle Haggard rose from the ashes of a family farm. His parents, James and Flossie Haggard, were farmers who lost everything in a 1933 fire in eastern Oklahoma. The blaze destroyed their barn, their new Model-A Ford, cows, horses, and feed and seed grains. To compound the crisis, a drought scorched the Oklahoma plains the next year and the Haggards made no money from crops.

"In those days, insurance wasn't around," said Haggard, "so they decided to go to California in 1935 to see if it was actually 'the Promised Land.' They told me about the trip. [Haggard was born in April 1937.] They said it took seven days to go from [Checotah,] Oklahoma [south of Muskogee] to Oildale [California, near Bakersfield]. They had been there in 1927, I believe, and the roads weren't even blacktopped. Sometimes the sand would blow across and you'd lose the road altogether. In 1935, my dad drove a 1926 Chevy, and they had everything they owned in the cargo trailer. There was a guy with a bicycle climbing a long hill. My family had stopped for water. My dad said, 'Hey, throw that bicycle on top of the trailer.' And the guy hung on the side of the car on a running board. Dad took him up that hill. And after he got up the hill, the guy got on the bike and rode along the back while holding on to the trailer. He pulled him nearly all the way to California." Of course the Haggards would lend a helping hand. They were farmers.

Flossie Haggard brought along an Empire box camera she used to document the journey. Merle Haggard held on to her snapshots of the Chevy, cargo trailer, and scenes from the new Route 66. She also kept a diary in which she wrote, "We packed canned meats and fruits, also filled a fifty-pound lard can with cured bacon, and loaded a two-wheel trailer with a bit of bedding, my faithful Singer sewing machine, some pots and skillets, and headed West." Flossie Haggard's beloved camera, handwritten diary, and sewing machine are now part of the permanent collection at the Smithsonian National Museum of American History, in Washington, D.C.

Once the Haggard family arrived in Oildale, they moved into an abandoned refrigerated railroad boxcar. James Haggard remodeled the boxcar into a home, adding windows and indoor plumbing. Flossie planted flowers in the front yard. The entire family of four (Flossie, James, and Merle's older siblings, Lillian and Lowell) found temporary work on a dairy—milking by hand forty Holstein cows. They were paid $50 a month. After two months, James Haggard was hired as a car carpenter for the Santa Fe Railroad, which led to Merle's lifelong passion for trains. "My family was fortunate," Haggard said. "They didn't come to California for the same reason as others. They had a fire and got wiped out. They were doing all right in Oklahoma, as hard as the times were."

Merle spent his teenage years on farms in the unforgiving orchards near Bakersfield. In her 1968 collection *Slouching Towards Bethlehem*, Joan Didion described the white-line fever that runs from Bakersfield to Sacramento. She wrote, ". . . U.S. 99 passes through the richest and most intensely cultivated agricultural region in the world, a giant outdoor hothouse with a billion-dollar crop." Haggard quit school, got married, and found work in that hothouse. "I was eighteen, nineteen years old," he recalled in 2005. "I picked cotton, I picked peaches, I picked strawberries. Strawberries are the worst of all, getting on your hands and knees and crawling around. You squeeze them and they fall apart before you get them to the bag."

These roots are embedded in Haggard's soul. In 2001, Haggard and his fifth wife, Theresa, sold Merle Haggard–brand oranges to the military from a citrus ranch they ran in Porterville, California. Haggard appeared at the first Farm Aid in 1985. He had planned a weeklong fifteen-car Amtrak train trip from Bakersfield to Champaign, Illinois, where the concert was held. At a press conference announcing the journey, Haggard declared, "There's nothing America can't do. We've [shown that] in the past. We walked on the moon. It seems we can figure out this [farm] problem." However, insurance costs derailed Haggard's train plans. But "Farm Aid Express" did transport farmers, politicians, and activists from Carroll, Iowa, to Champaign, Illinois. That train was sponsored by the *Des Moines Register* and donated by the Chicago and North Western Railway.

Haggard also wrote the ballad "Amber Waves of Grain," which he sang at the first Farm Aid concert: "If the amber waves of grain should disappear/And there were no wheat and barley anywhere/Would we buy our bread and butter from the Toyota man?/Would an Idaho spud be stamped MADE IN JAPAN?"

Haggard will never forget his Farm Aid experience. "I loved being around people I admired and rubbing shoulders with all my heroes," he said in 2005. "I watched everybody perform. Plus Willie is just a neat guy to be around. I love him. I've been his brother since the early 1960s. Farm Aid is like a family reunion on Thanksgiving Day."

Before the first Farm Aid, in 1985, Haggard told reporters it was necessary to look inward as never before. In 2005, Haggard suggested the importance of taking an even deeper look. He said, "We are at a serious pivot point in our stage of history. There's going to be some drastic changes in weather. Ice is going to melt, oceans are going to rise. [This is] not going to happen over a period of thousands of years, like we thought. We are at the end of the curb on oil resources, everybody is fighting for what is best. There are ways to save the planet—if there's time left."

—DAVE HOEKSTRA

"THIS LAND IS YOUR LAND"

Woody Guthrie

This land is your land, this land is my land,
From California to the New York island;
From the redwood forest to the Gulf Stream waters:
This land was made for you and me.

As I was walking a ribbon of highway,
I saw above me that endless skyway:
I saw below me that golden valley:
This land was made for you and me.

I've roamed and rambled and I followed my footsteps
To the sparkling sands of her diamond deserts;
And all around me a voice was sounding:
This land was made for you and me.

When the sun came shining, and I was strolling,
And the wheat fields waving and the dust clouds rolling,
As the fog was lifting a voice come chanting:
This land was made for you and me.

As I went walking, I saw a sign there,
And on the sign it said "No Trespassing."
But on the other side it didn't say nothing,
That side was made for you and me.

In the shadow of the steeple I saw my people,
By the relief office I seen my people;
As they stood there hungry, I stood there asking
Is this land made for you and me.

Nobody living can ever stop me,
As I go walking that freedom highway;
Nobody living can ever make me turn my back,
This land was made for you and me.

Opposite: Cattle graze in California. Above: Woody Guthrie (2nd from left) and his family: son Jody, wife Marjorie, daughter Nora, and son Arlo, 1960

"The Farm Aid concert is a wonderful thing because it gets the nation to stand up and say, 'We're behind you, farmers.' I've been part of Farm Aid consistently for years and years. Always proud to show up. I think my dad would approve, you know. He had a special affinity for people who were living on the land. His ancestors had been booted off essentially because of hard times or Wall Street—or sort of the convergence of Mother Nature and business together. So I've always had a special place in my heart for those families that wake up early in the morning and work all day."

—ARLO GUTHRIE, FARM AID ARTIST

"Farmers [need] to raise less corn and more hell!"

—KANSAS POPULIST MARY ELLEN LEASE, CA. 1890

The American Farmers' Experience: A Brief History

Howard Zinn

As an iconic figure, the American family farmer has, throughout our history, represented the heroic yeoman, tamer of the wild, and provider of our bounty. Less remembered are the struggles to hang on to the land, and the endless pursuit of economic justice in the heartland. The roots of family farmers' current battles against bad government policy, unfair lending practices of banks, and monopoly control by big corporations go back as far as the European conquest of the new continent.

Just a few years after the end of the American Revolution, in the counties of western Massachusetts, thousands of small farmers, burdened by high taxes and unable to pay their debts, faced the auctioning of their land, their livestock, their homes. The year was 1786, and many of them were veterans of the war against England. They took up guns, surrounded the courthouses, and refused to allow the auctions to take place. This became known as Shays' Rebellion, after one of their leaders, Daniel Shays, who had been a captain in the revolution.

There were pitched battles, and when the farmers laid siege to an arsenal in Springfield, Massachusetts, the militia used artillery against them, killing four and wounding twenty. But the rebels would not give up. They targeted the general they held responsible for what they called the "Springfield Massacre," burned his fences and woodlands, and mutilated two of his horses. They released debtors from prison and kidnapped prominent people. The bloodiest battle of the whole rebellion took place in early 1787, resulting in the deaths of thirty farmers and three soldiers. Shays' Rebellion was finally put down by an army sent from Boston. Several of the rebels were hanged, but Shays escaped to Vermont.

Similar protests and uprisings of beleaguered farmers took place in Maryland, New Jersey, Virginia, South Carolina, and Pennsylvania. When, in the summer of 1787, the delegates met in Philadelphia to draw up the Constitution, fear of rebellion was very much on their minds. James Madison said that Shays' Rebellion offered "new proofs of the necessity of such a vigor in the general government as will be able to restore health to any diseased part of the Federal body." The convention created a strong central government, one that could secure slave owners and large landowners against possible insurgency.

Still, in the decades after the revolution, tensions persisted between large landowners and poor farmers, leading to conflict. In the Hudson Valley of New York, a few families ruled like lords over enormous tracts of land; tenants and small farmers, oppressed by taxes and rents, organized anti-rent associations. In 1839, at a Fourth of July gathering, an orator, fresh from revolutionary agitation in Ireland, told the assembled farmers: "If you permit unprincipled and ambitious men to monopolize the soil, they will become masters of the country. . . ."

Twenty-five thousand small and tenant farmers signed a petition for an anti-rent bill, but the bill was defeated by the New York legislature in 1845. A kind of guerrilla warfare ensued, involving thousands of farmers. When a deputy sheriff tried to sell the livestock of a farmer who owed $60 rent on ten stony acres, there was a fight and the deputy was killed. Other attempts to take over livestock for rent payments were blocked, again and again. Soon almost a hundred anti-renters were in jail. Ultimately, the anti-rent movement was crushed, so the dissidents turned their attention to the voting booth and elected fourteen members to the state legislature. Proposals to break up huge estates following the death of the owners were defeated. But the legislature voted to make illegal the selling of tenant property for nonpayment of rent, and a constitutional convention outlawed new feudal leases.

Opposite: An Arthur Rothstein photograph of a Montana farm couple taken for the Farm Security Administration (FSA), May 1939. Above: A homesteader in Pie Town, New Mexico, photographed by Russell Lee for the FSA in 1940

Above: A Russell Lee photograph of a New Mexico homesteader named Mrs. Norris in her cabbage patch, taken for the FSA in October 1940. Opposite: Another Russell Lee FSA photograph of a Pie Town, New Mexico, farmer harvesting corn, 1940

The class of small landowners was thus enlarged, but the basic structure of rich landowners and poor farmers remained intact up to the Civil War and beyond. In 1862, in the midst of the Civil War, Congress passed the Homestead Act, which offered 160 acres of unoccupied and publicly owned land in the West to anyone who would cultivate it for five years. At $1.25 an acre, most people did not have the $200 necessary, so speculators moved in and bought up much of the fifty million acres of Homestead land.

During the Civil War years, the national government gave one hundred million acres of land to various railroads, free of charge. It was a dramatic example of government callousness to poor farmers and generosity to the rich. As for the newly freed slaves, their hopes for land came to naught; the dream of "forty acres and a mule," which they hoped would give reality to their freedom, died. They were now legally free but still bound to the land, often as tenants to the same plantation owners who had owned them as slaves.

In the decades after the Civil War, farmers suffered from high fees they had to pay to railroads and banks, and from uncertain weather conditions. In 1887, Texas farmers, facing a terrible drought, asked Congress to help them buy seed grain, and Congress appropriated $100,000. President Grover Cleveland, however, with a huge surplus in the treasury, vetoed the bill, saying, "Federal aid in such cases . . . encourages the expectation of paternal care on the part of the government and weakens the sturdiness of our national character." That same year, Cleveland used part of his surplus to pay off wealthy bondholders beyond the value of their bonds—a gift of $45 million.

Between 1860 and 1910, the U.S. Army, wiping out the Indian villages on the Great Plains, paved the way for the railroads to move in and take the best land. Then the farmers came for what was left. During that period, the population of the country doubled to seventy-five million, with twenty million people now living west of the Mississippi, and the number of farms grew from two million to six million.

Farming became increasingly mechanized—steel plows, mowing machines, reapers, harvesters, improved cotton gins, and then giant combines. In 1830, a bushel of wheat had taken three hours to grow. By 1900, it took ten minutes. But the new machines cost money. Farmers had to borrow, hoping the prices of their harvests would stay high, so they could pay the bank for the loan, the railroad for transportation, the grain merchant for handling their grain, and the storage elevator for storing it.

Two Iowa farmers during the 1985 farm crisis

rural communities. Soon Alliances spread all over the state and then all over the country. By 1897, there were four hundred thousand members in thousands of suballiances. By 1892, farmer lecturers had gone into forty-three states and reached two million farm families.

In 1890, the Alliances elected thirty-eight people to Congress and elected governors in Georgia and Texas. That year they met at a national convention in Kansas and formed the People's Party, or Populist Party. The great Populist orator from Kansas, Mary Ellen Lease, told the assemblage: "Wall Street owns the country. It is no longer a government of the people, by the people, and for the people, but a government of Wall Street, by Wall Street, and for Wall Street. . . . We want money, land, and transportation. . . . We want the accursed foreclosure system wiped out. . . . We will stand by our homes and stay by our firesides by force if necessary, and we will not pay our debts to the loan-shark companies until the government pays its debts to us."

The People's Party ran a presidential candidate in 1892, James Weaver, an Iowa Populist and former Union army general. But uniting the farmers' movement was not easy. In the South, there was a Colored Farmers National Alliance and a White Farmers National Alliance. There were moments of unity and solidarity, but white farmers owned land, while black farmers were mostly tenants or hired workers.

In the presidential election of 1896, the People's Party threw its support to the Democratic Party candidate, William Jennings Bryan, who promised farmers to go off the gold standard and thus make more money available. But Bryan was defeated by William McKinley. In the attempt to elect a sympathetic president, the Populist movement lost much of its independent spirit and its vitality. With McKinley, big business was firmly in power.

Farmers continued to struggle against great odds through the early twentieth century, and into the years of the Great Depression of the early thirties. In 1932, at the height of the economic crisis, there was a wave of foreclosures on small farms that could not pay their debts. In Oklahoma, with the soil turning dry as dust, farmers saw their land sold under the auctioneer's hammer. The great migration to California began, of hundreds of thousands, described so vividly in John Steinbeck's *The Grapes of Wrath*.

The election of Franklin D. Roosevelt in 1932 led to a barrage of legislation intended to stem the economic crisis and give some help to the poor and the unemployed. The New Deal farm legislation included passage of the

At the height of the national economic depression of 1877, white farmers in Texas, unable to pay their debts, were losing their farms to the merchants or banks who held their mortgages. They formed a Farmers Alliance—a populist political movement to address the needs of farmers and

Agriculture Adjustment Act in 1933. The new law gave the secretary of agriculture broad powers to raise prices and reduce production. Farmers received cash payments for cutting the acreage used to produce commodities, all financed by a tax levied on food processors. The goal of the legislation was to raise farm prices through cutting production.

Another cornerstone of the New Deal farm legislation was passage of the Commodity Credit Corporation (CCC) in 1933. Through the CCC, the government created a mechanism to guarantee a fair price for the farmer; if the price of a crop went above the value of the loan, the farmer sold it to buyers and pocketed the profit. However, if market price fell below the value of the loan, the farmer could sell his crop to the government at the value of the loan and thereby not go into debt. The government then sold the commodities at either a profit or a loss. Unfortunately, the loan rate was set too low over the years, thus diminishing the value of the program for family farmers. Roosevelt's New Deal legislation established farm policies that could have secured a floor price for family farmers akin to a minimum wage.

In 1935, the federal government established the Resettlement Administration to manage loans to distressed farmers. Two years later this was replaced by the Farm Security Administration (FSA) and a series of programs designed to help the poor farmer, lending money to buy land, setting up camps for migratory workers, and setting up a few experimental cooperative farms. The scale of such programs, however, was too small to deal with the immense problems of the nation's poorest farmers. The FSA was attacked by powerful lobbyists of the American Farm Bureau Federation, representing the affluent farmers, and by 1941, it had expired for lack of funds.

Ironically, it was the nation's entrance into World War II that saved many farm families. Their sons found employment in the armed forces, and although it was a bitter bargain for so many families that lost their sons, those who came back alive could get veterans' benefits. During the war, the lowered production of agricultural products had caused prices to rise, and farm mortgage debt declined.

With the end of the war, however, the fundamental problem of small farmers remained: the domination of the nation's agriculture by powerful commercial and banking interests intent on increasing profits and control. It was clear that those who till the soil would have to depend on their own resources, their own collective power.

In the decades that followed, the introduction of new farming technologies—improved seeds, synthetic fertilizers, and modern machinery—coupled with a deepening faith in scientific advancement, led to rapid increases in farm productivity. In the 1960s the so-called "Green Revolution," which purported to eliminate hunger by increasing food production with chemical fertilizers, pesticides, irrigation, and mechanization, sold the myth of ever-expanding yields without consequences. The "revolution" went hand in hand with America's industrial capitalism—maximize production and profits at all cost. By and large, American farmers bought the myth of the Green Revolution.

To keep up with the rapidly developing technologies and egged on by Nixon's Secretary of Agriculture Earl Butz to increase production, farmers took on more debt to buy new inputs and farm machinery. Without access to credit, however, small farmers could not compete, and many went under and sold out to their larger brethren. Farms grew larger and fewer, and more became locked into the industrial treadmill of more and more inputs to keep yields high. Greater production created surpluses of basic commodities, driving prices down. For many farmers, the sole way to keep up was to plant more, which only exacerbated the price problem. Ironically, even as large-scale monocrop agriculture—highly dependent on chemical inputs—produced record yields, hunger around the world, and social instability at home, grew.

The federal farm policies of the 1980s and 1990s chipped away at the regulatory controls of supply management and price stability of the New Deal legislation, leaving farmers at the mercy of the "free market," increasingly controlled by giant global corporations. The 1996 "Freedom to Farm Act" passed by Congress became quickly known among farmers as the "Freedom to Fail" bill, and many derided the bill as "the best farm bill corporate agribusiness could buy."

Tens of thousands of small and medium-sized farmers were forced off their land during the 1980s farm crisis. The "crisis" dragged on, producing persistent poverty throughout much of rural America. Once again, family farmers bore the brunt of misguided federal policies designed to serve the interests of large-scale agribusiness. Realizing the powerful interests controlling policy makers on Capitol Hill and at the statehouse, family farmers looked to themselves for survival. And it is family farmers who are at the forefront today, advocating and agitating for a new vision of American agriculture based on economic justice and environmental sustainability.

The Human Toll of a Chronic Farm Crisis

John Hansen, President, Nebraska Farmers Union

Twenty years ago, as family farmers and ranchers were being forced out of business and off their land, rural America needed help—lots of different kinds of help. Farmers and ranchers were beat up financially and beat down emotionally. They needed financial aid, advocacy, and moral support. Many people saw what was happening, felt bad about it, but shrugged their shoulders, and walked on by.

Rural America was becoming a poverty culture. The long-term, chronic lack of basic farm and ranch profitability began taking its human and economic toll on the infrastructure of both production agriculture and rural communities. As the economic viability of agriculture goes, so go most rural communities. Increasingly, rural and farm youth were heading toward hoped-for economic opportunities in cities. Schools, churches, and small-town Main Street businesses began to struggle with depopulation.

As rural populations began decreasing overall, the remaining population was increasing in age and poverty. Rising health-care and energy costs hit rural people disproportionately hard. While people loved their rural communities, they were becoming more depressed about their future.

Today, a drive through rural America shows abandoned farmsteads, livestock yards overgrown with weeds, rundown fences, and buildings in need of new shingles and paint. Many small towns are losing or have lost their hospitals, schools, drugstores, grocery stores, recreation programs, lumberyards, hardware stores, motels, and even their local diner. Rural poverty can be masked because of the hardworking, self-reliant nature of rural people. But if you know what to look for, it is all too easy to find—in fact, impossible to miss.

Twenty years ago, a few individuals saw the growing crisis in rural America, and instead of walking on by, they stood with America's family farmers and ranchers. They acknowledged they couldn't fix all that was wrong in rural America, but they knew that was no excuse for doing nothing. Thanks to the hard work, commitment, and dedication of Willie Nelson, Neil Young, and John Mellencamp, Farm Aid was born. Many hoped that Farm Aid would be a short-term effort to help bring healing and help to rural people in crisis, and the need for Farm Aid would go away.

At least one family farmer who attended that first concert knew better. He knew the problems that plagued rural America were long-term and would not quickly or easily go away. He knew the real test of the entertainers' commitment would be in the years to come when the problems did not vanish. He hoped the Farm Aid folks would stand with family farmers, ranchers, and the rural community for the long haul.

Twenty years ago, my father, Merle Hansen, made the long drive from our family farm in the hills of northeast Nebraska to Champaign, Illinois, to attend the first Farm Aid concert. My father knew that farm and ranch families were in crisis and they needed help. He knew that when your friends and neighbors are in need, you are under moral obligation to lend a helping hand. Farm Aid was, and still is, a helping hand. My father knew that unless farm policies were changed, agriculture markets would continue to get more concentrated, and less competitive, accessible, and fair. He knew that if our nation's food and fiber policy makers did not step in to provide more economic fairness, an ever-increasing number of farm and ranch families would continue to be driven off the land they loved. As someone who believed in the values and virtues of our traditional system of independent family farmer agriculture, my

Opposite and above: A 1986 farm protest in Chillicothe, Missouri

father wanted to do his part to support any and all efforts to heighten public awareness of the need for consumers and agriculture producers to work together to create a better future for families who farm and ranch.

My father rightly believed that the public policy battles over who grows our nation's food and fiber is about economic and social justice, responsible soil and water stewardship, and the kind of food production that is most consistent with our values as a democracy. My father realized the struggle over family farm agriculture is also the heart-and-soul battle over the culturally defining relationship between people and land that goes to the very core of our values as a society and a nation.

In the twenty years since Farm Aid was founded, the public-policy battles go on. The latest data on the concentration of agricultural markets from Dr. Mary Hendrickson and Dr. Bill Heffernan at the University of Missouri Department of Rural Sociology show that agriculture processors and retailers continue to increase their market-distorting concentration. Four companies now control 83.5 percent of all beef processing, 64 percent of pork processing, 56 percent of broiler processing, 51 percent of turkey processing, 63 percent of flour milling, and over 71 percent of soybean processing.

In the last twenty years, our nation's trade and farm policies have become increasingly controlled by the powerful agriculture-processing sector of the

Family farmers in Dodge County protest factory farming encroachment.

food economy, at the expense of family farmers and ranchers. The price the farmer can get for most crops goes down, while the processors' and retailers' share of the food dollar goes up.

In 2004, farm and ranch families earned 88 percent of their net income from off-farm jobs used to supplement their farm and ranch income. Farmers and ranchers pay what the mostly noncompetitive agriculture supply sector charges them for the inputs they need to produce their crops, and take what the mostly noncompetitive agricultural markets will pay them for their year's work. Farmers and ranchers as a sector, unlike the other players in the food economy, cannot pass along their higher operating costs to their customers. As a result, they continue to get squeezed off their farms and ranches.

Twenty years since the first Farm Aid, while farm and ranch families face many of the same challenges, there are some very promising and positive things happening. An increasing number of family farmers and ranchers are using direct marketing to consumers to earn more equitable incomes. Increasingly, farm and ranch families are growing and marketing their products in new ways. There has been a resurgence of farmer-owned cooperatives and a return to more sustainable and conservation-friendly production systems that use less energy.

Most important, urban consumers are learning what Europeans have known for a long time: It really does matter who you buy your food from. An increasing number of consumers want to know who grew their food and how it was grown, and they are willing to pay a fair price for food that tastes better and is safer. Consumers and family farmers and ranchers are beginning to work together to find a way around the conventional food system to their mutual advantage.

Twenty years later, I asked my father, now eighty-five years old and struggling with Parkinson's disease, what he thought about those first Farm Aid concerts and the Farm Aid folks. He looked up, smiled, and said, "They have done a world of good. They have stuck with us over the long haul." Then, always the farmer, always looking ahead, he said, "We still have a lot of work left to do."

Many thanks to all the folks involved in Farm Aid over the last twenty years. As my father likes to say, "You are good folks to ride the river with."

Children protest the foreclosure of their grandparents' farm in Gove, Kansas, ca. 1985

"Farm Aid is 365 days a year. As long as there are corporate hog farms and the rivers are being polluted, and there are so many chemicals in our food, we have a serious problem we need to work toward solving."

—DAVID AMRAM, FARM AID ARTIST

"Farmers have a tremendous impact on the quality of food that we eat. But it takes a lot of effort from the consumer to make that work. The consumer and the family farmer have to work together."

—JOHN MELLENCAMP

Born in a Small Town: John Mellencamp

Dave Hoekstra

Like gazing into a mirror, you can see your reflection in the still waters of Lake Monroe in central Indiana. You appear to stand alone. There is no valance of redwood trees, white pines, and blue mountains. This isn't fancy terrain, but it is true.

John Mellencamp will always be from these parts. Mellencamp's independent roots go back to a family of Dutch farmers who settled in Seymour, about forty-five miles south of the Lake Monroe residence that he shares with his wife Elaine Irwin and sons Hud, 11, and Speck, 10. Their home grows from the soul of a former village known as Paynetown. "On the other side of our driveway stands the foundation of the general store," Irwin said during a conversation in a metal barn where she explores photography and Mellencamp pursues painting.

The U.S. Army Corps of Engineers reconfigured the lake in 1960 as a reservoir to minimize flood damage from a dam about ten miles southeast of Bloomington. Lake Monroe became operational in 1965. It is Indiana's largest lake. "They flooded the town," Irwin said. "If you walk along the lake you see remnants of what used to be the town. There's an old garage. Old cars. We've kept them. They've grown over with vines. But this was a rural town. In the woods you find old fences and stumble across things that tie the story together for you."

The clues are more obvious in Mellencamp's life. Mellencamp is deeply rooted here. Driving up a gravel road from their house to the barn in a small John Deere Gator—the tiny tractor moving to a faithful beat—Mellencamp explains: "I come from a humble place, and it's important a person stays in that place and not become something else."

Mellencamp's recording studio is anchored in Belmont, fifteen miles from Lake Monroe. At the turn of the twentieth century, an art community

known as "The Hoosier Group" worked in Belmont. During spring some artists painted in the open air among the peonies, irises, and daffodils of the Indiana hills. "A famous impressionist painter named T.C. Steele [1847–1927] came out of there," Mellencamp said in his studio, awash with books of the works of Thomas Hart Benton, Max Beckmann, and Henri Matisse. "He believed there was something magical in [Belmont], that there was some sort of creative and psychic power. And it turned out I built my recording studio there." Irwin added, "There is a type of tree there that loses the needles, and when they rot they create this blue mist." Mellencamp laughed. "I was impressed with that, but then all my songs don't always make sense. Maybe I should have some more trees planted."

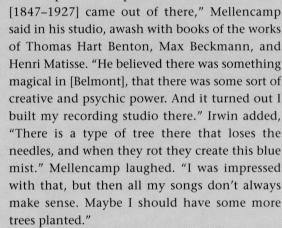

The 1941 Works Progress Administration (WPA) book *Indiana: A Guide to the Hoosier State* wrote of a roadside attraction outside of Belmont that was known as the "House of the Singing Winds" (admission: twenty-five cents), "named for the pleasant sound of the wind blowing through the evergreen trees near the house." This house was T.C. Steele's home.

A gentle Texas breeze brought Mellencamp into the Farm Aid family. Mellencamp wrapped up his 1985 album *Scarecrow* in Belmont at the same time Willie Nelson was organizing the first Farm Aid concert. *Scarecrow*, dedicated to his grandfather, Harry "Speck" Mellencamp, examined Mellencamp's rural roots and the hard times hitting those small towns. A feed

Opposite: Onstage at Farm Aid 1986, Austin, Texas. Above: John Mellencamp greets fans at a farmers protest in Chillicothe, Missouri, 1986.

John Mellencamp and Elaine Irwin outside their Indiana studio, 2005

mill had closed near Lake Monroe. The family farm of his great-grandfather John Mellencamp was sold after his sudden death. In the title track, "Rain on the Scarecrow," Mellencamp sang, "Scarecrow on a wooden cross, blackbird in the barn/Four hundred empty acres, that used to be my farm/I grew up like my daddy did, my grandpa cleared this land/When I was five I walked the fence, while Grandpa held my hand."

"Willie was out here playing golf," Mellencamp said as he sat hand-holding distance from Elaine. "He was with some guys I knew here in town. He was talking about the [first] concert, and one of the guys was a good friend of mine. He said, 'John Mellencamp made a record called *Scarecrow,* and in it is exactly what you're talking about.' They played nine holes, and Willie called me from the clubhouse, I think. He said, 'Do you want to do this?' We talked about farming and how I felt about it. I said I'd try to get some rock bands to come and play."

Mellencamp was the first artist Nelson recruited. "Willie has a certain kindness and understanding that I don't have," Mellencamp said as a Lamar Sorrento portrait of Johnny Cash looked over his left shoulder. "I remember having a heated discussion about corporate sponsors with Willie in a meeting about the first Farm Aid. I didn't want them there. I didn't want any sponsorship. I didn't want politicians to come. My favorite Willie Nelson story comes from that same meeting. After we announced the concert [at a press conference], I ran back to the trailer with Willie. There were hundreds of people around. He signed autographs for an hour and a half. I sat in the trailer, waiting, and finally I asked him, 'What are you doing?' And he said, 'Something you should think about doing.' It was a good point. He's thoughtful."

Between May 1982 and December 1983, Mellencamp had Top Ten hits with "Hurt So Good," "Jack and Diane," "Crumblin' Down," and "Pink Houses." This earned Mellencamp an invitation to perform at Live Aid, the July 13, 1985, concert that raised money for African famine relief. He turned it down. "Live Aid was different," Mellencamp said. "I knew it was going to be on [inter]national TV, satellite linkup, and it was all about that. Being here in Indiana I felt weird about it. With Farm Aid, I was directly involved with the first one—that's all I thought was going to happen, the first one. Nobody thought about the second one or the twentieth. But I only want to be involved in stuff if I feel it's really going to make a difference. There were so many bullshit things that happened in the eighties, but I thought Farm Aid would be an honest effort."

Mellencamp has stuck with the Farm Aid cause for twenty years. "Willie is the decision maker," he said. "I can't speak for Neil or Dave, but we're just helpers. If I feel I can help Willie and the family farmer, then every year I will do so. But as far as Farm Aid being part of my life, I can't say that it is."

Irwin looked at her husband. Mellencamp fidgeted like a bird on a fence. He pecked at his blue pack of cigarettes. "John's being humble again," she said. "He grew up in an agricultural area. His sister Laura has a family farm with her husband, Mark, near Seymour, Indiana. He understands the struggle and the difference between each family farm and a corporate farm. Most people don't. My kids go by the little old man who is out every morning at the crack of dawn driving his tractor on the highway. He's going back-and-forth and he must be in his eighties. It touches your life in a different way [than in the city]. John understands that. He has a heartfelt connection to wanting to see change."

Mellencamp's history with Farm Aid also belies his statement: He's been there more than just one day a year on concert day. In the spring of 1986, Mellencamp traveled to Chillicothe, Missouri, to participate in a rally in support of farmers staging an action at a USDA office. At the time, family farmers were feeling the heat. Land values were tumbling, farmers were seeing equity eroded, and the USDA, watching as collateral lost value, began foreclosing on farmers with outstanding loans. A group of Missouri farmers led by Bill Christison and his wife Dixie organized a farmer blockade of the local Farmers Home Administration [FmHA] office in Chillicothe to protest unfair lending practices. Mellencamp appeared at a rally of more than fourteen thousand farmers, sang songs from the back of a flatbed truck, and wrote a check for $15 thousand for the farmers group that organized the blockade, the Missouri Rural Crisis Center, an entity Farm Aid funded from the get-go and still works with today.

"I remember it," Mellencamp said. "That event made a real connection. I remember how many people showed up."

Mellencamp is still fighting authority, but he's also become an authority on the issues affecting farmers and rural communities across America. He has a profound understanding of the political complexities unfolding today. And Mellencamp doesn't hesitate to act on his beliefs. In 2003, Mellencamp called the Farm Aid office, all ticked off. He had been watching *Real Time With Bill Maher,* and Maher had referred to farmers as "the biggest welfare queens in America." Mellencamp's demand to Farm Aid was to "straighten him out on the facts." Farm Aid staffers urged Mellencamp to go on the show and educate Maher himself. A week later, he and Nebraska Farmers Union president John Hansen appeared on Maher's show. Both were ready to explain that as a result of current farm policy, which is heavily influenced by corporate interests, most family farmers never see a dime from government subsidies. Lucky for Maher, he'd done his research, and immediately after introducing his guests, he retracted his earlier statement. You could see the disappointment in Mellencamp's face: He had been ready for a good fight.

Another confrontation came about at the September 7, 2003, Farm Aid, in suburban Columbus, Ohio. Mellencamp had been backstage watching President George W. Bush's TV press conference where he asked Congress for $87 billion for the war in Iraq. When Mellencamp took the stage, he mentioned Bush's request and said, "Think about what that money could do for the family farmer." Some of the twenty thousand fans booed Mellencamp, while others cheered. "Can you imagine?" Mellencamp asked later. "One of the founders gets booed at Farm Aid? I hadn't been booed in twenty years. I felt like, 'How can you people be so wrong?' Then, when I sang 'To Washington,' that went down *really* good." Originally recorded by Charlie Poole in 1926, "To Washington" is a political song that has become a bluegrass standard. Mellencamp's version, which he recorded on 2003's *Trouble No More,* was clearly inspired by issues surrounding the Bush administration. "I was just pointing out that 'you people are the ones who will have to go fight this war. You people are going to have to pay for it. You are the people who

Mellencamp in his studio, with his painting of Ernest Hemingway on the easel behind him, 2005

"RAIN ON THE SCARECROW"

John Mellencamp and George Michael Green

Scarecrow on a wooden cross, blackbird in the barn
Four hundred empty acres, that used to be my farm
I grew up like my daddy did, my grandpa cleared this land
When I was five I walked the fence, while Grandpa held my hand

Chorus:
Rain on the scarecrow blood on the plow
This land fed a nation this land made me proud
And son I'm just sorry there's no legacy for you now
Rain on the scarecrow blood on the plow
Rain on the scarecrow blood on the plow

The crops we grew last summer weren't enough to pay the loans
Couldn't buy the seed to plant this spring and the farmers bank foreclosed
Called my old friend Schepman up to auction off the land
He said John it's just my job and I hope you understand
Hey calling it your job ol' hoss sure don't make it right
But if you want me to I'll say a prayer for your soul tonight
And grandma's on the front porch swing with a Bible in her hand
Sometimes I hear her singing take me to the promised land
When you take away a man's dignity he can't work his fields and cows

There'll be blood on the scarecrow blood on the plow
Blood on the scarecrow blood on the plow

Well there's ninety-seven crosses planted in the courthouse yard
Ninety-seven families who lost ninety-seven farms
I think about my grandpa and my neighbors and my name
And some nights I feel like dyin' like that scarecrow in the rain

Chorus:
Rain on the scarecrow blood on the plow
This land fed a nation this land made me proud
And son I'm just sorry they're just memories for you now
Rain on the scarecrow blood on the plow
Rain on the scarecrow blood on the plow

Rain on the scarecrow blood on the plow
This land fed a nation this land made me so proud
And son I'm just sorry they're just memories for you now
Rain on the scarecrow blood on the plow
Rain on the scarecrow blood on the plow

John Mellencamp, Irving, Texas, 1992

will make the sacrifice.' I felt kind of shitty onstage, but I remember Neil Young came up to me and said, 'I bet you don't even know what you're doing, but just keep doing it.'"

Irwin added, "All John was doing was pointing out the path we were on. It wasn't like he was making stuff up and yelling obscenities. He was recapping facts." Mellencamp was only talking in classic Indiana plainspeak, popularized across America from Larry Bird to David Letterman.

It seems Mellencamp is always speaking out for someone. His favorite Farm Aid moment was at the April 7, 1990, concert at the Hoosier Dome in downtown Indianapolis. Mellencamp lobbied to get Guns n' Roses, a band that many thought was controversial, on the bill. The gig turned out to be the final performance of the original version of the group. Drummer Steven Adler was fired shortly after Farm Aid IV. Mellencamp said, "I got calls from everybody, but so what? They're young kids finding their way through the world. They had a song called 'Down on the Farm,' and at the time there were two guys in the band from Indiana [Axl Rose and Izzy Stradlin are from Lafayette]. And they went out there, and they were great. That was such a great Farm Aid."

A year later, Mellencamp met Irwin, a model who was hired to appear on his *Whenever We Wanted* album cover. Ten weeks later they were engaged. In March 1992, she attended her first Farm Aid concert in Dallas. Mellencamp said, "We smooched all the way from Indiana to Texas. The guys in the band kept looking at us and saying, 'Would you stop that?'"

Mellencamp and Irwin work hard to maintain a healthy quality of life in their neck of the woods. "I do the best I can about what I bring into the house," Irwin said. "Our kids drink a gallon of milk a day, and I make sure it's organic. But they're little kids. They go to school and trade off stuff. I try to sneak in as many wholesome things as I can. If they don't complain, I know it's working." Although his children were not around, Mellencamp still whispered, "We have one kid who eats organic chicken nuggets. He doesn't know the difference." Irwin added, "He drinks chocolate soy milk. He thinks it's great. I can't protect them entirely, but we make the effort."

It is a different world than the one in which Mellencamp, 53, grew up. "Nobody had discussions of what was healthy," he said. "The government presented a phony-baloney food group thing that consisted of something red, something green, and we ate it. My mom used to keep hog-fat grease to make gravy right off the stove. My brother used to walk up and dip bread in there." Irwin groaned. Mellencamp smiled and said, "I did that myself. It was pretty good."

Irwin, on the other hand, was reared in a progressive household outside of Allentown, Pennsylvania. "My stepfather was kind of a hippie guy who made sure we didn't have junk food," she said. "My mom put egg and vanilla in a blender. That was our milk shake."

Mellencamp shook his head and said, "She never had a Big Mac until she met me." Irwin has not strayed from her political upbringing. In 2004, she was a delegate to the Democratic National Convention in Boston. "Sadly, the family farm was not one of the biggest issues," she said. "Farmers were there, and they asked questions, but more of the questions were about the economy in general."

Mellencamp's father, Richard, was executive vice president of an electrical company that wired Disney World and the Superdome in New Orleans (ironically, the site of the only Farm Aid Mellencamp has missed, due to illness). Mellencamp grew up around music. He recalled his father bringing home Woody Guthrie records. "When I was eight, Dad was only twenty-eight," Mellencamp said. "We had the stereo, and we had the Four Freshmen, Odetta, and Woody Guthrie. He may not even know why he had Woody Guthrie. My dad and a bunch of friends used to have 'bongo parties' where they played bongos to the records. Can you imagine being a six-year-old kid and having six drunk adults beating on bongos all night? It left quite an impression. But getting the Woody Guthrie award is the proudest thing that has happened to me." In October 2003, Mellencamp was honored at the seventh Annual Guthrie Awards Dinner by the Huntington's Disease Society of America (HDSA) for "the embodiment of Woody Guthrie's ideals." Mellencamp joined previous award winners such as Harry Belafonte, Paul Simon, and Odetta.

The honor came a month after Mellencamp was booed at Farm Aid. The world turns in strange directions, but one thing is certain: John and Elaine Mellencamp will be found wherever the truth stands as tall as old trees.

John Mellencamp, 1991

John Prine grew up knowing the power of mass appeal. His late father, Bill Prine, spent a decade as president of the United Steelworkers Union local in Maywood, a lucky penny's throw outside of Chicago. Bill Prine was from the western Kentucky coal-mining town of Paradise, which his son popularized in song. When the elder Prine migrated north, he found work as a tool and die maker at the American Can Company, at the same time they were organizing the union. He got in on the ground floor. "It was a good deal of his life put toward the union," John Prine said. "I used to go hang out with him at the union hall. I figured that's what everybody did when they grew up—they went to the union hall."

John Prine's working-class empathy has made him a natural friend to Farm Aid. Prine appeared at the first four Farm Aids. In 1983, Prine and John Mellencamp collaborated on the salty ballad "Jackie O" for Mellencamp's album *Uh-Huh*. "We had just written that song, and we were talking about doing the movie [*Falling From Grace*, starring Mellencamp, 1992]," Prine said. "Dwight [Yoakam] was around then, too. Me and him and John [Mellencamp], Joe Ely, and James McMurtry did a thing called Buzzin' Cousins.

[The Buzzin' Cousins sing Mellencamp's "Sweet Suzanne" on the *Falling From Grace* soundtrack.] Mellencamp was awesome. I used John's band most of the times I played Farm Aid. He gave them to me and gave me rehearsal time so we could have it together, which was great." Also in 1983, Mellencamp and Prine wrote "Take a Look at My Heart," which appears on Prine's *The Missing Years*, with Bruce Springsteen adding backing vocals.

"I may've called Willie's people when I heard about Farm Aid," Prine continued. "With the [Nelson Fourth of July] picnics, all you had to do was call Willie and put your hat in the ring. He's so quick to include people and make something come together. I was just glad to be a part of it.

"You can't get more salt of the earth than the farmers, so when you hear they're in trouble, you feel it. As little as I could help, I wanted to do what I could. I was so glad to see so many people standing up for the farmers, because as a country, if you don't support the family farmers—well, it's everything this country was founded on."

Prine was born October 10, 1946, in Maywood, Illinois, but he has deep recollections of the family's summertime visits to Paradise. Prine's grandfather on his mother's side was John Luther Hamm, a Kentucky guitar-picker. His paternal grandfather was a carpenter who traveled through Kentucky, Indiana, and Illinois and inspired the Prine song "Grandpa Was a Carpenter." Prine still remembers the smell of the tobacco farms around Paradise. "I didn't know too many farmers," he said. "My relatives grew stuff for their own use, for produce and things. But where they were from, people pretty much grew tobacco. My dad's steelworkers union was aligned with the coal miners. But working people—people who labor like that—are all joined together. Dad's hero was John L. Lewis [United Mineworkers of America president from 1920 to 1960]. That says everything."

A keenly appointed songwriter, Prine has several detailed Farm Aid memories. "Meeting Debra Winger [at the first Farm Aid] was music to my ears," he said. At Farm Aid III, Prine followed John Kay and Steppenwolf and Lou Reed with a set that included "Saddle in the Rain" and "Spanish Pipedream." Prine will never forget talking to Reed. "It was in Lincoln, 1987," Prine recalled. "He and Mellencamp were starting to hang out, they were doing something. Lou had just done the *New York* record, which I thought was really great. He told me he liked 'Hello in There.' I told him I liked 'New York,' and we decided we should write a ballad together. Haven't seen him since.

"But the concert was just good stuff, running into people you knew and didn't know. Willie's people were in the forefront of organizing all that stuff. John and Neil's people really pulled the production together. It was wonderful to see everyone work together like that to help out the farmers. It was always difficult to hear and see from the side of the stage, so everybody would be backstage watching on the monitors, and there were always so many people there. The hotels were equally interesting. To be with all those bands in hotels was just neat. It was like folk festivals were when I was starting out. People everywhere, playing music, telling stories all night long. It was good for me. I have a hard time sleeping anyway."

—DAVE HOEKSTRA

"Playing Farm Aid was amazing. The first one, in Champaign, we backed up seven different artists. We were the house band for the first two Farm Aids and at the one in Indianapolis. Some of the great artists we got to back up include John Prine, Bonnie Raitt, Dwight Yoakam, and Lou Reed. It was great!"

—TOBY MYERS, FORMER MELLENCAMP BASSIST

Farm Aid Live!

Iggy Pop, 1990

Kid Rock and Allison Moorer, 2002

Steve Earle, 1992

Billy Joe Shaver, 1994

Paul Simon, 1992

Beck, 1997

Paul English, 2004

Patrick Simmons of the Doobie Brothers, 2001

Susan Tedeschi, 2001

Marty Stuart, 1993

John Mellencamp, 2002

Willie Nelson and Dennis Alley, 2001

Billy Joel, 1985

Darius Rucker of Hootie and the Blowfish, Trick Pony's Heidi Newfield and Ira Dean, and Willie Nelson, 2003

Garth Brooks, 1990

Billy Bob Thornton, 2003

Suzy Bogguss, 1990

Glen Campbell, 1985

Dave Matthews, 2004

Crazy Horse guitarist Frank Sampedro, bassist Billy Talbot, and Neil Young, 2003

Willie Nelson, 1995

Richard Marx, 1992

Trisha Yearwood, 1999

Little Adam at Angelic Organics farm, Caledonia, Illinois

"If you get a tomato that's grown with care . . . where someone is trying to produce something they want to eat, the difference is profound. You can eat a good tomato like an apple. And people will go, 'What do you mean?' Yeah, you can, because it tastes that good. Because food, when it's grown with care, tastes better."

—DAVE MATTHEWS

"HOMEGROWN TOMATOES"
Guy Clark

There's nothin' in the world that I like better than
Bacon, lettuce, and homegrown tomatoes
Up in the morning and out in the garden
Pick you a ripe one, don't get a hard 'un
Plant 'em in the springtime, eat 'em in the summer
All winter without 'em's a culinary bummer
I forget all about the sweatin' and the diggin'
Every time I go out and pick me a big 'un

Refrain
Homegrown tomatoes, homegrown tomatoes
What'd life be without homegrown tomatoes
There's only two things that money can't buy
That's true love and homegrown tomatoes

You can go out and eat 'em, that's for sure
But there's nothin' a homegrown tomato won't cure
You can put 'em in a salad, put 'em in a stew
You can make your own, very own tomato juice
You can eat 'em with eggs, you can eat 'em with gravy
You can eat 'em with beans, pinto or navy
Put 'em on the side, put 'em on the middle
Homegrown tomatoes on a hot cake griddle

Refrain

If I could change this life I lead
You could call me Johnny Tomato Seed
I know what this country needs
It's homegrown tomatoes in every yard you see
When I die don't bury me
In a box in a cold dark cemetery
Out in the garden would be much better
Where I could be pushin' up homegrown tomatoes

Refrain twice

Words From a Shepherd

"Farmers are dreamers of the first order. The most romantic of dreamers. Feet in the soil, head in the clouds, backs bent even in today's tractors. They are most wishful of all of those who have inherited the earth as their legacy and work with their bodies as well as their minds. Who else depends so strongly on the unknown and goodwill of the unexpected as a farmer does? The impending birth of calves inspires dreams of the calf being the right calf and growing into being the right cow. The planning, the haying, even the milling, all being controlled by forces within the realm of knowledge and experience and yet controlled by a force far stronger than one can even begin to imagine. There are years when only steadfast grim concentration can carry one's step to the barn. And days when all goes so well that life is as close to perfection as is possible on this earth."

—SYLVIA JORRIN
FROM *SYLVIA'S FARM:*
THE JOURNAL OF AN IMPROBABLE SHEPHERD

The Story Economy David Mas Masumoto

Dear Baachan/Grandma,

I remember watching you eat the perfect peach. You'd close your eyes, breathe in the aroma, and slip a juicy slice past your lips. With first bite, the nectar exploded and flavor drenched your taste buds. A satisfying glow gently spread across your face. A moment of savoring. Soothing, content, perfection.

I believe the flavors transported you—memories of peaches in Japan as a child or working a lifetime in the orchards of California and the building of an industry as a farmworker. Now your memories have became part of our family farm and the work we do.

I'm driven by these haunting memories. Not just of the flavor of a peach but the stories of how they're grown and who grows them. Beyond lifeless commodities, human relationships lie at the core of great produce, adding to the flavors we enjoy. I call it "the story economy" that journeys with wonderful foods. Powerful, intimate, personal narratives about food; insight into the faces behind our meals. I also think it's how our businesses and communities need to be developed.

The story economy incorporates the power of memory and traditions—not nostalgia for the "good old days" that can no longer be (and for some were never that great). Rather, I refer to work that takes the best from the past as motivation to build and invest in a better future.

Think of the new significance placed on taste and flavor in the organic marketplace. Baachan, could you have imagined our peaches in gourmet restaurants or becoming the prized centerpiece of an evening dinner? We've become part of the new California cuisine, emphasizing fresh, local, and in-season food—it's the link of people with a place, and the story becomes part of a summer meal.

Think of the growing success of community-supported agriculture where consumers become direct subscribers and supporters of farmers by ordering a share of weekly harvests. The story of foods evolves into personal relationships between consumer and farmer.

Think of the revival of farmers markets that bring farmers and communities together. Often placed in downtowns, these gatherings help connect people and serve to revitalize an area. The blend of flavor and people combines with the feel of a real place, a neighborhood, a city center; something authentic is created and enjoyed.

I value stories that go beyond economic and monetary relationships. A search for that perfect memory adds meaning to my life's work—a quest for that tale I'm proud to pass down to generations.

Of course, not all products and places work in the story economy. I'm not sure we have much memory of mass-produced goods like fast foods that people consume but can't remember what they ate a few minutes later. Commuters pass through nameless places because they don't need to remember them; they're oblivious that such neighborhoods may be home to others who remain faceless. People pay for entertainment that blurs together, so one action movie or reality TV show more or less looks like another. Consumers take comfort in not being challenged; passive entertainment works because they're lazy thinkers. Most will forget these anonymous moments when they don't attach significance.

Baachan, your perfect peach story works because it's authentic: I employ all my senses. I can see the harvest glow in a peach with early morning light and feel the soft flesh; I breathe in the aroma while salivating as I think about the flavor; I anticipate hearing the smacking of lips over and over after each bite.

By thinking in stories, I'm forced to slow down and reflect, attaching words to the moment and committing feelings to memory. The story economy works because I can use these terms to help me recall the experience later and relive something pleasurable. Advertising tries to do this, but it's not the same: These are my expressions for my memories, remembrances of things past.

But I fear we're losing stories because we choose not to remember; we forget too quickly and easily. This is how great-tasting peaches are lost: farming in a system that regrettably rewards great-*looking* fruits. As if, at the point of sale, only what's on the outside matters, with little consideration and memory of what's good on the inside.

Responsibility comes with remembering. It requires work, it burdens us with thought. If we don't care about the future, it's simple to overlook stupid decisions in the present.

Consider the urban sprawl of the Central Valley of California: Poor planning decisions are now too easily forgotten and forgiven, no one is willing to take responsibility for how this valley will look twenty years from now. We need to organize city summits and community forums to plan and claim our futures. Historical amnesia may be the greatest threat to our stories. If we forget our quest for things good, we forgo things that will be great.

Vision comes from our ability to look to the future because we value stories of the past. I honor all the flavors of this valley we call home—I respect what we *are*, not what we are not—from blossom trails to fresh-fruit road stands to folk artists and valley poets; from immigrants arriving with their traditions and festivals, to the swap meets and flea markets that speak to our own culture. We need an annual Highway 99 (the main road linking many of the Central Valley towns) swap meet festival—celebrating the stories found in people's stuff, the gems and junk from our attics and garages: up and down the valley, as our stories go public, our own brand of cultural tourism.

Baachan, your story helps make this farm a home. We shared a peach memory that continues to motivate today. I close my eyes, too, as I eat a great peach. I can see and hear and feel you, and the stories continue to live. Perfection for generations. Priceless.

Your grandson,
Mas

"TO BE OF USE"
Marge Piercy

The people I love the best
jump into work head first
without dallying in the shallows
and swim off with sure strokes almost out of sight.
They seem to become natives of that element,
the black sleek heads of seals
bouncing like half-submerged balls.

I love people who harness themselves, an ox to a
  heavy cart,
who pull like water buffalo, with massive patience,
who strain in the mud and the muck to move things
  forward,
who do what has to be done, again and again.

I want to be with people who submerge
in the task, who go into the fields to harvest
and work in a row and pass the bags along,
who stand in the line and haul in their places,
who are not parlor generals and field deserters
but move in a common rhythm
when the food must come in or the fire be put out.

The work of the world is common as mud.
Botched, it smears the hands, crumbles to dust.
But the thing worth doing well done
has a shape that satisfies, clean and evident.
Greek amphoras for wine or oil,
Hopi vases that held corn, are put in museums
but you know they were made to be used.
The pitcher cries for water to carry
and a person for work that is real.

Opposite: Aunt Mossie, Mississippi. Above: Picking cucumbers at the Angelic Organics farm, Caledonia, Illinois

"PICKIN' TIME"
Johnny Cash

I got cotton in the bottom land
It's up and growin' and I got a good stand
My good wife and them kids of mine
Gonna get new shoes, come Pickin' Time
Get new shoes come Pickin' Time.

Ev'ry night when I go to bed
I thank the Lord that my kids are fed
They live on beans eight days and nine
But I get 'em fat come Pickin' Time
Get 'em fat come come Pickin' Time.

The corn is yellow and the beans are high
The sun is hot in the summer sky
The work is hard til layin' by
Layin' by til Pickin' Time
Layin' by til Pickin' Time.

It's hard to see by the coal-oil light
And I turn it off purty early at night
'Cause a jug of coal-oil costs a dime
But I stay up late come Pickin' Time
Stay up late come Pickin' Time.

My old wagon barely gets me to town
I patched the wheels and I watered 'em down
Keep her in shape so she'll be fine
To haul my cotton come Pickin' Time
Haul my cotton come Pickin' Time.

Last Sunday mornin' when they passed the hat
It was still nearly empty back where I sat
But the preacher smiled and said that's fine

The Lord'll wait til Pickin' Time
The Lord'll wait til Pickin' Time.

Lily's Chickens

Barbara Kingsolver

My daughter is in love. She's only five years old, but this is real. Her beau is shorter than she is, by a wide margin, and she couldn't care less. He has dark eyes, a loud voice, and a tendency to crow. He also has five girlfriends, but Lily doesn't care about that, either. She loves them all: Mr. Doodle, Jess, Bess, Mrs. Zebra, Pixie, and Kiwi. They're chickens. Lily likes to sit on an overturned bucket and sing to them in the afternoon. She has them eating out of her hand.

It began with coveting our neighbor's chickens. Lily would volunteer to collect the eggs, and then she offered to move in with them. Not the neighbors, the chickens. She said if she could have some of her own, she would be the happiest girl on earth. What parent could resist this bait? Our life style could accommodate a laying flock; my husband and I had kept poultry before, so we knew it was a project we could manage, and a responsibility Lily could handle largely by herself. I understood how much that meant to her when I heard her tell her grandmother, "They're going to be just *my* chickens, Grandma. Not even one of them will be my sister's." To be five years old and have some other life form entirely under your control—not counting goldfish or parents— is a majestic state of affairs.

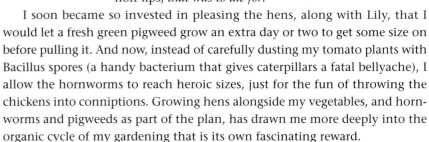

So her dutiful father built a smart little coop right next to our large garden enclosure, and I called a teenage friend who might, I suspected, have some excess baggage in the chicken department. She raises championship show chickens, and she culls her flock tightly. At this time of year she'd be eyeing her young birds through their juvenile molt to be sure every feather conformed to the gospel according to the chicken-breeds handbook, which is titled, I swear, *The Standard of Perfection*. I asked if she had a few feather-challenged children that wanted adoption, and she happily obliged. She even had an adorable little bantam rooster that would have caused any respectable chicken-show judge to keel over—the love child of a Rose-comb and a Wyandotte. I didn't ask how it happened.

In Lily's eyes *this* guy, whom she named Mr. Doodle, was the standard of perfection. We collected him and a motley harem of sweet little hens in a crate and brought them home. They began to scratch around contentedly right away, and Lily could hardly bear to close her eyes at night on the pride she felt at poultry ownership. Every day after feeding them she would sit on her overturned bucket and chat with them about the important things. She could do this for an hour, easily, while I worked nearby in the garden. We discovered that they loved to eat the weeds I pulled, and the grasshoppers I caught red-handed eating my peppers. We wondered, would they even eat the nasty green hornworms that are the bane of my tomato plants? *Darling*, replied Mrs. Zebra, licking her non-lips, *that was to die for.*

I soon became so invested in pleasing the hens, along with Lily, that I would let a fresh green pigweed grow an extra day or two to get some size on before pulling it. And now, instead of carefully dusting my tomato plants with Bacillus spores (a handy bacterium that gives caterpillars a fatal bellyache), I allow the hornworms to reach heroic sizes, just for the fun of throwing the chickens into conniptions. Growing hens alongside my vegetables, and hornworms and pigweeds as part of the plan, has drawn me more deeply into the organic cycle of my gardening that is its own fascinating reward.

With the coop built and chickens installed, all we had to do now was wait for our flock to pass through puberty and begin to give us our daily eggs. We were warned it might take a while because they would be upset by the move

Opposite: An heirloom chicken. Above: Joshua and a favorite chicken at his family's homestead, Phoenicia, New York

125

and would need time for emotional adjustment. I was skeptical about this putative pain and suffering; it is hard to put much stock in the emotional life of a creature with the IQ of an eggplant. Seems to me you put a chicken in a box, and she looks around and says, "Gee, life is a box." You take her out, she looks around and says, "Gee, it's sunny here." But sure enough, they took their time. Lily began each day with high hopes, marching out to the coop with cup of corn in one hand and my twenty-year-old wire egg-basket in the other. She insisted that her dad build five nest boxes in case they all suddenly got the urge at once. She fluffed up the straw in all five nests, nervous as a bride preparing her boudoir.

I was looking forward to the eggs, too. To anyone who has eaten an egg just a few hours' remove from the hen, those white ones in the store have the charisma of day-old bread. I looked forward to organizing my family's meals around the pleasures of quiches, Spanish tortillas, and soufflés, with a cupboard that never goes bare. We don't go to the grocery very often; our garden produces a good deal of what we eat, and in some seasons nearly all of it. This is not exactly a hobby. It's more along the lines of religion, something we believe in the way families believe in patriotism and loving thy neighbor as thyself. If our food ethic seems an unusual orthodoxy to set alongside those other two, it probably shouldn't. We consider them to be connected.

Globally speaking, I belong to the 20 percent of the world's population—and chances are you do, too—that uses 67 percent of the planet's resources and generates 75 percent of its pollution and waste. This doesn't make me proud. U.S. citizens by ourselves, comprising just 5 percent of the world's people, use a quarter of its fuels. An average American gobbles up the goods that would support thirty citizens of India. Much of the money we pay for our

fuels goes to support regimes that treat their people—particularly their women—in ways that make me shudder. I'm a critic of this shameful contract, and of wasteful consumption, on general principles. Since it's nonsensical, plus embarrassing, to be an outspoken critic of things you do yourself, I set myself long ago to the task of consuming less. I never got to India, but in various stages of my freewheeling youth I tried out living in a tent, in a commune, and in Europe, before eventually determining that I could only ever hope to dent the salacious appetites of my homeland and make us a more perfect union by living *inside* this amazing beast, poking at its belly from the inside with my one little life and the small, pointed sword of my pen. So this is where I feed my family and try to live lightly on the land.

Once upon a time, when I had my first baby, I believed that if I took care not to train her to the bad habits of sugar, salt, and fat, she would grow up not wanting those things. That delusion lasted exactly one year, until someone put a chocolate-frosted birthday confection in front of my sugar-free child and—how can I say this delicately?—she put her face in the cake. We humans crave sugar, fat, and salt because we evolved through thousands of years in which these dietary components were desperately scarce; those members of the tribe who most successfully glutted on them, when they found them, would store up the body fat to live through lean times and bear offspring. And now we've organized the whole enchilada around those latent biochemical passions—an early hominid's dream come true, a health-conscious mom's nightmare. If my cupboards were full of junk food, it would vanish, with no help from mice. We have our moments of abandon—Halloween, I've learned, is inescapable without a religious conversion—but most of the time my kids get other treats they've come to love. Few delicacies

Below: Willie Harrison, Mathiston, Mississippi. Pages 130 to 131: Gerlean in the garden, Mathiston, Mississippi

compare with a yellow-pear tomato, delicately sun-warmed and sugary, right off the vine. When I send the kids out to pick berries or fruit, I have to specify that at least *some* are supposed to go in the bucket. My younger daughter adores eating small, raw green beans straight off the garden trellis; I thought she was nuts till I tried them myself.

The soreness in my hamstrings at the end of a hard day of planting or hoeing feels good in a way that I can hardly explain—except to another gardener, who will know exactly the sweet ache I mean. My children seem to know it, too, and sleep best on those nights. I've found the deepest kind of physical satisfaction in giving my body's muscles, senses, and attentiveness over to the purpose for which they were originally designed: the industry of feeding that body and keeping it alive. I suspect that most human bodies have fallen into such remove from that original effort, we've precipitated an existential crisis that requires things like shopping, overeating, and adrenaline-rush movies to sate that particular body hunger.

And so I hope our family's efforts at self-provision will not just improve the health and habitat of my children but also offer a life that's good for them, and knowledge they need. I wish all children could be taught the basics of agriculture in school along with math and English literature, because it's surely as important a subject as these. Most adults my age couldn't pass a simple test on what foods are grown in their home counties and what month they come into maturity. In just two generations we've passed from a time when people almost never ate a fruit out of season to a near-universal ignorance of what seasons mean. One icy winter I visited a friend in Manhattan who described the sumptuous meal she was making for us, including fresh raspberries. "Raspberries won't grow in the tropics," I mused. "And they sure don't keep. So where would they come from in the dead of winter?" Without blinking she answered, "Zabar's!"

Apparently, the guys running the show don't know much about agriculture, either, because the strategy of our nation is to run on a collision course with the possibility of being able to feed ourselves decently (or at all) in twenty years' time. I can't see how any animal could be this stupid; surely it's happening only because humans no longer believe food comes from dirt. Well, it does. Farmers are not just guys in overalls, part of the charming scenery of yesteryear; they are the technicians who know how to get teensy little seeds to turn into the stuff that comprises everything, and I mean *everything*, we eat. Is anybody paying attention? For every farm that's turned over to lawns and housing developments, a farmer is sent to work at the Nissan plant or the Kmart checkout line. What's lost with that career move is specific knowledge of how to gain food from a particular soil type, in a particular climate—wisdom that took generations to grow.

I want to protect my kids against a dangerous ignorance of what sustains them. When they help me dig and hoe the garden, plant corn and beans, later on pick them, and later still preserve the harvest's end, compost our scraps, and then turn that compost back into the garden plot the following spring, they are learning important skills for living and maintaining life. I have also observed that they appreciate feeling useful. In fact, nearly all the kids I've ever worked with on gardening projects get passionate about putting seeds in the ground, to the point of earnest territoriality.

"Now," I ask them when we're finished, "what will you do if you see somebody over here tromping around or riding a bike over your seedbeds?"

"We'll tell them to get outta our vegables!" shouted my most recent batch of five-year-old recruits to this plot of mine for improving the world one *vegable* at a time.

Maria Montessori was one of the first child advocates to preach the wisdom of allowing children to help themselves and others, thereby learning to feel competent and self-assured. Most of the teachers and parents I know agree, and they organize classrooms and homes that promote this. But in modern times it's not easy to construct opportunities for kids to feel very useful. They can pick up their toys or take out the trash or walk the dog, but all of these things have an abstract utility. How useful is it to help take care of a dog whose main purpose, as far as they can see, is to be taken care of?

Growing food for the family's table is concretely useful. Nobody needs to explain how a potato helps the family. Bringing a basket of eggs and announcing, "Attention, everybody: FREE BREAKFAST" is a taste of bread-winning that most kids can attain only in make-believe. I'm lucky I could help make my daughter's dream come true. My own wish is for world enough and time that every child might have this: the chance to count some chickens before they hatch.

Farm Aid Backstage  Taj Mahal

Ethnomusicologist Taj Mahal, who appeared at Farm Aid II and Farm Aid IV, brought a full plate of knowledge to the Farm Aid table. Taj Mahal holds a degree in animal husbandry from the University of Massachusetts in Amherst. Between 1957 and 1963, he worked on a dairy farm in Palmer, a small town outside Springfield, Massachusetts.

"The first day I came to work on the farm, I had just turned sixteen," Taj Mahal said before the 1990 Indianapolis Farm Aid, where he performed a mule-driving version of Howlin' Wolf's "Sitting on Top of the World." "There were fourteen people covering four generations living in this house. They didn't leave their folk behind just because they got up in years. The father had made his money in textile mills, and he bought the farm for his son. It was a big old farmhouse with lots of old clocks, an old pump organ, and a piano."

By the time Taj Mahal turned nineteen, he was farm foreman. "I'd get up at quarter past four in the morning, and I ran the farm," he said. "I milked anywhere between thirty-five and seventy cows a day. I set up the breeding schedule. I clipped udders. I grew corn. I grew Tennessee redtop clover. Alfalfa." Taj Mahal soon found an equal passion for farming and music. He explained, "Farming is where I wanted to go for a while. But then my idea of a real good farm is a turn-of-the-century farm where you have horses, sires, and Clydesdales do your heavy pulling. They don't tear up the land like tractors do. They don't use any nonrecoupable energy sources. You take good care of them, and they work a lot better on the land. They're much more efficient, and it gives you a lot more to do that's really closer to the soil in a traditional way. By the turn of the century, 80 percent of Americans had some kind of agrarian thing in their background. Now it is down to less than 1 percent. Even the farm I worked for can't afford to keep cows."

Vocalist-guitarist Taj Mahal (born Henry St. Claire Fredericks) has spent forty years embracing traditional blues music and expanding the form with Caribbean, Hawaiian, and Latin seasonings. In the mid-sixties, he and fellow musicologist Ry Cooder cofounded a bluesy folk-rock band called the Rising Sons. Taj Mahal's mother was a gospel singer, and his father was a West Indian jazz arranger and pianist. But Taj Mahal will never forget his long days on the farm.

"I got a close-up look at the family farm," he said. "And I'm a strong believer that's something that should be presented to young people with a future to it. If you want star wars up in the air, you better deal with something going on on the ground. You have a whole generation of kids who think everything comes out of a box and a can, and they don't know you can grow most of your food. Nobody has a right to take away eight or nine generations of people working the land. The land is like the mother. It's very important to get that in perspective in how you live your life."

—DAVE HOEKSTRA

Using horses to plow at the Farm School in Massachusetts, 2004

"When I was a kid, I had an aunt and uncle who had a dairy farm. I spent some summer vacations out in the fields, swimming in the pond. I remember all the wonderful things about farm life . . . the richness of the food . . . just the way the milk tasted when it came right from the cow. There was something really wonderful about that, to be able to grow up with more of nature around, more of an idea of what the whole cycle of the earth was about."

—EMMYLOU HARRIS, FARM AID ARTIST

Understanding Farm Policy

Keeping the Farm Movement Moving

Jim Hightower

"As through this world I travel
I see lots of funny men,
Some'll rob you with a six-gun,
Some with a fountain pen"

—WOODY GUTHRIE, "PRETTY BOY FLOYD, THE OUTLAW"

The "fountain pens" are the ones doing the serious stealing in our society today. Whether it's downsizers and globalizers knocking down America's working families or corporate greedheads and political boneheads squeezing out America's family farmers—the moneyed elites are using their "fountain pens" (their lobbyists, campaign checks, lawyers, judges, politicians, PR agents, etc.) to rob us of fair wages, fair prices, fair credit, health care, pensions, bargaining power, educational opportunities, political sovereignty, and other essential components of America's middle-class framework. In so doing they are stealing the Big Idea of America, which is the egalitarian notion that we're all in this together, all striving for the Common Good.

In a cabal of arrogance and ignorance, Wall Street and Washington are out to supplant our democratic ethic of "fairness and justice for all" with their plutocratic ethic of greed: "I got mine, you get yours . . . *adios, chump*." The good news is that a grassroots rebellion is building against this all across the country. While it's politically fashionable these days to declare that Americans are "conservative," that label is as bad a fit as trying to put socks on a rooster. The true political core of our body politic is not Republican, Democrat, conservative, or liberal—but maverick. We're a nation of nonconformist mutts, mad-as-hellers, and anti-establishment rebels, and when push comes to shove (as it frequently has in our history), folks will shove back.

Today, you can see this shove-back in burgeoning movements of workers in city after city who're pushing and winning "living wage" campaigns, or who're building effective coalitions to confront the Wal-Martization of our economy. But there's also been a shove-back in the countryside, where farmers have been refusing to go quietly, as bankers, speculators, chemical peddlers, genetic manipulators, global commodity traders, monopolistic processors, and retailers—as well as the politicians of both parties they own—combine to shove the family farm out of existence, leaving our food supply in the grasping hands of a few globalized, industrialized, agribusiness profiteers. This modern-day farm rebellion began in the 1970s and has followed two distinct paths.

The first was a path of confrontation, which farmers were forced to take when agribusiness interests and government policies pushed them to the economic breaking point. Earl Butz, agriculture secretary under Nixon, had led an effort in the early seventies to bust the farm price for grain and other basic commodities. He urged farmers to expand their production dramatically, promising that this increased output would be gobbled up by an ever-growing export market. "Get big or get out," he coldly instructed.

Sure enough, our nation's productive farmers borrowed money to plow more land, and they produced record crops. But Uncle Earl had lied to them. The export market was awash in grain and unable to absorb the new bounty from the United States—so world grain prices plummeted. This was good for Cargill, ADM, and the other global grain buyers (who were the real

Opposite and above: Farmers take to the streets of Chicago in protest during the 1985 farm crisis.

135

Above: Willie Nelson has often traveled to Washington on behalf of American farmers. Here he discusses farm policy in the chambers of Senator Tom Daschle, 1995. Opposite: Farmers protesting in Chicago, 1985.

constituency that Butz was serving), but it saddled family farmers with a crushing debt. Soon, the bankers began demanding payment, and tens of thousands of good farmers found themselves face-to-face with auctioneers come to sell off their equipment and land.

At first, farmers tried the conventional outlet of politics, with many voting in 1976 for Jimmy Carter, who promised to help them. But he lied, too, instead raising the interest rates on their debts. In the Carter years, with farm prices staying low and the cost of everything from tractors to fuel skyrocketing, it was a good time to be a farm auctioneer.

STRIKE!

That's when bucolic rural America erupted in deep, seething anger. "You just can take so much of this, then you've got to do something," said Jay Naman, president of the Texas Farmers Union in 1977. That summer, the American

Agriculture Movement (AAM) sprang from our country's farmlands, quickly spreading throughout the plains states, the Midwest, the South, and eventually to the Northeast and California. Far more militant than the established agriculture groups, AAM's hard-hit farm families declared that they would go on strike in 1978, curtailing their plantings until Washington responded to their plight.

These were not the meek farmers of the American Gothic image. They were mostly young, college educated, and upwardly mobile. Many were Vietnam vets. They had taken over the family farm from Dad and Mom just as Butz & Gang were exhorting them to expand. Now they felt suckered, and they were not going to take it. They knew three things: (1) They were about to lose what had been in their families for generations; (2) They were going under not because they were inefficient, but because they were trapped in a farm policy designed by and for corporate agribusiness rather than farmers; and (3) they were a political minority . . . and it was time for them to act like one.

They chipped in to hire organizers and open local strike offices (131 in Texas alone). They mailed tractor keys to members of Congress, saying "You try farming under your farm bill." They sent thousands of letters to Carter, enclosing enough money in each to buy the wheat in a loaf of bread: three cents. Then they hit the highways and byways with tractorcades—caravans of tractors blockaded food processing plants, encircled state capitols, and shut down rush-hour traffic for days in Washington, D.C.

They also learned that dissent can be a hard road. When a large group organized a protest on the Texas-Mexico border against pesticide-drenched commodities being brought into the United States, they were granted a permit by authorities to march onto an international bridge near McAllen. Once the farmers were all on the bridge, however, the police sealed it off, tear-gassed the farmers, flailed them with clubs, and jailed them. For these middle-class sons of the soil, this raw treatment was a shocking eye-opener, and "McAllen" became a symbolic cry that energized and radicalized AAM members across the country.

It was assumed that the movement would peter out when it came time for spring planting, but the farmers kept pushing and reaching out. In Texas, for example, the AFL-CIO endorsed the strike, and ACORN (Association of Community Organizers for Reform Now) chapters in Houston and Dallas sent

Farmer Judith Redmond with organic produce from her Full Belly Farm at the Berkeley Farmers Market, California

delegations to rally with the farmers. Local and national media showed up, too, focusing both on the colorful protests and the roiling farm crisis. Feeling the rising political heat, skittish politicians were soon rushing out to hug a farmer and declare allegiance to the cause.

Hugs, of course, don't raise farm prices, and farmers knew they would have to keep up the pressure by organizing for the long haul. A major break came in 1985, when Willie Nelson, Neil Young, John Mellencamp, and others held the first Farm Aid concert and committed not merely to an ongoing series of high-visibility concerts but more importantly to funding a Farm Aid organization that would help give the movement structure, focus, and endurance.

As we know, however, the establishment is expert at hunkering down in political storms to outlast the fury of people's movements. Twenty-five years after the launch of this agriculture movement, family farm activists certainly cannot claim to have won their legislative battle for an agriculture policy that works for them. But neither have they lost, for they have built alliances, skills, programs, and goodwill that have saved thousands of farmers and allowed the movement to persevere in the face of a determined global corporate assault on the family farm's very existence. The farm crisis has not gone away . . . but neither has the movement.

A NEW SPROUTING

The other path of rebellion has been quieter but no less daring and determined than political confrontation, and it is steadily changing the food economy to the benefit of farmers and consumers alike. This is what I call the "Good Food" movement, though it flies such other flags as "Sustainable," "Organic," "Locally Grown," "Beyond Organic," and "Pure Food." This very broad-based coalition has become a mass movement involving farmers, consumers, entrepreneurs, local community leaders, independent marketers, chefs, food activists, and others.

These are folks who have realized that the corporate and political powers that have been in charge of our food policy have turned dinner into an industrialized, conglomeratized, and globalized substance—when food, by its very nature, is agrarian, small-scale, and local. According to some agriculture economists, the industrial model returns as little as 9 percent of the food dollar to the farmer; is exterminating America's efficient family-farm system and depleting entire rural towns; requires massive taxpayer subsidies; dumps eight billion pounds of pesticides on cropland each year; ships the typical food product to market from 1,500 miles away; fosters monopoly pricing; makes America increasingly dependent on foreign production; compromises on taste and nutrition—while also delivering foodstuff riddled with fecal contamination, antibiotic-resistant bacteria, artificial growth hormones, genetically altered organisms, an overdose of fats and sugars, and a toxic stew of chemical additives and residues.

The rebellion is intent on bringing this perverse system back to Earth, taking grass-roots control of our food economy and food culture. The pioneers have been farmers—a mix of traditional farmers seeking a way out of their downward spiral of debt (including some of the AAM protesters), along with some of the early back-to-the-land families that persevered, plus a new breed of agricultural entrepreneurs. While this movement has been political when necessary, its real battleground has been the marketplace.

Twenty-five years ago, there were only a few organic farmers operating in a fringe market through a scattering of funky health food stores. Today, organic production tops $12 billion in annual sales and is growing 20 percent a year. By diversifying the production on their farms, focusing on some higher-value niche crops, slashing costs by using organic and sustainable practices, and selling as directly as possible to consumers—these farmers have found a new and profitable model that delivers an abundance of fresh, delicious, nutritious food at fair prices to their communities, plowing their income back into the local economy.

Their Good Food model makes all kinds of sense, but as Woodrow Wilson once noted: "If you want to make enemies, try changing something." All these farmers are trying to change is sixty years of corporatized agriculture. At every step, they've had to battle the bankers, agriculture colleges and extension agents, the big wholesalers and retailers, bureaucrats and politicians at all levels, farm media—the whole establishment, which first tried to ignore these farmers, then ridiculed them, then tried to block them, and now are out to co-opt them. But the farmers have a secret that the entrenched agriculture powers have long forgotten: They're producing exactly what the larger public wants.

A new marketplace has evolved since the 1970s to link Good Food producers with consumers. Restaurateurs, led by Alice Waters of Chez Panisse in

"I was brought up on a 160-acre farm in Feasterville, Pennsylvania, which is now completely cemented, plasticized, and condoed over. Today, more and more people are losing their farms and have no other place to go to continue what they are doing to feed us and our children."

—DAVID AMRAM, FARM AID ARTIST

Spring rhubarb and chives at a Massachusetts farm stand

"When I first started to work at the National Save the Family Farm Coalition, it was November 1987 in the midst of the intense debate on the Agricultural Credit Act. Farm Aid was the concert, the vision, and the source of funding for the enormous challenges we were tackling. Farm Aid provided much of the energy that bolstered the work we were doing—regional training, meetings, conference calls, materials, manuals, and some communication through MCI mail. This all was pre-fax, pre-e-mail, and pre-Internet, but the connections across and among member groups and farm activists in the countryside were strong. There have been many events—Capitol Hill rallies with Paul Wellstone, presidential debates, Capitol Hill meetings with Senate leaders, town hall meetings, farmer summits on genetic engineering, Farm Aid and Willie's support of efforts against [the agribusiness] Premium Standard Farms. These events are the threads woven through the family farm movement. Farm Aid has been there for all of us, and we deeply appreciate their commitment and vision."

—KATHY OZER, EXECUTIVE DIRECTOR,
NATIONAL FAMILY FARM COALITION

Eggplant at the Angelic Organics farm, Caledonia, Illinois

Berkeley, California, became Good Food foragers, seeking out farmers and creating a market for them. Some three thousand farmers markets have sprung up coast to coast with twenty thousand farmers selling at them. Co-ops and independent processors were established to provide a bulk market for Good Food commodities. Good Food groceries now exist in practically every city, and even supermarket giants are compelled to offer some organic and locally produced items. Various cities are encouraging new Good Food distribution systems: the purchase of organic, local food for schools and other government institutions; and the certification of food stamps and WIC coupons for Good Food purchases by poor families.

Ultimately, the ongoing farm movement is not about farmers but about us: What kind of society do we want? The "fountain pens" want to turn food into nothing but another profit center for global corporate elites, but we don't have to let them. If We the People can't take charge of our dinner, can we take charge of anything? The folks who have made the farm movement work are not merely striving for their own good but also for the common good, advancing America closer to its democratic ideals. By making dinner better, we can make life better for all of us. That's a worthy struggle.

"FLAG [Farmers Legal Action Group] was able to start up in 1986 because of the visionary and generous support of Farm Aid. Providing funding to lawyers may have been a bit of a stretch, but Willie Nelson saw that farmers were struggling across the country, because they could not get help understanding and enforcing their rights. With Farm Aid's support, FLAG came to win important victories for family farmers in law-reform litigation, to work as the legal 'back office' for farm community organizations, and to distribute plain-language legal-education booklets throughout the countryside. I remember being at my first Farm Aid concert with the new FLAG staff, right after FLAG started up. When Arlo Guthrie sang 'This Land Is Your Land,' we felt very fortunate to be part of a fine team that was working to make the words of the song a reality."

—RANDI ILYSE ROTH, FLAG EXECUTIVE DIRECTOR, 1993–2003

Tomatoes at the Ferry Plaza Farmers Market, San Francisco

In early 1986, Farm Aid took a grand step toward unifying the many and varied voices being raised in rural America. Farm Aid and Willie Nelson invited farmers to participate in the innovative United Farmer and Rancher Congress (UFRC).

Through the hot summer of that year, organizers for the UFRC working with grass-roots organizations all over the country staged special farm county meetings where family farmers offered their ideas and solutions to the ongoing farm crisis. Farmers also elected delegates to the upcoming Congress, and on September 11, 1986, nearly two thousand family farmers and ranchers converged on St. Louis, Missouri, for the three-day gathering that was sponsored and coordinated by Farm Aid.

At the Congress, delegates hammered out resolutions that offered a farsighted blueprint for fair farm policy reform. It included hard-hitting statements on a fair price for farmers, food assistance, quality, and safety; conservation and environmental protection; as well as other key issues including strong, clear demands for reform within the government's antagonistic farm credit system.

In fact, the credit resolutions approved at the congress became the foundation for the Agricultural Credit Act of 1987.

While the farmers and ranchers who attended the Congress came with serious business in mind, there was some time for high jinks and a symbolic demonstration of unity when a young Senator Tom Harkin from Iowa rose to the podium on Saturday afternoon. Quoting President Harry Truman, Harkin addressed the throng. "You know as well as I, when the price of wheat goes up, the price of bread goes up; when wheat has fallen, the price of bread didn't go down a bit," Harkin said. "There you have it. That's the policy of big business. Low prices to the farmer, cheap wages for labor, and high profits for the big corporations. And, my friends, that is the essential problem with America today."

At a predetermined point in Harkin's speech, the entire delegation made a clear declaration of their unity. Nearly every farmer had arrived that morning in his or her own battered seed cap. In one smooth movement, each farmer replaced the hat, which was a personal statement of each farmer's self, with a United Farmer and Rancher Congress cap, sending a wave of white rippling through the hall.

The unity wasn't easily won. There were disparate voices in the room; different factions represented. But they had come together to find one voice, and somehow they did. In the eyes of Ralph Paige, leader of the Federation of Southern Cooperatives and a member of the steering committee that created the Congress, Farm Aid gets the credit: "Farm Aid pulled together some of the most unbelievable matches in this world during crisis. It didn't always line up, but to help farmers, it was pulled together. That's the beauty of Farm Aid."

"I grew up in a very small town in Northern California. My family have been farmers and ranchers for many, many generations. But we lost our ranch and farm on the courthouse steps about ten years ago, to corporate America. I was in Nashville working and got that phone call, and it was one of the worst days of my life."

—FARM AID ARTIST HEIDI NEWFIELD OF TRICK PONY

Opposite: Farmer delegates at the September 1986 gathering of farmers and ranchers in St. Louis, Missouri

"I'm the son of a sharecropper. My father was a farmer, raising cotton, watermelons, and tobacco in the South Carolina area. My mother had seven children, and farming has always been in my life. My parents always wanted to own their own land, but under the share-cropper system, they were never able to come out ahead, they were never able to pay the bills. Most of my siblings had to work; they couldn't go to school. But we always had food, because the only thing we didn't raise on the farm was sugar or salt. We had good meals, we had grits and eggs and ham, that kind of stuff. My mother was born in 1910, and my dad is passed now. The thing I remember most about my dad—and I think about this all the time—is that during those days, people would travel on foot, and they would always stop by the house, and my dad would always feed them. He'd say, 'Come on in, I can't give you any money, but I can give you a meal.' And my mom would always say, 'You'll take in anybody.' And so, that's the way I am.

"Actually, when I was young, I wanted to get away from farming because it was just too much work for me, and I tried a number of things. That's how I ended up in Vietnam—I just wanted to get away. I thought I'd be treated differently once I served in Vietnam, but, unfortunately, it didn't work that way. Once I got back, I tried it as a policeman in Philadelphia, and that didn't work. And when my mom got sick, I moved back home to Florence, South Carolina, to help her. I've been farming there for well over twenty-five years now. My brother was farming, and I started farming with him. I loved the land, it was just a feeling. I love to feel the land under my feet, I love to be out there with no shoes and feel the soil, and I tell my friends that I can actually smell the watermelon growing.

"It can be difficult, too—to plant something and watch it grow, and especially when you don't have irrigation, you can't get water to it all the time. There's no paid vacation. And after you've put in all your work and all your time, you just have to hope the price is right. In 2003, I received twenty-four cents a pound for a watermelon. In 2004, I got twelve cents a pound. So there's no guarantee you're going to make money.

"I try to grow all of my stuff pesticide-free, chemical-free. I've been doing that now for probably five years. I've been trying to use manures, cover crops, and to keep the grass down I use mulches. I started doing it this way because I like to eat what I grow and I like to know what I'm eating, and I just got tired of paying those high prices for those fertilizers and pesticides. You can tell the difference in the taste of the product—and from the soil itself. Because at one time we were using chemicals in our row crops, and you'd stick a shovel in the ground and never come up with an earthworm, but now with mulches and different manures, you can find earthworms."

"The friendships that develop thanks to Farm Aid are really special. I can't wait until the next time I have an opportunity to see farm friends from all over the country. It recharges you, it gives you energy, because there are so many people still out there doing the work. Farm Aid has provided a neutral turf where people can come together and work for the good of family farmers without worrying about who belongs to what organization. That's the unique thing about Farm Aid. It's not a turf thing; Farm Aid provides a platform for groups to come together."

—DAVID SENTER, FARM ACTIVIST

When Willie Nelson staged the first Farm Aid concert, farmers were in the grip of a farm crisis as bad as most could remember. A big part of the problem stemmed from a downturn in the economy and some unfair lending practices at the USDA's FmHA.

Farmer allegations of mistreatment by FmHA had been validated two years earlier when a federal judge in Bismarck, North Dakota, ordered the agency to stop foreclosing on family farmers until it started treating farmers fairly. That order prevented an estimated eighty thousand farm foreclosures.

"We saved a lot of farms and farmers' lives," says Sarah Vogel, a lead attorney in the challenge. "I still run into people who tell me that but for that case they would not be farming."

While the judge's order temporarily halted some of the economic bleeding in farm country, the USDA dragged its feet about changing its practices. That angered farmers but also inspired them to fight back. They got so mad, they took their grievances straight to Congress and mounted a massive campaign for farm credit law reform. Among the leaders of the effort were the National Save the Family Farm Coalition (later renamed the National Family Farm Coalition), the Western Organization of Resource Councils (WORC), and the Farmers Legal Action Group (FLAG), all organizations receiving Farm Aid grant funds.

The political climate was ripe for reform, and farmers were so energized that Congress moved with unusual speed to pass the Agriculture Credit Act of 1987. Theresa Keaveny, one of the key strategists in its winning passage, says the new law played a huge role in saving farms: "It was a significant policy victory, one of the biggest in the last twenty years. It kept people on the land, gave them rights, and ensured that these rural communities would not get plowed under."

Much of the work to win reform fell to Farm Aid–funded organizations, like the National Save the Family Farm Coalition. Helen Waller, the coalition's first president, credits Farm Aid with helping to build strength and confidence within those groups. Says Waller, "One of the things that Willie and the Farm Aid board did that was so right was to evaluate existing organizations and use those structures to funnel money through rather than set up a whole new organization. It was the key to keeping administrative costs down and to activating people who were really out there struggling and working. Willie made it very clear that Farm Aid was there to help, but the burden for getting the job done was on us. He really helped us help ourselves."

With passage of the Agricultural Credit Act, Farm Aid stepped up once again to send a special letter to nearly ninety thousand FmHA borrowers, telling them about their rights under the new law, and a list of Farm Aid–funded organizations ready to help. The letter came straight from Willie Nelson, and it ended with this observation: "I know that farmers are not to blame for the 'farm crisis,' and those of us at Farm Aid will continue to do everything we can to help."

That's a promise that has not been broken.

"I grew up on a farm in Kansas that has been in my family for three generations and will someday be handed to me and hopefully handed down to my children. It was ingrained in me as a child that it was very important that we hold on to this farm no matter what. And I felt firsthand the pride that my grandfather and father took in working the land, raising the livestock. And I also recall the struggles and hardship they faced and still face. And it's a way of life. I know that growing up on a farm taught me all kinds of things and instilled in me the values that I carry with me every day and the values I hope to pass on to my children."

—MARTINA McBRIDE, FARM AID ARTIST

Homegrown: Neil Young

Dave Hoekstra With Jennifer Fahy

Every time Neil Young sings "Four Strong Winds" at a Farm Aid concert, his voice finds hope in changing conditions. Toward the end of Farm Aid 2004, Young stood in the face of a cool, damp breeze and framed every nuance of the ballad, written in 1963 by fellow Canadian Ian Tyson.

A song about recognizing the truth, "Four Strong Winds" describes a world left behind and the necessity to face the future. Before singing the song, Young told the audience of 20,000, "Go out and buy some food from family farms . . . Go to a place where they have some food grown by some people and not by factories . . . grown by some families and not by some board of directors." He reminded the crowd that Farm Aid turns twenty in 2005 and that when the organization began, America was losing more than a thousand farms a week. Young said that number is down to 330 a week, but that Farm Aid cannot and will not stop. There is still work to do.

Young is Farm Aid's truth teller. He thinks Farm Aid is different from other concerts because Farm Aid fans look for the truth to be told to them. He explains, "At my own shows, I don't really go off on things like that, because people have come to hear music—that's what they've paid for. But when people buy a ticket to Farm Aid, they're coming for Farm Aid, and that's what this is all about. So I've got a license to tell, actually. I take it as my responsibility to make sure people don't forget what they're doing, what they're supporting, and don't get carried away, having a good time so much that they forget why we're here." He goes on: "Sometimes it's a very strong picture that needs to be painted. Sometimes we need to be graphic, which is something people usually don't get at a concert."

Young gets graphic, all right. From the Farm Aid '97 stage in Illinois, he described in vivid detail the polluted rivers and streams destroyed by factory farms. He told the audience, "North Carolina's got a river in it called the Neuse River. This river is dying. The people who work in this river and fish in it have got lesions on their body. They've got bacteria growing in cuts all over their body. The fish have got massive distortions in their shapes, things growing from the inside." He described the massive pools of manure, euphemisti-

cally called "lagoons," that characterize a factory farm. These lagoons leach hog waste into our rivers and pollute our groundwater—to say nothing of their stench, which travels throughout the countryside.

Young seems to relish his role of truth teller, onstage and off. "I feel that I *should* do that. Not being the number one guy, I can be on the edge and go a little further than Willie can. Willie's the one who's gonna try to make things happen, and all I'm trying to do is to point out why we're trying to do all these things—that's my part in it." Willie Nelson appreciates that Young tells it like it is. In David Crosby's 2000 book *Stand and Be Counted,* Nelson said, "At every Farm Aid concert, I count on Neil to speak his mind. Neil doesn't hold back when he blasts factory farms for polluting the water and soil. He's not afraid to point out Washington's farm policy failures. He's got courage."

The farmers count on Young, too: Corky Jones, a Nebraska farmer who has been to every Farm Aid concert, says, "I love to see Neil get fired up. It gives farmers like me the extra fight we need to stay on another season. It gives us hope."

Young's been giving farmers hope each year since Farm Aid's beginning. In August of 1985, Young was in Texas working with Nelson on the video for their duet, "Are There Any More Real Cowboys?" for Young's *Old Ways* album. The video was being filmed at the Old West town of Luck, which Nelson created for his film *Red Headed Stranger. Old Ways* was an artistic precursor to Farm Aid, with guest appearances from Nelson, Waylon Jennings, and Spooner Oldham, augmenting Neil's band, the International Harvesters. Young agreed with Nelson that America desperately needed Farm Aid, and they got to work on planning the concert.

Young—along with Bob Dylan, the Beach Boys, Tom Petty and the Heartbreakers, and Daryl Hall—is one of the few performers who appeared at

If I was Bill Clinton
I'd be shakin in my boots
I'd straighten out the answers and give them back the truth
Then I'd save the family farmer ~~devote I still~~
a lu ~~for the power~~
lick or somethin good
behind
Tryin to ~~stop~~ keep America
from losing all its roots
Then I'd ride off in ~~sun set~~ to...

Young wrote this poem at Farm Aid on the back of a postcard in 1993 and titled it "Poem for Bucks."

both Live Aid and the first Farm Aid. At Live Aid, Young performed solo, with the International Harvesters, and he also played his first set with Crosby, Stills and Nash since 1974. (Crosby, Stills, Nash and Young would reunite again at Farm Aid in 1990 and 2000.) At the first Farm Aid, Young sang "Heart of Gold" and a torrential version of "Hey, Hey, My My (Out of the Black)," and he duetted with Waylon Jennings on the *Old Ways* track "Get Back to the Country," which Jennings would later cover.

On October 4, 1985, Young took out a full-page ad in *USA Today* with an open letter he had composed and read at the Farm Aid concert. It began with a story similar to that of many farmers in the mid-eighties: "His great grandpa worked the farm. His grandpa worked it and his daddy worked it. He's thirty years old. His wife and children at his side, he stands in the window of the old farmhouse. A car comes up the driveway. A man in a suit is at the wheel, his briefcase at his side. Today is the last day for this family farm. Tomorrow is foreclosure day." Young also spun the ballad "This Old House" out of the emotion he put into the letter. The track landed on the 1988 Crosby, Stills, Nash and Young album *American Dream*. The letter asked President Reagan to consider, "Will the family farm in America die as a result of your administration?"

It would become the first of many appeals from Young to politicians for justice for family farmers and pointed criticisms of their lack of response. At Farm Aid VI, Young admonished the new Clinton administration and Secretary of Agriculture Mike Espy. Before launching into an impassioned version of his song "Helpless," Young told the crowd, "I'd like to do this song for the Secretary of Agriculture. Mr. Espy, this song is for you. Too bad you couldn't make it. You know, we've been talking to farmers for seven or eight years now. Traveling around the country, all over the place, meeting farmers, and somehow I thought this year was going to be different. Somehow I thought people from the government were going to be here in force to see what they could do for the American farmer. Where is the change?" The administration got the message, and the next year Secretary Espy came to Farm Aid in New Orleans. The year after that, his successor, Dan Glickman, came to Farm Aid in Louisville and also participated in a town hall meeting, where he listened to farmers' testimony and attempted to address their concerns.

Young's passion comes from his love of the earth, of nature—a love he's had since he was a child. He spent the spring of 2005 in the studio recording a new album, which he says is about the prairies, where he spent his teenage years when he moved with his mother to Winnipeg. He says, "Out in the prairie there's so much space, you can see for fifty to sixty miles down the road. You can see the top of a grain elevator, and you can seem to be walking all day and still never get close enough to read what's written on the side of it. And, you know it says 'co-op' or something, but you can't quite read it." Before he moved to those wide-open spaces, Young lived with his family in the very different landscape of Ontario. He remembers, "I lived in a rural town of seven hundred people, surrounded by farms. Half of the kids I went to school with lived on farms. I lived in town but I still knew the way of life and I knew the farmers. We used to get our eggs from a farm—honey, too." As a kid, Young raised chickens and sold the eggs to earn cash. He even thought he'd grow up to be a "scientific farmer." Members of Young's family on his father's side were farmers, but they were musicians as well. And once Young had a ukulele (followed by a guitar) in his hands, all other career options went out the window.

Still, Young says, the countryside is "a big part of my life—that's where I come from and why it's easy for me to relate to rural people and that way of life. It's really the basis of so many things I believe in." It's what drives Young's dedication to Farm Aid; the people are not abstract to him. He says, "We're doing this because we're about the kind of people that we're doing it for. I can talk to farmers and look them in the eye and understand some of what they're saying to me, and they know that I care about them, even though my life is different from theirs—I've been really lucky. That's something we have in Farm Aid, relating at the person-to-person, human being-to-human being level. In my life, that's been very unique."

Farm Aid, and what it represents, is part of Young's everyday life, not just once a year. Offstage, Young and his wife, Pegi, have cultivated a deep relationship with American agriculture. "We buy our food at places where they sell good food. We try to get good organic food and those foods that we know are healthy, without the antibiotics and chemicals. We look at labels."

At Broken Arrow Ranch, their home in the hills south of San Francisco, the Youngs raise oats and barley and Scottish Highland cattle, a heritage breed known for its good temper and lean but flavorful meat. Following in his dad's footsteps, Young's son Ben raises chickens and has an organic egg business. Young says, "It's not a big business, but it shows what we believe in, and Ben's

Neil Young onstage at Farm Aid with sister Astrid Young (left) and wife, Pegi Young, 2001

"Wilco got to play at Farm Aid with the likes of Neil Young and Brian Wilson. It was great sharing the stage with those performers and hearing Brian Wilson and his band do an a cappella 'In My Room' from the next dressing room. I was moved by Neil's 'After the Gold Rush' that night, for sure. And it was inspiring to hear about the fight against factory farming, as well as learn about the difficulties independent farmers face."

—FARM AID ARTIST JOHN STIRRATT OF WILCO

"Land really is the best art."

—ANDY WARHOL, 1985

Opposite: A family farm in West Virginia. Above: Young doing an acoustic performance at Farm Aid 2001, Noblesville, Indiana

proud of it." He explains, "There's no better feeling than producing your own food and eating and selling it to others. Everybody gets a good hit from it. We get letters from people who love the eggs so much. They talk about the color, they talk about how good they taste, and how they gave somebody one of Ben's eggs, and they went out of their minds going, 'What kind of egg is this?' You know, it's just a *real* egg."

The Youngs are working to get their 1,800 acres certified organic. Young echoes the complaint of many family farmers when he talks about his difficulty in finding a local, organic processor for his beef: "Organic processing of meat is where the deficit is right now because there's a lot of beef that is grown and raised organically, but when it comes to processing, there's a shortage of places that can process it." But organic food, something close to Young's heart and often the subject of his Farm Aid rants, has become much more common than it was when Young first started talking about it. "I remember talking about organic food and really stressing how important it was, and we were worried about the conventional farmers in the audience—that I was going too far and that I was not speaking for all of them. And yet, as the years have gone by, there's more and more organic food, and we've been pushing to go in directions that other people have been realizing are a good way to go. It's not that we're responsible for these things happening, but we have shown a way for people to say, 'Hey, I could do that and I can make a difference.'" It's almost as if Young is rejoicing in a battle won when he says, "It's not such a goofy thing to want to have organic vegetables as it used to be."

Young's longtime bus driver and confidant Joe McKenna was an organic farmer in Florida. During the late 1970s, McKenna and his father purchased about twenty acres in Orange County, outside Orlando. After several hard freezes, McKenna put his farm on hold until the mid-1990s, when he was diagnosed with cancer. McKenna reestablished the farm as a certified organic operation to produce food for his own consumption and to share with others. He believed nutrition played a major role in extending his life. McKenna died in January 2003, but the farm, now being run by Joe's friends Kim Buchheit and Mike Robinson, will continue to grow good food.

Young describes good food choices as irrevocable. "Once you start down the path to good food, you don't want to go back. You feel better about what you're doing, and eventually you feel like your health is better. You feel

Young during a solo performance, Farm Aid 2001, Noblesville, Indiana

better about yourself in general. It's just good to take care of your own and take care of yourself and try to help the people who are working hard in your own country by buying the things that they're capable of making . . . that are grown in a responsible way. It makes you feel good. There's just no way around it, it's like, it's better than any of the drugs you see advertised all night on TV—I know that."

Although Young has repeatedly pronounced from the Farm Aid stage, "I'm not happy to be here . . . Farm Aid shouldn't have to be here," he concedes that there are things to celebrate. He calls Farm Aid a subtle thing, a grassroots movement with huge momentum. "It's not sensational, but it's very strong, and it moves in a very deliberate way. We didn't know where we were going to end up, we didn't know we were going to do twenty of these now. But it's just getting better and better. It's not like it's not a problem—it still is a problem, but we're making so much progress that it's giving us fuel to continue. It's not a dead-end street. We make a difference, there's no doubt about that. We do it, and we just don't go away."

Ever mindful of his role, Young cautiously ends, "There are things to celebrate. But there are things to remember, too. So you have to celebrate with good conscience." Young's good conscience has led him to take a stand for American family farmers. His voice, from the Farm Aid stage and in his everyday life, has been a strong wind for change.

"Willie Nelson and my family who farm inspired me to play at Farm Aid. My relatives have farmed for many generations in Louisiana, Arkansas, and Mississippi. Farm Aid was so empowering. Neil Young was awesome."

—DEANA CARTER, FARM AID ARTIST

"MOTHER EARTH"

Neil Young

Oh, Mother Earth,
With your fields of green
Once more laid down
  by the hungry hand
How long can you
  give and not receive
And feed this world
  ruled by greed
And feed this world
  ruled by greed.

Oh, ball of fire
In the summer sky
Your healing light,
  your parade of days
Are they betrayed
  by the men of power
Who hold this world
  in their changing hands
They hold the world
  in their changing hands.

Oh, freedom land
Can you let this go
Down to the streets
  where the numbers grow
Respect Mother Earth
  and her giving ways
Or trade away
  our children's days
Or trade away
  our children's days.

Respect Mother Earth
  and her giving ways
Or trade away
  our children's days.

Farm Aid Live!

Boyd Tinsley and band mate Dave Matthews, 1995

Arlo Guthrie, 1990

Nelson, Joe Walsh, and Bon Jovi, 1986

Tracy Chapman, 1992

Neville Brothers, 1994

Bonnie Raitt, 1990

Kris Kristofferson, 1992

John Hiatt, 1990

Lucinda Williams, 2004

Neil Young, 2001

Nelson onstage with Tom Arnold and Roseanne Barr, 1993

John Fogerty, 1997

Nelson and Billy Ray Cyrus, 1997

Tim McGraw, 1996

Lorrie Morgan, 1992

Slash and Axl Rose of Guns n' Roses, 1990

CSN&Y reunion: Stephen Stills, David Crosby, and Neil Young, 2000

Alan Jackson, 1990

Townes Van Zandt, 1993

John Mellencamp, 1998

Brian Wilson, 1998

Dave Matthews, 2002

The (Agri)Cultural Causes of Obesity

Michael Pollan

Sometimes even complicated social problems turn out to be simpler than they look. Take America's obesity epidemic, arguably the most serious public-health problem facing the country. Three of every five Americans are now overweight, and some researchers predict that today's children will be the first generation of Americans whose life expectancy will actually be shorter than that of their parents. The culprit, they say, is the health problems associated with obesity. You hear several explanations. Big food companies are pushing supersize portions of unhealthful foods on us and our children. We have devolved into a torpid nation of couch potatoes. The family dinner has succumbed to the fast-food outlet. All these explanations are true, as far as they go. But it pays to go a little further, to look for the cause *behind* the causes. Which, very simply, is this: When food is abundant and cheap, people will eat more of it and get fat. Since 1977, an American's average daily intake of calories has jumped by more than 10 percent. Those two hundred or so extra calories have to go somewhere. But the interesting question is, "Where, exactly, did all those extra calories come from in the first place?" And the answer takes us back to the source of all calories: the farm. The underlying problem is agricultural overproduction, and that problem (while it understandably never receives quite as much attention as underproduction) is almost as old as agriculture itself. Even in the Old Testament, there's talk about how to deal not only with the lean times but

also with the fat: The Bible advises creation of a grain reserve to smooth out the swings of the market in food. The nature of farming has always made it difficult to synchronize supply and demand. For one thing, there are the vagaries of nature: Farmers may decide how many acres they will plant, but precisely how much food they produce in any year is beyond their control.

The rules of classical economics don't operate very well on the farm. When prices fall, for example, it would make sense for farmers to cut back on production, shrinking the supply of food to drive up the crop's price. But in reality, farmers do precisely the opposite, planting and harvesting more food to keep their total income from falling, a practice that of course depresses prices even further. What's rational for the individual farmer is disastrous for farmers as a group. Add to this logic the constant stream of "improvements" in agricultural technology (mechanization, hybrid seed, agrochemicals, and now genetically modified crops—innovations all eagerly seized on by farmers hoping to stay one step ahead of falling prices by boosting yield)—and you have a surefire recipe for overproduction, another word for way too much food.

All this would be bad enough if the government weren't doing its best to make matters worse, by recklessly encouraging farmers to produce even more unneeded food. Absurdly, while one hand of the federal government is campaigning against the epidemic of obesity, the other hand is actually subsidizing it. We have been hearing a lot lately about how our agricultural policy is undermining our foreign-policy goals, forcing third world farmers to compete against a flood tide of cheap American grain. Well, those same policies are also undermining our public-health goals by loosing a tide of cheap calories at home.

While it is true that our farm policies are making a bad situation worse, adding mightily to the great mountain of grain, this hasn't always been the case with government support of farmers, and needn't be the case even now. For not all support programs are created equal, a fact that has been conveniently overlooked.

In fact, farm programs in America were originally created as a way to shrink the great mountain of grain, and for many years they helped to do just that. The Roosevelt administration established the nation's first program of farm support during the Depression, though not, as many people seem to

Loading corn, Perrysville, Ohio

think, to feed a hungry nation. Then, as now, the problem was *too much* food, not too little; New Deal farm policy was designed to help farmers reeling from a farm depression caused by what usually causes a farm depression: collapsing prices due to overproduction. In Churdan, Iowa, recently, a corn farmer named George Naylor told me about the winter day in 1933 when his father brought a load of corn to the grain elevator, where "the price had been ten cents a bushel the day before," and was told that, suddenly, "the elevator wasn't buying at any price." The price of corn had fallen to zero.

New Deal farm policy established a system of price supports, backed by a grain reserve, that worked to keep surplus grain off the market, thereby breaking the vicious cycle in which farmers have to produce more every year to stay even. It is worth recalling how this system worked, since it suggests one possible path out of the current subsidy morass. Basically, the federal government set and supported a target price (based on the actual cost of production) for storable commodities like corn. When the market price dropped below the target, a farmer was given an option: Rather than sell his harvest at the low price, he could take out what was called a "nonrecourse loan," using his corn as collateral, for the full value of his crop. The farmer then stored his corn until the market improved, at which point he sold it and used the proceeds to repay the loan. If the market failed to improve that year, the farmer could discharge his debt simply by handing his corn over to the government, which would add it to something called, rather quaintly, the "ever-normal granary." This was a grain reserve managed by the USDA that would sell from it whenever prices spiked (during a bad harvest, say), thereby smoothing out the vicissitudes of the market and keeping the cost of food more or less steady—or "ever normal."

This wasn't a perfect system by any means, but it did keep cheap grain from flooding the market and by doing so supported the prices farmers received. And it did this at a remarkably small cost to the government, since most of the loans were repaid. Even when they weren't, and the government was left holding the bag (i.e., all those bushels of collateral grain), the USDA was eventually able to unload it and often did so at a profit. The program actually made money in good years. Compare that with the current subsidy regime, which, as of 2004, costs American taxpayers about $19 billion a year and does virtually nothing to control production.

So why did we ever abandon this comparatively sane sort of farm policy? *Politics*, in a word. The shift from an agricultural support system designed to discourage overproduction to one that encourages it dates to the early 1970s— to the last time food prices in America climbed high enough to generate significant political heat. That happened after news of President Nixon's 1972 grain deal with the Soviet Union broke, a disclosure that coincided with a spell of bad weather in the farmbelt. Commodity prices soared, and before long so did supermarket prices for meat, milk, bread, and other staple foods tied to the cost of grain. Angry consumers took to the streets to protest food prices and staged a nationwide meat boycott to protest the high cost of hamburger, that American birthright. Recognizing the political peril, Nixon ordered his secretary of agriculture, Earl (Rusty) Butz, to do whatever was necessary to drive down the price of food.

Butz implored America's farmers to plant their fields "fence row to fence row" and set about dismantling forty years of farm policy designed to prevent overproduction. He shuttered the ever-normal granary, dropped the target price for grain, and inaugurated a new subsidy system, which eventually replaced nonrecourse loans with direct payments to farmers. The distinction may sound technical, but in effect it was revolutionary. For instead of lending farmers money so they could keep their grain off the market, the government offered to simply cut them a check, freeing them to dump their harvests on the market no matter what the price.

The new system achieved exactly what it was intended to: The shelf price of food hasn't been a political problem for the government since the Nixon era. Commodity prices have steadily declined, and, in the perverse logic of agricultural economics, production has increased, as farmers struggle to stay solvent. As you can imagine, the shift from supporting agricultural prices to subsidizing much lower prices has been a boon to agribusiness companies because it slashes the cost of their raw materials. That's why Big Food, working with the farm-state congressional delegations it lavishly supports, consistently lobbies to maintain a farm policy geared toward high production and cheap grain.

But as we're beginning to recognize, our cheap-food farm policy comes at a high price: First, there's the $19 billion a year of taxpayer dollars the government spends to keep the whole system afloat; there's the economic

Corn harvest, Big Rock, Iowa

misery that the dumping of cheap American grain inflicts on farmers in the developing world; then there's the almost immeasurable cost of environmental pollution and depletion, which takes more taxpayer dollars to address; and, finally, there's the obesity epidemic at home—which most researchers date to having started in the mid-seventies, just when we switched to a farm policy consecrated to the overproduction of grain. Since that time, farmers in the United States have managed to produce five hundred additional calories per person every day; each of us is, heroically, managing to pack away about two hundred of those extra calories per day. Presumably, the other three hundred—most of them in the form of surplus corn—get dumped on overseas markets or turned into ethanol.

Cheap corn, the dubious legacy of Earl Butz, is truly the building block of the "fast-food nation." Cheap corn, transformed into high-fructose corn syrup, is what allowed Coca-Cola to move from the svelte eight-ounce bottle of soda ubiquitous in the seventies to the chubby twenty-ounce bottle of today. Cheap corn, transformed into cheap beef, is what allowed McDonald's to supersize its burgers and still sell many of them for no more

than a dollar. Cheap corn gave us a whole raft of new highly processed foods, including the chicken nugget, which, if you study its ingredients, you discover is really a most ingenious transubstantiation of corn—from the corn-fed chicken it contains to the bulking and binding agents that hold it together.

Such cheap raw materials also lead to more and more highly processed food, because the real money will never be in selling cheap corn (or soybeans or rice) but in "adding value" to that commodity. Which is one reason that in the years since the nation moved to a cheap-food farm policy, the number and variety of new snack foods in the supermarket has ballooned. The game is in figuring out how to transform a penny's worth of corn and additives into a $3 bag of ginkgo biloba–fortified brain-function-enhancing puffs, or a dime's worth of milk and sweeteners into Swerve, a sugary new "milk based" soft drink to be sold in schools. It's no coincidence that Big Food has suddenly "discovered" how to turn milk into junk food: The government has made deep cuts in the dairy-farm program, and as a result milk is nearly as cheap a raw material as water. As public concern over obesity mounts, the focus of

Farm Aid Backstage  Kris Kristofferson

At Farm Aid VI, Kris Kristofferson, a veteran of the previous five FA concerts, got a kick out of an incident that occurred between Neil Young and Roger Clinton. The president's brother was onboard to sing, hang out, and promote an upcoming album. "At the press conference," Kristofferson later recalled, "everybody was saying they were so glad to be back at Farm Aid. They got to Neil Young, and he said something like, 'I'm not glad to be back here. This is the sixth one, and we don't have one person from the government here repre-

senting the people.' I guess Roger Clinton took offense to that. He said something very condescending to Neil, and if looks could kill, Roger would have been dropped in his tracks."

At Farm Aid VI, Kristofferson sang "Vietnam Blues," his first songwriting hit, recorded in 1966 by Dave Dudley. Kristofferson later joined his fellow Highwaymen for a set. (After one of the first Highwaymen sessions in 1985, Kristofferson

walked into the studio complaining that something was wrong with his voice. "How would you know?" asked his buddy Willie.)

Kristofferson, a native of Brownsville, Texas, said, "I've been trying to carry on the same tradition as John [Cash], providing a voice for some people who don't have one. . . . When popular heroes are consistently generous and compassionate, it's a powerful example for the people who love

them. Maybe we're on the verge of a spiritual revolution."

At the first Farm Aid, Kristofferson did an early-afternoon set that included "Me and Bobby McGee," "Shipwrecked in the Eighties," and "They Killed Him," a ballad about the deaths of Mahatma Gandhi and Martin Luther King Jr. "The problem is still there today," Kristofferson said recently. "The small family farmers are dying out against the big corporations. I can't believe it's been twenty years."

—DAVE HOEKSTRA

political pressure has settled on the food industry and its marketing strategies—supersizing portions, selling junk food to children, lacing products with trans fats and sugars. Certainly Big Food bears some measure of responsibility for our national eating disorder—a reality that a growing number of food companies have publicly accepted: Kraft, McDonald's, and Coca-Cola have vowed to change marketing strategies and even recipes in an effort to help combat obesity and, no doubt, ward off the coming tide of litigation.

There is an understandable reluctance to let Big Food off the hook. Yet by devising ever more ingenious ways to induce us to consume the surplus calories our farmers are producing, the food industry is only playing by a set of rules written by our government. (And maintained, it is true, with the industry's political muscle.) The political challenge now is to rewrite those rules, to develop a new set of agricultural policies that don't subsidize overproduction—and overeating. For unless we somehow deal with the mountain of cheap grain that makes the Happy Meal and the Double Stuf Oreo such "bargains," the calories are guaranteed to keep coming. 🚜

"I was flattered that Willie asked the Supersuckers to be involved in Farm Aid. I had never thought about our band being able to help with anything until we did Farm Aid for the first time, in Louisville, in 1995. Then we thought, 'Well, you know, we have some fans and we might influence some people and they might influence some people, and who knows?' So you do feel like you're rocking for a higher purpose, which is a good thing for everybody. It's good for a band to forget about themselves once in a while and do something for a reason other than furthering their career. All of the experiences with Willie and Farm Aid have been really heady and great, and a lot of crazy, magical things have happened for us. It's got such a great energy."

—EDDIE SPAGHETTI OF THE SUPERSUCKERS

Farm Aid Backstage  Nanci Griffith

The spacious Hoosier Dome in Indianapolis was the right setting for Nanci Griffith to sing "From a Distance," a beautiful ballad she discovered from New York songwriter Julie Gold that went on to become a hit for Bette Midler. Griffith performed the song before forty-five thousand people at Farm Aid IV. She sang, "From a distance there is harmony/And it echoes through the land/It's the hope of hopes, it's the love of loves/It's the heart of every man." Griffith also sang her topical farm ballad "Trouble in the Fields." Both tunes were from her 1986 album *Lone Star State of Mind*.

"I remember the familial grace of being there," Griffith said. "I was so excited to do it. I enjoyed doing panels with the farmers. That was important because my family were all farmers out in West Texas. They survived the Dust Bowl and the Great Depression on their farms. I felt I was carrying on in the footsteps of my family."

Farm Aid IV found Griffith being followed by the likes of Iggy Pop, Was (Not Was), and John Prine. "I remember that well," Griffith said of the eclectic lineup. "Alan Jackson played the year I was there, and it was right before he really hit," she said. "He came up and introduced himself. That was sweet. I'll always remember that. It made me curious, so I watched his segment when he played." Early in the day, Jackson sang "Here in the Real World" and "Blue Blooded Woman."

Griffith remains politically involved today. She is active with the Campaign for a Landmine Free World and has traveled to Indochina with the Vietnam Veterans of America. "My parents were beatniks," she said. "They were both very political and very left wing. It's impossible to not be political when you grow up in Austin, Texas."

—DAVE HOEKSTRA

A Bright Future for "Farmers of the Middle"

Frederick Kirschenmann

"One of [Benjamin] Franklin's goals in life was to provide useful advice for aspiring middle-class shopkeepers and tradesmen. He was America's godfather of self-help business books. By creating what he called a strong "middling class," he hoped to lay the foundation for his vision of a stable civic society in America . . . the 'middling people' should be the proud sinews of the new land."

—WALTER ISAACSON, *A BENJAMIN FRANKLIN READER*

The notion that the middle class forms the bedrock of American civic society has deep roots in our culture. In fact, as early as 1774, Benjamin Franklin wrote that the very survival of the Province of Pennsylvania depended on "the middling people"—the "farmers, shopkeepers, and tradesmen of this city and country." In *Plain Truth,* he argued that "mistaken principles of religion" combined with "a love of worldly power," exercised by a few elite in positions of power, threatened to undo the good life envisioned by the majority in the middle. America's modern day middling people, especially the farmers of the middle, are once again under siege.

According to data from the 2002 Census of Agriculture, in just five years (1997–2002), the United States lost 14.5 percent of its midsize farmers, those with gross sales ranging from $50,000 to $500,000. In many Midwest states where farming anchors the state's economy, those midsize operator losses were even higher: Iowa, 18.5 percent; Michigan, 18 percent; and Illinois, 16.5 percent.

There are many reasons for these dismal statistics. Ever increasing concentration in the industrial food sector forces farmers to expand their operations to maintain access to these markets. Large firms prefer doing business with large farms because it reduces their transaction costs. Constant increases in fossil fuel costs (the basis of almost all industrial farm inputs) put undercapitalized farmers at a competitive disadvantage. The predominant business culture in our society insists that in a market-based economy, efficiency of scale is the *only* important social and economic "good," and therefore the loss of the midscale farms is simply an "inevitable" outcome of free market

forces at work. Furthermore, current federal farm policies have tended to favor large farms.

During this same five-year period that farms of the middle have been disappearing, the number of mega farms (over $500,000 in gross sales) has been *increasing*. But, so has the number of the very small farms (those with less than $5,000 in gross sales). These trends reflect growth in direct market sales (mainly by small farms) and highly concentrated, bulk commodity farm sales (mostly by megafarms, which tend to produce one or two commodities under contract to highly concentrated firms).

What emerges is a bipolar food system that offers consumers only two food choices: buying directly from small farmers through farmers markets, Internet sales, and other direct-marketing arrangements; or buying mass-produced (usually highly processed) foods that travel through supply chains dominated by megafood firms offering virtually no traceability or differentiated characteristics.

These changes have placed America's independent family farm in the middle in a very vulnerable position. Pushed out of the bulk, mass-production commodity market by economies of scale, and largely prevented from direct marketing due to the lack of adequate infrastructure to accommodate their productive capacity, the middling farmers are disappearing rapidly.

During the past decade, most Americans seemed unconcerned about these trends. As long as a constant flow of branded products continued to show up in local supermarkets at reasonable prices, customers seemed to be satisfied. *Fast, convenient,* and *cheap* became the siren call of the marketplace.

Fortunately, that is changing. While these grim farm statistics have been playing themselves out, an unprecedented new market has emerged—a market uniquely suited to the farms in the middle. This new market features rising demand for highly differentiated food products, which are distinguished by quality characteristics, by accompanying food stories, and by new supply chain relationships. *Fast, convenient,* and *cheap* are being challenged by *memory, romance,* and *trust.* And, now, a few Benjamin Franklin types are issuing the clarion call to help shape a new business culture to meet the growing demands of this new market.

Restaurant chefs have mounted the bully pulpit declaring that they are no longer satisfied with the usual humdrum fare. They still wish to provide their customers with great-tasting food, but they also want to tell diners where the food came from, what kind of environmental stewardship was practiced in producing it and bringing it to their tables, how the animals that provide the meat on their plates were treated, and how the farmers and farm workers who produced the food were compensated.

In addition, health care providers have taken a new interest in the kind of food being fed to patients in hospitals. Should they really be serving meat from animals that have been fed subtherapeutic levels of antibiotics when antibiotic resistance is a mounting health care problem? And nursing homes and other long-term care facilities are beginning to explore whether an additional investment in health-promoting foods could actually decrease the cost of long-term care for their clients.

The dramatic increase in obesity and diabetes among children is compelling local school boards to take a more critical, health-based look at the food being served in school lunch programs. College and university students are putting pressure on school administrators to provide better tasting, locally grown, more nutritious food in campus cafeterias.

These emerging markets place new demands on food-service providers for highly differentiated food products. These new-market consumers want fresh fruits and vegetables that are grown nearby; grass-fed beef and dairy products that are raised without antibiotics or growth hormones; food products that travel through a fully transparent supply chain that provides for complete traceability; and food that was produced by local family farmers and farm workers who are adequately compensated. And visionary CEOs of food service corporations are beginning to reshape the business culture of their companies to meet these growing demands and take advantage of these new market opportunities.

The emergence of this highly differentiated food market is consistent with sound free-market theory and provides unique opportunities for the farmers in the middle. More than a decade ago, Michael Porter of the Harvard Business School argued that there are two ways to be competitive in a global economy: being the lowest cost supplier of an undifferentiated commodity, or being the supplier of a product that commands higher value by virtue of its differentiation. Each can be equally competitive and therefore successful in the marketplace. Porter also argues that, while not impossible, it is extremely difficult for the same firm to be the supplier of *both* undifferentiated and differentiated products.

Farmers of the middle possess a comparative advantage in producing these highly differentiated products. Small farmers, who use direct market channels to pass their products to consumers, lack the capacity and effective distribution channels to meet the rising market demands of restaurants, hospitals, schools, and nursing homes. The megafarms, which mass-produce large quantities of undifferentiated commodities at the lowest possible price, will find it hard to efficiently target their operations to produce products with these special features. Furthermore, large-commodity farms will find it much harder to promote the kind of food story that the market wants to hear. The farmers in the middle have the precise productive capacity, the innovative management potential, and the compelling kinds of food stories to meet the market demand.

Of course, there are challenges. It is always difficult to change an entrenched business culture. Most farmers have been conditioned to believe that the only way to be competitive in today's global economy is to be the lowest cost supplier of a mass-produced commodity. The economic pressures of the past half-century have left us with an aging farm population where there are almost three times as many farmers over age sixty-five as under age thirty-five. It also is difficult for food firms in a supply chain (that have long operated on the business principle of competition with other players in the chain) to begin operating as farming partners within a new system to produce a product of unique value.

Inadequate infrastructure poses an additional challenge. Most of today's processing and packing firms are designed to manufacture undifferentiated products as cheaply as possible. These firms were not designed to process differentiated products that retain their identity from farm to table. But developing the enterprises to meet this demand offers many opportunities for rural economic development. Constructing moderate-size, efficient, multi-species meat-processing facilities similar to some of the new-generation abattoirs in Europe might be a unique opportunity to generate and retain wealth within rural communities throughout the United States.

Of course, these efforts will require investment capital. Farmers will need capital to make the transition from being undifferentiated commodity producers to becoming producers of unique, highly differentiated products. Investments in such food-related enterprises traditionally have not been as attractive as investments in the development of new technologies. But it may be possible to attract local investors to support enterprises that have the potential to improve the health and well-being of their own communities. There also is a small but growing group of socially conscious investors more open to considering unique, environmentally friendly food enterprises as targets for their investment dollars.

Farmers and other partners involved in the new values-based, value chain enterprise need reliable information upon which to base their business decisions as they enter this new business world. Accordingly, the agricultural research and education communities need to take a fresh look at their research and extension activities. For example, if farmers are to be compensated adequately for their role in the value chain, reliable data are needed on the cost of production for the many new, differentiated food products. Food customers who want to buy particular food products because such purchases "support local family farmers" will need assurances that this claim is au-thentic. The Fair Trade Coffee enterprise may serve as a model. Farmers also may require unique seeds to produce plants with specific qualities of taste and nutrition. The research community may need to work with farmers to develop new varieties.

To bring these new products into the marketplace in an efficient manner, farmers will need to develop marketing networks. Each network could feature its own brand promoting its own unique differentiated product, but all the networks would be united in a national program. This program would guarantee that common environmental and social standards had been met and verified through a third-party certification system and the process would be identified by a common seal. Already, such networks are evolving in various regions of the country, and systems are in place to certify farms that adhere to organic and crop improvement standards. This same system will be employed to certify the farmers of the middle who produce these unique products, as well as identifying their other partners in the value chain.

Finally, we will need new government policy options so that the farmers in the middle who produce these unique products are not discriminated against by policies that were designed primarily to meet the needs of farmers producing undifferentiated commodity products.

Fortunately, a national "Agriculture of the Middle" program already has begun to address many of these issues. The program includes farm, university, industry, government agency, and nonprofit organization leaders. There is reasonable optimism that these challenges can be addressed successfully.

Market demand is a powerful economic driver, and as long as the public continues to demand these unique products, entrepreneurs will find a way to meet that demand. And hopefully our middling farmers will benefit from that market demand.

Diversity Needed in U.S. Agriculture

Edward "Jerry" Pennick, Director, Land Assistance Fund,
Federation of Southern Cooperatives/Land Assistance Fund

We farmers know that diversification is key to survival because it lessens dependence on one crop while increasing market potential. And for African-American farmers, the need for diversity goes far beyond what's in our fields. To build a sustainable and just agricultural system, there must also be racial diversity. Racial diversity in U. S. agriculture is the only way for every community to have the opportunity to create a significant degree of local control over food production.

Unfortunately, African-Americans are in serious danger of being forced out of America's agricultural production system altogether. The National Agricultural Statistics Service (NASS) estimates that today, African-Americans own 7.8 million acres of rural land, which has an estimated value of $14.4 billion. Studies by the Federation of Southern Cooperatives/Land Assistance Fund indicate that African-American–owned rural land is being lost at the rate of one thousand acres per week. That translates into $2 million in real wealth that is drained from the African-American community each week, not to mention the additional millions in potential land-related economic activity, both agricultural and nonagricultural.

One of the main reasons for African-American farm and land loss may well be actions of the government itself. After denying blatant evidence of racial discrimination for years, in 1997 the USDA settled the largest class-action lawsuit in U.S. history brought by African-American farmers (*Pigford v. Glickman*). While the case brought the experience of African-American farmers to the public's attention, it will do very little to slow down the pace of African-American land loss unless it goes hand in hand with the political will and action needed to ensure racial diversity and equality within the USDA.

Thomas Jefferson equated land ownership with citizenship. History shows that the more African-Americans are able to own and sustainably develop their land, the more active participants they are in the social, economic, and political evolution of the country. The ultimate success in reversing the trend of African-American land loss will be determined by the level of commitment, from both the public and private sector, to a diverse food and agriculture system that leaves no farmer behind.

"There's a respect for the farmers from country artists that is profound, and to think that the farmers are going to be displaced from their homes . . . is enough to incite these great artists to riot on their behalf. There's something essentially noble about the American farmer."

—MARK ROTHBAUM, FARM AID BOARD MEMBER

"Our organization, the Federation of Southern Cooperatives, was created during the civil rights movement to help rural communities and African-American farmers find a way for us to hold on to the land. Over the years, we have worked with fifteen to twenty thousand farmers who have traditionally not had access to markets, to capital, or to resources. We work in one hundred of the poorest communities in the South, in Georgia, Alabama, Mississippi, South Carolina, Louisiana, and Arkansas—the black belt. And those farmers own fifty, seventy-five acres; they are not of scale to compete with the larger farmers, nor do they get the resources that large farmers get, like subsidies. Most of our farmers have a small acreage of vegetables.

"We realized that we needed to team up with Willie and Farm Aid because the same problems that are hitting every family farmer in this country hit black farmers double. Farm Aid has been instrumental in helping us meet some of the challenges by forming a coalition with other farm groups from around the country. It's more than money that is needed to save family farmers. It's the awareness that Farm Aid has brought—it's the activism that they have brought to the movement. I think part of the battle is going to be won through that."

—RALPH PAIGE, DIRECTOR, FEDERATION OF SOUTHERN COOPERATIVES

Mississippi farmer Tommy Harmon

A New Farm Policy for Good Food From Family Farms

Mark Smith, Campaign Director, Farm Aid

Imagine the countryside dotted with many small farms on the land, contributing to strong and vibrant local economies. Imagine our streams and waterways clean and protected for future generations. Imagine that the food you buy is fresh, grown locally, and free of unnecessary additives and chemicals. All of these "imaginings" are within our reach—but

they will not be realized without our determined insistence for a new direction of food and farm policy to guide how our food is to be grown, and by whom.

The *new* American agriculture that is the basis for the Good Food movement needs the support of policy makers to ensure that these family farm–centered food production models continue to grow and expand.

The federal Farm Bill, which Congress debates and passes every five to seven years, must put the interests of America's family farmers, consumers, and the environment above those of the giant agribusiness corporations that now dominate our food industry. For too long, corporate interests have steered our federal food and farm programs to their own benefit at the expense of all other interests. All of us eat; therefore, all of us have a stake in the next farm bill. *We the People* must demand a new direction for our national food and farm policy, one that serves our interests rather than a handful of multinational food giants.

Farm Aid's vision for a fair and just food and farm policy for America would:

• Provide farmers a fair market price for their products in fair and competitive marketplaces.

• Support incentives in federal farm programs that encourage and support the transition of American agriculture from the currently chemical-dependent industrial practices to more diversified and sustainable methods of production for food, fiber, and crops used for renewable energy.

• Increase support for programs that expand family farm–centered food systems, including farm-to-school programs, farmers markets, Community Supported Agriculture farms (CSAs), and programs that increase access to fresh, nutritious, and locally produced food.

• Stop factory farms and provide incentives to increase production and marketing of sustainable livestock production.

• Expand programs that support young people to become farmers, including long-term low- or no-interest loans.

• Increase conservation measures to avoid wasteful overproduction and to improve environmental stewardship of our natural resources.

• Create a farmer-owned reserve to ensure food security in times of scarcity and price stability in times of plenty.

• Implement mandatory country of origin labeling on food products so that consumers know where their food comes from and can choose their food accordingly.

• Enforce, and if necessary overhaul, existing antitrust laws to stop the growing corporate consolidation and control of the food industry.

• Put an end to export and import dumping of agricultural commodities that push small-scale producers around the world off their land.

• Support fair-trade agreements that place domestic food sovereignty— the right of each country to develop farm programs that meet the needs of their citizens—above the interests of the multinational food corporations. Support international trade policies that place family farm agriculture, sound resource management, safe food, and viable rural communities above the excessive profits of the multinational food corporations.

Organic Farming: A Solution Story

Bob Scowcroft, Organic Farming Research Foundation

By most estimates, sales of organically labeled products represented about 2 percent of our nation's food economy in 2004. This means that America's consumers spent about $11 billion on certified organic products. This is especially significant when one realizes that twenty years ago the organic economy probably amounted to less than $100 million. Today, America's organic farmers provide us with just about everything from asparagus to zucchini, milk to cotton, beef to flowers.

Farmers have made the transition to organic production systems for any number of reasons: Environmental protection, avoiding dangerous pesticides, and the high quality of organically grown products all fit into the mix. But let's face it, the primary reason is the public's ever-expanding commitment to pay the real cost for the food they eat. Simply put, more consumer demand equals more organic acreage, and more organic farmers.

We estimate that as many as ten thousand organic farmers—the vast majority sole proprietors or family farmers—will plant and harvest their organic acreage in 2005. They will do so to sell directly to consumers and also into an ever expanding market of processing and wholesale operations. Consumer surveys identify taste, freshness, and health benefits as the primary reasons more consumers are purchasing certified organic food.

But more must be done. The organic economy has expanded, despite any identifiable institutional or governmental support. Our nation's 69 agricultural university research institutions have just 496 certified organic research acres out of an estimated 886,000 available research acres. Congress has appropriated only $3.5 million of our total $1 billion Agricultural Research Service (ARS) budget for organic research—a mere 0.35 percent. At a minimum, since organic food currently represents 2 percent of our food economy, organic farmers should receive 2 percent of our land-grant and governmental-agricultural resources. We call it a fair-share standard for organic family farmers.

One place where we can generate additional resources for organic farmers is in Congress, where our representatives debate and determine our food and farming policies. Using the "fair-share" standard as a benchmark, Congress should appropriate $18 million annually for ARS organic research. But that's not enough. We need more farmers transitioning to organic production systems as well.

Everyone knows that farming isn't easy. Leaving conventional agriculture for an organic farming system—one that may take three or four years to achieve certified organic status—requires a quantum leap of faith in one's own farming and marketing skills, a new network of information sources, and the support of one's neighbors, who may not understand your change of heart. Some might define such a leap of faith as a "paradigm shift," while others imagine a perfect ear of organic sweet corn on a hot summer's day.

Suffice it to say, we know "organic" when we verify, see, and taste it. Consumers have created an opportunity for change in our nation's heartland. And family farmers, both young and old, are responding accordingly. There may be no other story where the power of one individual's shopping list can have so much of an impact on the very fabric of our rural culture and heritage. Personal responsibility goes a long way. Make your shopping list an organic one and bring the future of farming into your kitchen today. 🚜

"People who love the land, who want the land to give back to them forever, are the people who are going to produce the food that's good."

—DAVE MATTHEWS

The Consequences
of Industrial Agriculture

Factory Farms Pollute Our Water

Robert F. Kennedy Jr., President, Water Keeper Alliance

For three hundred years, America's family farmers produced more than enough pork chops, chicken, and dairy products for domestic consumers and export markets. They practiced traditional animal husbandry, rotating their animals with crops and recycling their manure so that pollution did not get into public waterways. These family farmers were proud stewards of their land, raising their animals in an environmentally sound and humane manner.

A few decades ago, a handful of industrialists devised a way to produce chicken, then pork and milk, in factories, often eliminating family farmers, and maximizing their own profits by housing their animals in crowded buildings and creating huge piles of manure or ponds of liquefied fecal waste, much of which has ended up in America's rivers and estuaries.

Uncontrolled pollution and odors from factory farms are contaminating hundreds of miles of American rivers and are destroying rural communities. Over the past dozen years, industrial pork, chicken, and dairy factories have killed billions of fish, put tens of thousands of farmers out of work, subjected billions of farm animals to unnecessary cruelty, and poisoned America's air and groundwater.

A couple of years ago, I met a farmer named Julian Savage, who has experienced this devastation firsthand. He and his wife live on a modest North Carolina farm that has been in his family since the Revolutionary War. Julian always raised a few crops, some chickens, and some hogs. He made a little money on the side by leasing out part of his farm to summer campers. Ten years ago, all of that came to an abrupt end when a hog factory moved in next door. The stench from the operation's liquefied hog waste was so overwhelming that both he and his wife have vomited from the fumes, and he once passed out in his yard. His doctor actually told him that to protect his health, he must stop working in his own fields. And, of course, no one came to his camping spot anymore. The odor permeates his entire property, and his fishing hole, now polluted, no longer produces any fish. This is just one family's story, but, unfortunately, it is typical.

Several years ago, after Rick Dove, the Neuse riverkeeper, showed me photos of devastation from hog and poultry factories in North Carolina, I wanted to see it for myself. In the mid-eighties, North Carolina saw an explosive growth in hog and poultry factories, which has led to it becoming the nation's number two hog-producing state and one of the top chicken- and turkey-producing states.

Rick Dove took me by boat and airplane to see North Carolina's rivers. On this tour, Rick threw a net over the side of his boat and pulled out fish with pustulating lesions. "These fish will die soon," Rick explained to me. "They have been exposed to a microscopic organism called *Pfiesteria piscicida,* which is giving them these sores." Researchers have learned that in recent years *Pfiesteria* has been infecting waters in North Carolina and the Chesapeake Bay. The toxic organism has been activated by extreme nutrient pollution, much of it from hog and poultry factories. Then Rick took me to meet some of the fishermen who had been working in the *Pfiesteria* infested waters; they had open sores on their arms and legs that would not heal. One, a man named David Jones, had experienced significant memory loss, another symptom of *Pfiesteria* exposure. Finally Rick and I flew in a small plane over North Carolina's rivers. When I looked down, I saw pollution-choked waters everywhere. Just two decades earlier, these rivers had been pristine.

While multinational food conglomerates build more animal factories, however, survey after survey demonstrates that Americans prefer food that comes from traditional farms, not industrial operations. Consumers consistently say that they believe food from family farms is safer, healthier, and tastier. They also care about the way animals are being treated and the environmental impacts of the food they are eating.

One company I really like is Niman Ranch, a network of family farmers and ranchers who all adhere to a strict animal husbandry protocol. Bill Niman, a cattle rancher and the company's founder, says that thirty years ago he "just wanted to raise animals the way nature intended." All of Niman Ranch's animals are raised without hormones, without antibiotics, and without being fed animal by-products. Niman Ranch's pig farming standards, created by the Animal Welfare Institute (AWI), require that all pigs have access to pasture or deep straw bedding and prohibit environmentally unsound practices like liquefied manure and inhumane practices like tail docking and metal sow crates (both of which are ubiquitous in the factory farm industry). AWI's standards also require that the animals be raised on true family owned and operated farms.

Like most Americans, I want my food to come from family farms, not factories. When I buy meat from Niman Ranch and other family farmers, I know that I am supporting environmentally friendly, humane farming. And that's the way I like it. 🚜

Factory-farm hogs are confined in cages that do not allow them to move about freely.

"It frightens me when farming becomes a big corporate business. I think that the food suffers, especially the way that animals are being raised in incredibly inhumane conditions. But beyond that, it's so unhealthy and so harmful to the environment—and then we put the stuff in our bodies and we wonder why we're getting sick. It's really horrific what the agribusinesses are doing to Mother Nature—and it's going to come back to bite us."

EMMYLOU HARRIS, FARM AID ARTIST

Neil Young joins family farmers protesting factory hog farms.

Farm Aid Program Campaign for Family Farms and the Environment

The fight against factory hog farms was launched on April 1, 1995, in Lincoln Township, Missouri. There, Farm Aid and family farmers desperate for economic justice banded together to oppose corporate agribusiness. More than three thousand family farmers stomped through snow from an early-spring storm to gather down the road from a huge factory farm complex known as Premium Standard Farms. These farmers knew well the economic and environmental damage the factory farm and others like it were wreaking all over the country. Family farmers, who have long viewed hogs as so-called "mortgage lifters," because they add value to crop production and mean cash to typically cash-strapped operations, were losing out to factory farms.

USDA statistics tell the hard story: In 1985, there were 388,570 farmers selling hogs, and the average farm sold 117 hogs a year. In 2003, only 73,600 U.S. hog farmers remained, and average sales were about 739 hogs per farm per year.

In the early 1990s, Farm Aid began hearing from farmers and farm groups about "factory farms" and the damage they were doing in rural areas. To counter industrial farming interests, Farm Aid supported the convening of planning sessions with farmers in Kansas City, Missouri, which resulted in the formation of the Campaign for Family Farms and the Environment (CFFE). Since then, Farm Aid has supported this dynamic collaboration of farm groups through grants to member groups and to a central organizing team. As is often the case with Farm Aid, added support came from Willie Nelson himself.

Willie brought Farm Aid's voice to the fight against factory farms in his typically down-to-earth way. He rode his tour bus from Austin, to the Lincoln Township rally, got up on a makeshift stage on a flatbed truck, and, backed by a group of local musicians, sang songs like "On the Road Again" and "Will the Circle Be Unbroken."

While the farmers at the rally loved the performance, Willie really electrified the throng when he told them, "This is what Farm Aid is all about. Stopping the big corporate guys from running over the little guys."

Missouri hog farmer Roger Allison MC'd the rally. "The crowd went absolutely wild when Willie said that," he recalled. "There were whoops and hollers and clapping and whistling. Willie's appearance and Farm Aid's support energized the campaign. When people get the crap kicked out of them over and over, sometimes it's a little hard for them to get up in the morning. But then you have Willie. He drives up from Texas to show his support, and people see that and say, 'By gosh, there is hope, because we have friends in high places,' and by that I mean Willie Nelson and Farm Aid. It just renewed people's spirits to fight back for economic, social, and environmental justice."

The Lincoln Township rally was only the beginning for the farmers. With Farm Aid support, family farmers staged rally after rally, challenged an unfair pork industry taxing system through a petition drive, and forced a successful vote on the tax that saw thirty thousand independent hog producers turn thumbs down on the factory farm system. When the USDA tried to pretend the vote never took place, the farmers and their campaign took the USDA to court and said, "This is America! There's no way we're going to let the USDA steal the results of a democratically conducted vote just because a handful of corporate agriculture interests have the government in their pocket." Though lower courts sided with the farmers, the U.S. Supreme Court handed them a severe setback when it declined to reverse the USDA action.

With Farm Aid's ongoing support, those same farmers and others like them intend to continue their efforts to gain economic, social, and environmental justice for family farmers.

Opposite: Grass-fed beef cattle on the Marin Sun Farm, Inverness, California

The Ugly Face of Soil Erosion

Gene Logsdon

If you pause at the top of the hillside in my pasture and look around, you might notice that there has been a decided movement of the earth's crust right under your feet. You can tell by looking at the woodlot that adjoins the pasture. The soil surface in the woods, which has never been cultivated, is about three feet higher than the pasture. Three feet of soil have eroded off my hillside between about 1885 and 1975, when I put a stop to it by turning the hill into permanent pasture. That's a little less a half-inch a year, seemingly negligible. But it adds up. And this is a little hill. Our area in north-central Ohio is described on soil maps as flat to gently rolling, not subject to severe erosion.

Throughout the country, the severity of soil erosion is evident—even though the National Resource Inventory (NRI) uses a hopeful tone to report the statistics. In 2001, "only" 103.8 million acres suffered severe soil loss, which was down from 172 million in 1982. But that's still 1.8 billion tons of lost soil, down from 3.1 billion. Though it may sound like progress, other millions of acres are suffering "moderate" soil loss that is still, in the long run, unacceptable.

Various statisticians try to put those numbers in meaningful terms. A California study indicates that we are losing four to six pounds of soil for every pound of food we eat. Whereas by employing biointensive, small-plot farming methods, we could add twenty pounds of soil for every pound we eat. In the Midwest, experts generally agree that the cornbelt is still losing four to five bushels of soil for every bushel of corn produced, the lost soil turning the Gulf of Mexico off New Orleans into a gigantic "dead zone."

The general assumption has been that with modern conservation methods we are licking the problem. Experts have declared that the worst days of soil erosion have passed, that there would be no more horrendous twenty-ton-plus losses of soil per acre per year. But even the experts admit that in some areas, when wind erosion is added in, soil losses still exceed fourteen tons per acre per year and more.

Is there any way to stop erosion? Yes. We could redistribute the structure of agriculture back into local economies. We could take the farm animals out of those miserable animal factories and take displaced farmers out of the miserable human factories and put them both back on the land. Then put at least 80 percent of the farmland back into permanent or semipermanent grass and legumes and let the animals do the harvesting by grazing. Scores of books and articles describe how it is done. This could reduce erosion to acceptable levels *if* the pastures are not overgrazed or mismanaged.

Could it happen? Yes. It already is. The number of grass, or pasture, farmers is increasing. They are proving that pasture farming can raise as much food per acre as can annual cultivation—and at far less expense.

Agribusiness counters by pointing out that farmers still produce, as in 2004, record-breaking crops. There is a short answer for that. Take away the fertilizer that produces those records, and yields on eroded land will drop precipitously. We just can't keep adding more petroleum-based fertilizer to make up for soil and soil nutrients lost to erosion, even if we had an unlimited amount of cheap fertilizer—which we don't.

Opposite: A deeply furrowed field in the Central Valley, near Fresno, California

"To forget how to dig the earth and tend the soil is to forget ourselves."

—MAHATMA GANDHI

Genetically Engineered Seeds: The Death of Agriculture

Martin Teitel

Agricultural genetic engineering (GE) is the manipulation of specific genes, moving them from one species and inserting them into another to create a specific trait. For example, a pesticide has been built into every cell of a GE corn plant. Resistance to an herbicide has been built into a GE soybean plant. A flounder gene has been inserted into a tomato plant to produce tomatoes with better freezing quality. These gene transfers from one species to another could not have occurred in nature.

Seeds aren't merely a part of agriculture—in many respects, seeds *are* agriculture. Twelve thousand years ago, people around the world invented agriculture by saving seeds that best met their community's needs and tastes, just as they selected animals for breeding that provided the best food and fiber. A community of people slowly shaping plants by seed saving is the core of agriculture and the basis for most of human civilization.

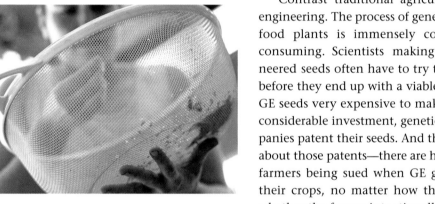

This is why the spread of genetically engineered food endangers agriculture. It is not because the technology has not been proven safe—although that is the case. It is not because biotechnology plants create living pollution that imperils organic agriculture around the world—although they do. It is not because this kind of technology creates a high-input global monoculture that reduces biological diversity and jeopardizes family farmers everywhere—although that happens every day.

Rather, in addition to those problems and others, genetically engineered food-producing plants threaten the very heart of agriculture: the creation and maintenance of interdependent life between people and the plants they eat. Without the plants that feed us and animals, we would die. Without farmers to tend those plants and save their seeds, most agricultural plants would quickly disappear. Yet it is precisely this intimate and indispensable relationship between plants and human communities that is most threatened by genetic engineering of food-producing plants.

Contrast traditional agriculture with genetic engineering. The process of genetically engineering food plants is immensely complex and time-consuming. Scientists making genetically engineered seeds often have to try thousands of times before they end up with a viable plant. This makes GE seeds very expensive to make. To protect their considerable investment, genetic engineering companies patent their seeds. And they are very serious about those patents—there are hundreds of cases of farmers being sued when GE genes are found in their crops, no matter how the genes got there, whether the farmer intentionally planted the seeds without permission or whether the wind blew the seeds in without the farmer's knowledge.

Aside from the ethical, economic, and political issues that arise when corporations claim ownership of the basis for all human life, the patenting of seeds also changes, and maybe ends, agriculture. Agriculture consists of living representations of community values, carried from generation to generation by seeds. That does not occur in genetic engineering of crops—communities don't have biotech labs in their grange halls! The values that inform the objectives and goals of corporations producing GE seeds are not good nutrition, community stability, deliciousness, or lovely appearance. Rather, the values that form the basis of engineered food-producing plants are economic gain. Turning humanity's food into patented industrial products breaks the ancient interdependence between plants and human communities. Genetic engineering makes seed saving, the source of all agriculture, unnecessary— and illegal.

Why should we care? Maybe agriculture has gone the way of buggy whips and silent movies. The problem is, if we permit distant companies to own the basis for human life, we are ceding control of our values and tastes, and we are also giving up the primordial relationship between food and human communities—and between farmers and families—that has shaped and sustained the human world for thousands of years.

Instead of local farmers knowing their markets and growing what people like and even love, we have industrial-scale producers signing technology contracts and functioning as fabrication units for distant corporations who tell the rest of us: If you want to live, eat what we sell.

If we fail to push back against the spread of corporate-owned, GE food plants, we will see the decline of individual food choices, the destruction of the community-based farming and market system, and the transformation of eating into an act defined by company profit needs.

We can, must, and will do better. Nothing less than agriculture itself is at stake. 🚜

An estimated 85 percent of soybeans, 75 percent of cotton, and 50 percent of corn produced in the United States is genetically engineered. Ingredients made from these crops are in most items of processed food.

Opposite: A family farmer carefully saves eggplant seeds.
Right: Eggplant seeds drying in the sun

The Ogallala Aquifer: Depletion of a Precious Resource

Darryl Birkenfeld, director of the Ogallala Commons

In the 1970s, as I was growing up on an irrigated farm in Texas, I remember asking adults, "Is it right for us to pump out all the water from the aquifer?" The general response to my question was: "If God didn't want us to use the water, He wouldn't have put it down there." Thirty years later, I'm still asking that question, and I wish more people would, too.

One of America's greatest natural resources is the High Plains–Ogallala Aquifer, which undergirds parts of eight Plains states: Nebraska, Kansas, Colorado, Oklahoma, and Texas, with small parts in New Mexico, South Dakota, and Wyoming. Farmers, ranchers, and townspeople across the 174,000 square miles of this north-south axis depend on the Ogallala to produce the food and fodder that feed Americans as well as people around the world. The Ogallala's subterranean beds are saturated with more than 3.2 billion acre feet of water (an acre foot of water is one acre of water that is one foot deep). However, the fossil waters of the High Plains aquifer were deposited across the eons of time since the Rocky Mountain Uplift occured more than 65 million years ago. Those sources have long since been cut off, and with aquifer recharge from annual precipitation at about 0.15 inches, the Ogallala must be considered nonrenewable, especially given that much of our agricultural production is heavily dependent on intensive irrigation. Between 1960 and 1990 alone, more than a half-billion acre feet of water was extracted from the Ogallala by farmers in southwest Kansas, the Oklahoma panhandle, and west Texas.

Currently, the Ogallala Aquifer has about half of its water reserves left in states where the greatest depletion has occurred. Having abandoned the responsibility to preserve the Ogallala for generations far into the future, we succumb to an accepted truth that "managed depletion" is the best rational option. In Texas, there is a state water plan that legislates having 50 percent of the Ogallala left by 2050. It has merit as a political solution, but does little to reverse the behavior that will cause the eventual total depletion of the Ogallala Aquifer.

Large-scale agriculture, based on maximizing yields above all else, locks us into the eventual depletion of the Ogallala Aquifer. Countering this mindset are alternative forms of agriculture striving to sustain the aquifer: local food systems, sustainable agriculture, and grass-based farming and ranching. These approaches give American society the possibility of choosing new patterns of living. But as long as we view our natural resources as commodities for extraction, we will not break the cycle that is leading to the rapid depletion of this precious gift.

The Dead Zone

A variation of Rachel Carson's groundbreaking book *Silent Spring*, which documented the impacts of DDT on birds and insects, could well be titled *Silent Ocean*, documenting the impact of soil runoff on our oceans. Each year in the Gulf of Mexico, a swath of up to seven thousand square miles becomes lifeless—completely void of shrimp, fish, and other marine life. The aptly named Dead Zone is an annually occurring phenomenon, caused mainly by runoff of fertilizers and chemicals that are used on farms across the United States. The Mississippi River watershed drains about 40 percent of U.S. land area, carrying soil, with its fertilizers, pesticides, and herbicides, from farms and fields stretching from the Appalachians in the east to the Rockies in the west into the Gulf. When these nutrients enter the Gulf, they cause hypoxia, a condition where all the oxygen in a body of water is depleted, making it incompatible for living creatures. In some places the sea is eerily empty of any life; in other places, dead fish, crabs, and worms litter the sea floor. The Dead Zone results in loss of income for fishermen, shrimpers, and crabbers; food chain alterations; loss of biodiversity; and the death of innocent sea animals.

The tragedy of the Gulf's Dead Zone is played out in other bodies of water around the world. The Dead Zone is a problem caused by human decisions and human practices, and therefore can be changed—if we choose to act before we cause the collapse of one of our largest fisheries.

Genetically engineered (GE) corn and soybean seeds were first offered to farmers on a massive scale in the mid-1990s, and it wasn't long before some family farmers started asking questions. Europe and Asia registered wave on wave of negative reaction to the seeds. Some countries closed their markets to GE corn and soybeans. Many farmers suspected the big companies that control the seeds through patents and economic pressure weren't telling them everything they needed to know. Looking for ideas and advice, farmers telephoned Farm Aid, and Farm Aid responded by sponsoring and planning informational meetings in conjunction with its two concerts in Bristow, Virginia, in 1999 and 2000. The gatherings drew interested farmers from all over the country. Among them was George Naylor of Iowa, who later became a sharp critic of engineered seeds. At the first summit meeting, he was merely interested in learning more. "I went to the summit not knowing much. I felt I didn't want to raise them, but I didn't really have a complete view of all the possibilities and the scientific issues," said Naylor.

The farmers heard from scientists, activists, economists, and journalists who gave them the straight story about some of the effects of using genetically engineered seeds. After much discussion, planning, and the crafting of a Farmer's Declaration on Genetic Engineering in Agriculture, the family farmers agreed

they needed to create a special campaign—a "truth squad"—to counter the advertising and public-relations statements coming from the seed and farm-chemical industry. The Farmer to Farmer Campaign on Genetic Engineering in Agriculture was the result.

"Farmers aren't generally being told the truth or the whole truth about these things," said Naylor. The campaign is a farmer-directed effort housed at the National Family Farm Coalition, where Naylor now serves as president. In its formative years, the campaign received strong organizational support and funding from Farm Aid.

"If it wasn't for Farm Aid's encouragement and support, I just can't imagine the campaign getting off the ground at such an early date," said Naylor. "To have people and groups like Farm Aid that understand where the farm movement is coming from and the absolute need for farmers to be educated and organized to protect themselves—why, that is invaluable. There are just not a lot of organizations in our society that understand and are willing to put money behind that kind of thing."

The Farmer to Farmer Campaign remains active, continuing to help farmers to understand the economic, legal, and political implications of the spread of genetically engineered seeds. Farm Aid remains a steady partner in these efforts.

Recombinant Bovine Growth Hormone (rBGH)

A 2004 poll conducted by the Food Policy Institute at Rutgers University found that roughly half (48 percent) of Americans realized that genetically engineered (GE) foods are currently available in supermarkets, while slightly less than a third of Americans believe that they have consumed GE food. Yet, experts estimate that between 60 to 70 percent of processed foods on American shelves contain genetically engineered ingredients.

One of the most widely consumed genetically modified ingredients today is in milk. Recombinant Bovine Growth Hormone (rBGH), a genetically engineered hormone produced by Monsanto, is injected into an estimated 30 percent of the U.S. dairy herd to boost production. Milk containing rBGH is mixed with ordinary milk during processing. Since the Food and Drug Administration (FDA) does not require dairy products from rBGH-treated cows to be labeled, consumers cannot be sure their favorite brand of milk is GE-free—unless it is explicitly labeled organic or rBGH-free.

The growth hormone rBGH was approved by the FDA for use in the United States in 1993. Since then, there has been much controversy surrounding it. Opponents of the milk-production booster claim it presents major health risks for dairy cows and for humans. The FDA, however, has rejected these claims, stating its research shows no such danger.

Evidence of health risks associated with rBGH came to light in 1998 while the Canadian government was reviewing an application to allow rBGH to be used in Canada. The Canadian government rejected the use of the growth hormone, pointing to scientific data showing dramatic increases in lameness, mastitis, and infertility among cows receiving doses of rBGH. This led to concern that cows receiving rBGH would be dosed with higher or more frequent amounts of antibiotics and other drugs that could be passed on to consumers.

In taking action to reject rBGH, Canadian government scientists also criticized the U.S. FDA for allegedly overlooking important information on the potential human health impact of rBGH when the U.S. agency approved the hormone.

Back in the early 1990s, Farm Aid began educating food buyers about the concerns surrounding rBGH. In a 1994 letter to its members, Farm Aid said, "We don't need rBGH. It is bad for family dairy farms. Many of your local family dairy farmers who refuse to inject their cows will be forced out of business.

"rBGH may be bad for your health. No long-term studies have been conducted on the effect of this drug on humans. What we do know is that cows get more infections with rBGH. When cows get infections, they need antibiotics, which might contaminate our milk. When we are exposed to antibiotics on a daily basis, they won't work when we are sick and really need them.

"So why on earth is this drug on the market? Because some powerful companies expect to profit enormously from rBGH—the chemical companies that developed this drug and the dairy processors who sell milk products to you."

Above: Soybeans

American Family Farmers:
Roger Allison and Rhonda Perry

In the early 1980s, the U.S. Department of Agriculture (USDA) started to illegally foreclose on thousands of Missouri farmers. Among those facing foreclosure were Missouri farmer Roger Allison's farm and his parents' adjoining one. Rather than sitting by and watching himself and his parents get put out of business, Roger decided to do something about it. He and his parents took their cases to federal court and eventually won based on lack of due process. Their cases were part of the national class action suit *Coleman v. Block,* which stopped government farm foreclosures across the United States.

In 1985, with the farm crisis in full swing, Roger pulled together a group of rural activists and area farmers going through foreclosure to address the immediate needs of struggling farmers around them. Within days, the Missouri Rural Crisis Center (MRCC) was born. According to Rhonda Perry, MRCC codirector and Roger's wife, "Roger was planning on doing activist work for a year, then going back to farming. Twenty years later, he's still doing it."

Rhonda's parents were among the activist farmers who were members of MRCC. Rhonda was living in Montana in the late eighties but kept abreast of her parents' activities in the farm movement. She recalls how the movement changed her parents' strict conservative views. "I tried to call them one week-end a dozen times, with no luck," she says. "Finally, I caught up with them, and they told me they were campaigning door-to-door for Jesse Jackson all weekend!" Rhonda was shocked and pleased to hear her parents talk about working with allies from the civil rights movement, Jewish community groups, and progressive politicians. "MRCC really brought people together and changed many people's lives," Rhonda recalls.

In 1990, as Rhonda passed through Missouri on her way from Montana to Arizona, where she planned to move, her parents persuaded her to come with them to the MRCC annual meeting. At the meeting, she says, "I knew this was what I was meant to do." Her destiny clear, Rhonda stayed in Missouri and helped Roger run the MRCC. Because farming ran common in their veins, they eventually became business partners, raising a few cows and pigs together. They were married in 1996.

Today Roger and Rhonda own 850 acres. Like many central Missouri farms, theirs is diversified. "Farmers are generally very smart," Rhonda explains. "The old way, and the way of the future, is to raise what's best, most profitable, most environmentally sound on the land you have." Roger and Rhonda farm using this philosophy of both traditional and progressive sustainable farming. They raise between ten and twenty sows and about seventy-five head of cattle on the land most suited for pasture. In the creek-bottom land, rich in nutrients, they grow 200 to 250 acres of row crops. The remaining forest is managed to provide habitat for wildlife that they hunt for food and let live naturally beside their home. "It's nice to know you're doing something right," Rhonda says, "even among all the chaos."

In the early nineties, when a factory hog farm operation moved into their backyards, independent family farmers in north Missouri got together with

> "It's important for us as adults to support [Farm Aid] and buy the right food, but don't forget to teach your kids . . . because they're the ones who will hold the future in their hands. Make sure you teach your kids these things, too."
>
> —LEE ANN WOMACK, FARM AID ARTIST

MRCC to talk about what they could do to fight back. The group put together an economic development committee and invited Shirley Sherrod from the Federation of Southern Cooperatives to speak. "Do what you know," she advised. Roger, Rhonda, and the other farmers knew hogs. Patchwork Family Farms was their solution.

Patchwork Family Farms enables independent hog producers to directly market their products to consumers who care about the welfare of animals, farm families, and rural communities. Along with direct sales to area restaurants, food co-ops, and institutions, Patchwork now sends its pork to people all over the country through a mail-order service.

"The name Patchwork Family Farms," Rhonda explains, "came from something Jesse Jackson said at a protest on the courthouse steps." Paraphrasing Jackson, a longtime voice for family farmers, she says, "By ourselves, we're not enough. My patch is not big enough. Your patch is not big enough. But together, we can make a quilt to keep us all warm." Today, Patchwork boasts eighteen member producers, including Roger and Rhonda, and sales have grown to $350,000 annually.

Roger, Rhonda, MRCC, and their project, Patchwork Family Farms, are not only challenging the corporate takeover of the food industry, they are also rebuilding the food system. They are working to create a democratic and efficient food system that provides healthy and affordable food for all people. Patchwork is keeping farmers like Roger and Rhonda on their land, guaranteeing good food from family farmers for all of us. —SKY DEMURO

Rhonda Perry on her Missouri farm

"I just can't imagine our nation without family farms. It makes me incredibly sad to picture that . . . The family farm is part of our history and our identity, and if we've got a chance to keep them around, we've got to do everything we can."

—GILLIAN WELCH, FARM AID ARTIST

"We eat every day, and if we do it in a way that doesn't recognize value, it's contributing to the destruction of our culture and agriculture. But if it's done with focus and care, it can be a wonderful thing. It changes the quality of your life. Every other culture devotes time to this. It's not a new idea. People have always foraged during the seasons for what was closeby. They picked it, and they brought it to the marketplaces, and they sold it to people in the neighborhood. People brought it home, cooked it, and ate it with their families. It's a ritual—a sacred ritual, I think—in most house-holds around the world."

—ALICE WATERS, CHEF, GOOD FOOD PIONEER

Family Farm Food vs. Factory Farm Food

Mark Smith

If you can appreciate the difference between a homegrown tomato and one you get at the supermarket in the dead of winter, then you can understand the dissimilar qualities between a family-raised ham and one shipped from the factory to the supermarket.

I did not learn this until well into my forties, when I decided to buy a ham from a family farm to celebrate the holidays. Only when I put the first bite into my mouth did I realize that I had never tasted a real ham before—the flavor my parents and grandparents tasted before factory livestock production took hold in this country. The flavor, texture, aroma, and color were nothing like the ham I had eaten all my life.

Taste and texture are only the tip of the iceberg when comparing the real but hidden differences between a family farm–raised ham and a factory-raised ham. Here's a look at the other differences between family and factory livestock production that you might consider the next time you want to purchase a ham or pork chops.

	FAMILY FARM–RAISED HAM	FACTORY-RAISED HAM
SOCIAL/ECONOMIC	Farm families are the engine for rural economic vitality and comprise a healthy tax base to support schools and Main Street businesses.	Each hog factory displaces 6-10 small-scale producers and decreases property values, weakening the fabric of rural communities and draining the local economy of needed resources.
HEALTH AND NUTRITION	Hogs are fed a natural diet and allowed to forage for food; meat is free of antibiotics and hormones used for growth promotion.	Hog feed is laced with antibiotics and hormones to promote rapid growth. Hormones and antibiotic-resistant bacteria are passed on to consumers in their meat.
ENVIRONMENTAL	Family farms compost manure and use it as a farm nutrient.	Manure lagoons bigger than football fields pollute the ground and surface water with fecal waste; air is polluted with harmful gases.
ENERGY	Food produced and sold locally needs less energy to get from farm to table.	Factory hams are shipped coast-to-coast, using massive quantities of energy. On average, each food item travels 1,500 miles before landing on your table.
ANIMAL WELFARE	Animals are treated humanely with good nutrition and animal husbandry practices, and allowed to live in healthy conditions and exhibit natural behaviors.	Tens of thousands of hogs are crowded into metal crates in factories, with no opportunity to live and behave naturally.
DEMOCRACY	Family farms make decisions about farm practices around the kitchen table and participate in their local community.	Hog corporations make decisions behind closed doors in distant boardrooms, with no consideration of the impact their decisions have on local communities.

The Pleasures of Eating

Wendell Berry

Many times, after I have finished a lecture on the decline of American farming and rural life, someone in the audience has asked, "What can city people do?" "Eat responsibly," I have usually answered. Of course, I have tried to explain what I meant by that, but afterward I have invariably felt that there was more to be said than I had been able to say. Now I would like to attempt a better explanation.

I begin with the proposition that eating is an agricultural act. Eating ends the annual drama of the food economy that begins with planting and birth. Most eaters, however, are no longer aware that this is true. They think of food as an agricultural product, perhaps, but they do not think of themselves as participants in agriculture. They think of themselves as "consumers." If they think beyond that, they recognize that they are passive consumers. They buy what they want—or what they have been persuaded to want—within the limits of what they can get. They pay, mostly without protest, what they are charged. And they mostly ignore certain critical questions about the quality and cost of what they are sold: How fresh is it? How pure or clean is it, how free of dangerous chemicals? How far was it transported, and what did transportation add to the cost? How much did manufacturing or packaging or advertising add to the cost? When the food product has been manufactured or "processed" or "precooked," how has that affected its quality or price or nutritional value?

Most urban shoppers would tell you that food is produced on farms. But most of them do not know what farms, or what kinds of farms, or where the farms are, or what knowledge or skills are involved in farming. They apparently have little doubt that farms will continue to produce, but they do not know how or over what obstacles. For them, then, food is pretty much an abstract idea—something they do not know or imagine—until it appears on the grocery shelf or on the table. . . .

When food, in the minds of eaters, is no longer associated with farming and with the land, then the eaters are suffering a kind of cultural amnesia that is misleading and dangerous. . . . The passive American consumer, sitting down to a meal pre-prepared or fast food, confronts a platter covered with inert, anonymous substances that have been processed, dyed, breaded, sauced, gravied, ground, pulped, strained, blended, prettified, and sanitized beyond resemblance to any part of any creature that ever lived. The products of nature and agriculture have been made, to all appearances, the products of industry. Both eater and eaten are thus in exile from biological reality. And the result is a kind of solitude, unprecedented in human experience, in which the eater may think of eating as, first, a purely commercial transaction between him and a supplier, and then as a purely appetitive transaction between him and his food.

And this peculiar specialization of the act of eating is, again, of obvious benefit to the food industry, which has good reason to obscure the connection between food and farming. It would not do for the consumer to know that the hamburger she is eating came from a steer who spent much of his life standing deep in his own excrement in a feedlot, helping to pollute the local streams, or that the calf that yielded the veal cutlet on her plate spent its life in a box in which it did not have room to turn around. And, though her sympathy for the slaw might be less tender, she should not be encouraged to meditate on the hygienic and biological implications of mile-square fields of cabbage, for vegetables grown in huge monocultures are dependent on toxic chemicals—just as animals in close confinement are dependent on antibiotics and other drugs.

The consumer, that is to say, must be kept from discovering that in the food industry—as in any other industry—the overriding concerns are not quality and health but volume and price. For decades now the entire industrial food economy, from the large farms and feedlots to the chains of supermarkets and fast-food restaurants, has been obsessed with volume. It has

Opposite: Green Gulch Farm, Muir Beach, California. Above: Enjoying a fresh organic fig

189

relentlessly increased scale in order to increase volume in order (presumably) to reduce costs. But as scale increases, diversity declines; as diversity declines, so does health; as health declines, the dependence on drugs and chemicals necessarily increases. As capital replaces labor, it does so by substituting machines, drugs, and chemicals for human workers and for the natural health and fertility of the soil. The food is produced by any means or any shortcut that will increase profits. And the business of the cosmeticians of advertising is to persuade the consumer that food so produced is good, tasty, healthful, and a guarantee of marital fidelity and long life. . . .

Eaters must understand that eating takes place inescapably in the world, that it is inescapably an agricultural act, and that how we eat determines, to a considerable extent, how the world is used. This is a simple way of describing a relationship that is inexpressibly complex. To eat responsibly is to understand and enact, so far as one can, this complex relationship. What can one do? Here is a list, probably not definitive:

- Participate in food production to the extent that you can. If you have a yard or even just a porch box or a pot in a sunny window, grow something to eat in it. Make a little compost of your kitchen scraps and use it for fertilizer. Only by growing some food for yourself can you become acquainted with the beautiful energy cycle that revolves from soil to seed to flower to fruit to food to offal to decay, and around again. You will be fully responsible for any food that you grow for yourself, and you will know all about it. You will appreciate it fully, having known it all its life.
- Prepare your own food. This means reviving in your own mind and life the arts of kitchen and household. This should enable you to eat more cheaply, and it will give you a measure of "quality control": You will have some reliable knowledge of what has been added to the food you eat.
- Learn the origins of the food you buy, and buy the food that is produced closest to your home. The idea that every locality should be, as much as possible, the source of its own food makes several kinds of sense. The locally produced food supply is the most secure, the freshest, and the easiest for local consumers to know about and to influence.
- Whenever possible, deal directly with a local farmer, gardener, or orchardist. All the reasons listed for the previous suggestion apply here. In addition, by such dealing you eliminate the whole pack of merchants, transporters,

processors, packagers, and advertisers who thrive at the expense of both producers and consumers.
- Learn, in self-defense, as much as you can of the economy and technology of industrial food production. What is added to food that is not food, and what do you pay for these additions?
- Learn what is involved in the *best* farming and gardening.
- Learn as much as you can, by direct observation and experience if possible, of the life histories of the food species.

The last suggestion seems particularly important to me. Many people are now as much estranged from the lives of domestic plants and animals (except for flowers and dogs and cats) as they are from the lives of the wild ones. This is regrettable, for these domestic creatures are in diverse ways attractive; there is much pleasure in knowing them. And farming, animal husbandry, horticulture, and gardening, at their best, are complex and comely arts; there is much pleasure in knowing them too. . . .

The pleasure of eating should be an *extensive* pleasure, not that of the mere gourmet. People who know the garden in which their vegetables have grown and know that the garden is healthy will remember the beauty of the growing plants, perhaps in the dewy first light of morning, when gardens are at their best. Such a memory involves itself with the food and is one of the pleasures of eating. The knowledge of the good health of the garden relieves and frees and comforts the eater. The same goes for eating meat. The thought of the good pasture and of the calf contentedly grazing flavors the steak. Some, I know, will think it bloodthirsty or worse to eat a fellow creature you have known all its life. On the contrary, I think it means that you eat with understanding and with gratitude. A significant part of the pleasure of eating is in one's accurate consciousness of the lives and the world from which food comes. The pleasure of eating, then, may be the best available standard of our health. And this pleasure, I think, is pretty fully available to the urban consumer who will make the necessary effort. . . .

Eating with the fullest pleasure—pleasure, that is, that does not depend on ignorance—is perhaps the profoundest enactment of our connection with the world. In this pleasure, we experience and celebrate our dependence and our gratitude, for we are living from mystery, from creatures we did not make and powers we cannot comprehend. . . .

Farm Aid Backstage Jason Ringenberg

"During the 1984–85 heyday of my band Jason and the Scorchers, I had a sticker on my guitar that read FARMING IS THE BACKBONE OF AMERICA. This was no attempt to latch on to a bandwagon; I did in fact grow up on an Illinois hog farm. I believed every word of that sticker, especially in those times when much attention was being focused on the farm crisis. My father never lost our farm, a homestead that my grandfather had built, but many of our neighbors, relatives, and friends did not make it. The commodity prices were—and still are—way out of proportion to land and production expenses. This was heartbreaking for me to watch.

"I had grown up in the perfect Norman Rockwell environment. All of our relatives and family friends were farmers. My entire ancestry is buried in two local cemeteries. Almost every farm in my home area had been worked by one of my people at one time or another. I had an idyllic childhood, wandering the countryside and helping on the farm. The memories of those times are too numerous to mention, but one I often wear out in my mind is how the farmers would stop in the middle of the road and talk endlessly about weather, crops, politics, and sports. When a rare car would approach, the driver would just make his way past on the side of the ditch. Now people would probably honk or yell obscenities.

"In the mid-1980s, I was traveling the world in a rock band but still kept very close with my homeland. The news was often depressing. This neighbor had to move, that relative was quitting. Another old farmer went to meet his maker—his farm sold and swallowed up by a larger operation.

My own father hung on to the older ways. At age eighty-two, he still farms with his quaint old tractors and corn pickers, but he is an anachronism now. I thank God every time I see him climb onto one of his old tractors.

"When the Farm Aid movement took root, I was delighted to see it blossom. We gave it our full support, played at the 1986 Austin Farm Aid concert, and in every interview, I spoke of the heritage and unique American farm culture that was fast disappearing. To this day, I still honor that heritage. I even have a small farm myself in Tennessee. Whenever I turn a piece of dirt, I think back to those farmers from the prairies of Illinois. They were, and some still are, the true backbone of America."

Farm Aid Backstage  Spooner Oldham

The thread of a common man runs through the soul of Lyndon "Spooner" Oldham. The legendary rhythm & blues keyboardist was born and reared around the cotton fields of Muscle Shoals, Alabama. He cut his chops at the Muscle Shoals Sound Studios in nearby Sheffield. Oldham, 61, created the signature organ riffs of Percy Sledge's "When a Man Loves a Woman," and in 1967 he played behind Aretha Franklin when Jerry Wexler brought her to Muscle Shoals. In 1977, Neil Young enlisted Oldham to play on the *Comes a Time* sessions in Nashville, and since then Spooner has often lent his sparse, soulful style to Young's band. Oldham also played on Willie Nelson's 1979 classic "Angel Flying Too Close to the Ground."

At the Farm Aid concerts you're liable to bump into a variety of characters backstage, and Farm Aid 2004 was no exception. There was Oldham, eating organic food and watching the concert on a backstage monitor. He wasn't in town to play keyboards with Young (who performed only with his wife Pegi) but rather with newcomer Kitty Jerry, whose debut country-soul album was produced by Young's steel guitarist Ben Keith.

As a teenager, Oldham, then a fledgling musician, was trying to figure out ways to score some pocket change. "I thought, 'Well, everybody cotton farms around here,' " he said. "My granddaddy had a vacant acre of land, and I asked him if I could borrow it for one season. I wanted to plant cotton, pick cotton, and harvest it. There was a cotton gin a half-mile down the road. It was convenient—if I had cotton to sell. You could sell a five-hundred-pound bale where they paid $3 per hundred pounds. I hired people to help me and still lost $40 that season. The boll weevils got the cotton, and I didn't use any poison to keep the varmints away. One of the first things I learned about farming was that you have to do a lot of work yourself."

At Farm Aid 2004, Oldham met for the first time his hero Jerry Lee Lewis, who also performed at the concert. "I had always respected his talents highly," Oldham said. "He was real generous with his time and gave me a hug. We got a picture of me and my daughter and him. But I don't have a clue if he knew who I was.

"Being at Farm Aid is interesting in a lot of ways. I've played three or four now. The [good] food stuff is ongoing, and I had never seen a rotating stage until I played a Farm Aid. The band would be setting up drums on the backside while you're out there playing. It rotates like a merry-go-round. And you keep playing that way." Oldham knows about keeping on. He was a farmer once.

—DAVE HOEKSTRA

The Good Food Movement

Here Comes the Future

Joan Dye Gussow

A quarter of a century ago, the idea that we should eat locally seemed absurd. It also seemed backward-looking: My generation had been brought up to eat vegetables grown in California and everything else grown somewhere in the great middle by Farmer Jones. Later generations were brought up to pay no attention at all to where their food came from—it was just there, in the grocery store. It was usually cheap, and there was lots of it. People who might have remembered the taste of food that came from nearby farmers were getting old or dying off. There was nobody to protest what was being called "progress." When, in 1980, I merely hinted at the idea of local eating, a nutrition professor stood up after my talk and asked me witheringly what I thought Iowans would do for vitamin C in the winter. I confess that I wasn't actually sure; I, too, had been fed from this rootless food supply.

What I was sure of was that something had to change in the way we got our food. Years of asking questions about how humans might produce enough food on a sustainable basis for the world's growing population had convinced me that the global industrial food system that fed us cheaply was not sustainable. Our food is the product of a variety of cooperative arrangements between humans and nature, which means its continued production requires, at a minimum, the continued availability of certain resources: topsoil, water, solar radiation, a predictable climate, and—most essentially—the skills of farmers. Among these necessities, farmers are presently under great stress because of various habits that make up our "way of life." Thus, one of the critical tasks of our time is figuring out how to live in a way that will allow our descendants to eat.

At this point, the farmers and ranchers who sell into the global food system are paid so poorly for what they do that many of them can afford to keep farming only if someone—sometimes everyone—in the family finds outside employment so they can stay on the land. It seems reckless beyond belief to allow our nation's food security to depend on the generosity of folks who often take a financial loss to keep producing. If farmers stop farming, we lose the capacity to feed ourselves and will necessarily depend on an often hostile world

to feed us—a fact that seems not yet to have alarmed those responsible for "homeland security." All these developments portend a future that seems anything but hopeful. But there *is* hope, and it flourishes in a small but vibrant movement working outside the global industrial food chain to make local eating a reality.

It's so encouraging to watch the breakdown of agricultural ignorance in communities across the country, as increasing numbers of eaters realize how unhappy they are with the things to eat that agribusiness has brought them. Alerted by frequent food-safety alarms, they urgently want to know where their food has come from, who is growing it, and what has been happening to it on its way to their tables. These enlightened eaters are finding ways to connect themselves—and their schools, hospitals, clubs, and other institutions—more directly to farmers, creating what Tom Lyson at New York's Cornell University has called a "civic agriculture." By this, he means an enterprise intended not just to reconnect farms and folks but to rebuild community in the process.

The civic agriculture initiatives Lyson lists include farmers markets, community and school gardens, small-scale farmers (organic and otherwise) who have formed "production networks," Community Supported Agriculture farms (CSAs), grower-controlled marketing cooperatives, community kitchens, specialty producers and on-farm processors, small-scale off-farm local processors, restaurant-supported agriculture, roadside stands, and more—all of them activities in which "the imperative to earn a profit is filtered through a set of cooperative and mutually supporting social relations."

So while there continues to be pain and grief and loss on farmlands across the nation, there is also hope and determination to make a different system, one

Above: Harvest from a backyard garden, Boston, Massachusetts

where vibrant local economies are based on thriving family farms, small-scale business enterprises, and markets featuring fresh local food year-round—economies that will make farming once again a desirable lifestyle, so that handing down the farm to one's children will no longer seem like a punishment but a privilege. If we level the playing field for producers by taking away the policies that support the present industrial food system—cheap fuel and water, public funding of high-tech agricultural research, massive public investments in infrastructure (including overbuilt highways to handle giant truckloads of traveling food)—we can invest the money saved in a food system that conserves soil, water, air, and human resources, and produces reasonably priced food.

We live in a "high-consumption, high-waste, growth-obsessed industrial/technological society," as one farmer wrote recently. But it is truly heartening to realize how much attitudes have changed in just a quarter of a century. And, as shortages of water, increasing energy costs, and contaminated-food scares forcibly remind us of the fragility of our food system on which we depend, we can grow more confident that eating what local farmers produce will be an increasingly attractive choice in the years to come. 🚜

Berries at a northeastern farm stand

"My family lives at the bottom of the San Joaquin Valley, so we have access to fresh food that's grown there. At our local independent grocery store they buy their stuff from the family farmers. The funny thing is, it's not in an organic or left-wing sort of way; it's just available, so they buy it. There's a huge family-owned, pasture-fed cattle ranch right near us, so all the store's beef is from that. My wife and I shame our children into not eating fast food. We don't mince words. We just say, 'No, I don't care if you're seventeen, you can't eat there.' And then my oldest daughter read *Fast Food Nation*, and she hasn't wanted to go to a fast-food place since."

—FARM AID ARTIST JOHN DOE OF X

Mike and Terra Brownback admit they didn't always do things in a way that is good for the earth. But they have had nothing but success since switching to organic methods of farming. In Loysville, Pennsylvania, the Brownbacks run Spiral Path Farm, where they grow sixty acres of organic vegetables. When the family began farming in 1978, they grew corn, hay, and grains, such as wheat and oats, using chemical fertilizers and sprays. They also raised hogs after learning the hard way that hogs brought in more money than cattle. By the mid-eighties, the Brownbacks had acquired 125 sows, which they raised "conventionally." They bought the promise of industrial agriculture that quantity is more important than quality. Mike believed he could maximize his income by raising a large number of hogs in a small area. The Brownbacks raised their hogs indoors in crates. Manure ran through slats in the floors and into "lagoons," a factory farm term for ponds that collect waste.

Then in the early nineties, Mike began suffering from "heart problems," in a spiritual sense. "I'd pluck a fresh ear of corn in early July when they're just ready, and I became conscious of the fact that I sprayed poison on the corn that I was feeding my sows." He felt guilty feeding his pigs contaminated corn when the family was eating healthy, organic vegetables from their garden. Mike realized, "I was not following my heart by doing one thing for myself and another for my livestock and the people who bought our meat." It got to the point where Mike couldn't even look his sows in the eyes. The family decided to make a change: They gave up hog farming and started growing vegetables, using sustainable, organic methods. Spiral Path Farm now sells wholesale organic herbs and vegetables and operates a 225-member CSA (Community Supported Agriculture) farm, where local customers become shareholders in their farm, paying in advance to cover the anticipated costs of the farm operations. In return, they receive shares of the farm's harvest throughout the growing season.

Spiral Path Farm has a diverse array of produce to increase opportunities for successful crops. "We grow A to Z—everything from asparagus to zucchini," says Mike. Terra adds, "Organic food has a better taste. A carrot tastes more carroty than what you're used to. A tomato tastes more tomatoey. There's a whole taste explosion."

The Brownbacks are very hopeful about the future of sustainable farming. "The opportunity for growth is astounding," Mike says. "There is this incredible group of farmers taking matters into their own hands and finding their own markets." He adds, "It's really important for the general customer to demand organic food, and it becomes the norm. Not from a business point of view, but because it's the right thing."

Back when he was a conventional hog farmer, scraping together enough income to survive, no one ever said to Mike, "I want to be a farmer when I grow up." Now that he's an organic farmer, all kinds of people ask him about his way of farming. Even Mike's son Will, who studied mechanical engineering, decided to return to the farm to carry it into the next generation. "People are going to feel the vibe," Mike says. "At the heart level, we all want to do the right thing, ahead of making money."

—SKY DEMURO

Opposite: Romano green beans and organic sage, chives, rosemary, and thyme
Above: Free-range, grass-fed beef cattle

The Craftsman: Dave Matthews

Dave Hoekstra

Dave Matthews and his wife, Ashley Harper, live in a modest frame home on the outskirts of downtown Seattle. It is an old house full of young ideas. Their front yard is surrounded by a brown fence made from recycled Douglas fir. The timber came from the floor of a nearby 1910 school building. There are still lessons to be learned here.

A Farm Aid board member since 2001, Matthews is a deeply thoughtful voice for his agricultural beliefs. In February 2002, he purchased five farms of the University of Virginia's treasured Kluge property. He has preserved agriculture and forest land on the 1,261 acres, with an emphasis on organic farming and supporting local farmer/food consumer relationships. Ashley is studying for her doctorate in naturopathic medicine (natural and nontoxic therapies) at Bastyr University, north of Seattle. Bastyr is one of the world's leading academic centers in natural health sciences. Dave and Ashley's backyard garden consists of lush herbs, flowers, and a majestic magnolia tree that casts no doubt.

Ashley and Dave have twin daughters, Grace and Stella. They were born a month before 9/11. The future is forever precious. The family eats organic. Dave and Ashley drive fuel-efficient cars, and as much as possible they walk to destinations. They buy recycled products. Ashley designed a laminated chart on recycling methods that she posted on the refrigerator door. The family walks the walk.

"Farm Aid interested me before I was involved," Matthews said during a talk with his wife on their back porch overlooking the sunny garden. "I was drawn to the struggles of a culture that's at the root of this country. Then, when the band played for the first time in [Louisville] Kentucky, I liked the whole sense of it. It had a festival vibe, but it had community. It didn't matter if you were new singers like us or a legend like Willie. There was a sense of purpose involved that I enjoyed. It also made me reflect on my life, my own involvement, and how I live."

The Dave Matthews Band made its major American-venue debut at the Farm Aid tenth anniversary concert on October 1, 1995, at Cardinal Stadium, in Louisville. The band preceded Hootie and the Blowfish, whose fans kept chanting "Hootie! Hootie! Hootie!" until about thirty seconds into the first song, whereupon the crowd stood awestruck. The Matthews Band played extended jazz-folk songs from its sophomore album, *Under the Table and Dreaming*.

The band returned in 1997 and 1999. In 2001, Willie Nelson personally asked Matthews to serve on the Farm Aid board. Matthews has been a loyal friend to the Red Headed Stranger. Matthews has appeared solo annually at Farm Aids 2001–2004, giving his fans a unique chance to see him alone and acoustic. "When I joined, it seemed like a good idea because this farming machine was attempting to take over every corner of our food supply," Matthews explained. "There was also this growing urge to sustain the family farmer. Those things became apparent to me in my interest in the quality of food I was eating and soon thereafter the quality of food my family was eating. I'm involved for the big picture, and it seems the natural battle to support. It is one that is concerned on so many different levels with things I am concerned with: the health of the environment, the health of citizens, the health of the farm, the health of our culture. All of those fall on a very basic level right at how we grow food and what we eat. I can't think of a more universal purpose than the support and nurturing of healthy food from healthy farms."

Matthews, 38, is the youngest of the four faces of Farm Aid. His popularity has brought a new crop of fans into the Farm Aid family fold. Every new generation finds it increasingly difficult to locate farmers living among them. "It is important to give a young edge to Farm Aid," Matthews said. "The number one thing that makes our country great is how knowledgeable young people are."

Matthews was born in Johannesburg, South Africa. In 1969, he moved with his family to New York when his late father, John, was hired by IBM. His mother, Valerie, is an architect. After living in Cambridge, England, and returning to Johannesburg to attend high school, Matthews settled in

Above: Australorp chickens raised for egg production at Dave Matthews's Best of What's Around farm in Scottsville, Virginia. Opposite: Matthews and Ashley Harper in the backyard of their Seattle home

Charlottesville, Virginia, in 1986. The Dave Matthews Band was formed there. "Being a physicist, my father was a great believer in progress," he said. "But he also loved nature. He was a photographer, and outside of taking the occasional family photographs, all he did was photograph nature. He loved birds. That meant a lot to me growing up. Healthy progress also means we have to be concerned for the environment. That may have something to do with what I believe about farming."

Ashley Harper, 31, is from suburban Atlanta. Her father, Carroll, grew up on a farm and her mother, Susan, gardened. Carroll Harper was a salesman, and Susan was an elementary school media specialist. "I got into [farming] in Charlottesville," Ashley said, "being interested in health and then being interested in organics and growing my own garden." In 1993, Matthews and Harper met in Charlottesville. They moved to Seattle in 1999 so Harper could study naturopathy. Harper is in her sixth year of medical studies. As her husband went off to get a bottle of Fat Tire beer, she said, "Dave has been an amazing 'Mr. Mom.' I'm gone before they wake up in the morning, and he reads to them downstairs. He'll put them to bed at night."

Naturopathic medicine is a new and demanding field. "We have philosophies that define our goal with our medicine," she said. "First do no harm. Treat the cause. Treat the whole person. Education is a huge part of what we do for our patients, help them make healthy lifestyle choices . . ." Her husband returned, sat down, and added, "While Dad lights a cigarette in the middle of the day. She *is* making progress; I don't do this very often."

Once they settled in Seattle, Matthews and his neighbor designed the family garden and patio. Matthews even built a brick wall: "It was back-breaking, but it makes me feel great when I look at it now," he said as he peered out at the garden. "The biggest reason was so we'd have more space to plant. We eat from our garden." Harper added, "Little greens and herbs. I'm obsessed with that. Herbal medicine is a big part of naturopathic medicine. I want to know how the herbs grow and what they look like in different stages. I'm also interested in growing things for birds, squirrels, whoever in the wild wants to eat it."

During her first year of school, Harper attended a lecture by Dr. Bill Mitchell, one of the founders of Bastyr University. His theme on that particular afternoon was that you cannot have healthy people without living on a healthy planet. "That totally hit home with me," she said. "And it connects with the idea of Farm Aid. We face challenges every day. We live in a toxic

Matthews during a solo performance at Farm Aid, 2003, Columbus, Ohio

environment, so detoxification is a big part of what we do for people, from basic liver cleanses to eliminating allergenic foods and talking to people about organic foods."

Where Harper attends school, the university's garden grows more than 250 species of Western and Chinese herbs, allowing for observation of plants year-round. "We've got vegetables, and we've been planting fruit trees," Harper said. "They sell it in the cafeteria [open to the public, with food priced by the pound], and people who work in the garden get some, too."

Seattle offers more of a wealth of quality food than most major cities in America. "There's more availability of locally farmed and organic supermarkets here," said Matthews, who was the unofficial host of Farm Aid 2004, held at the Muckleshoot Indian Reservation near Auburn, outside of Seattle. "I think sometimes people come to visit us just so they can go to the Whole Foods we have here. It is awesome. And the smaller market is thriving. There were concerns when Whole Foods started making headway in Seattle that it was going to damage the smaller organic and locally farm-based supermarkets and co-ops. In fact, it's done the opposite. They are growing. There is an awareness here that hopefully is a trend that will spread throughout the country. The only downside I see is that it is generally more expensive. As more organizations like Farm Aid promote healthy and locally grown foods, then the prices will begin to reflect what people can afford. As things become more available, the prices will come down."

Matthews does his own shopping and can get enthusiastic about what he finds in Seattle grocery stores. "Shopping is one of my favorite things," he said. "The more that people become aware of the health and social benefits of buying organic or small, locally farmed food, [they also discover it's] the taste. A tomato is a tomato until you taste a tomato that's grown organically. My wife actually hated tomatoes. Then we started eating organic food—because of her—and now she loves tomatoes. And meats, too. I know there are people who would say if you're eating meat it doesn't matter if it's organic or not, it's destructive to the environment. But food that is grown with care and animals that are raised and slaughtered with concern for their well-being, with the idea that if they're unhealthy and unhappy the food isn't going to be as good—I tell you the quality is a different flavor. It sort of multiplies."

Matthews's Scottsville, Virginia, farms are managed by Kevin and April Fletcher under the company name of Best of What's Around. Six full-time people work on the farm year-round. The business is named after a 2001 Matthews hit, in which he sings: "Whatever tears at us/ Whatever holds us down/And if nothing can be done/We'll make the best of what's around."

"In the early years we didn't want to say, 'Dave Matthews Farm,'" April Fletcher said in an interview from Scottsville. "We want it to be about something more than Dave Matthews, because we really believe in what we're doing. But at the same time, it would be stupid not to have some connection with this famous do-gooder. He came up with the name. He also liked the idea that the name reflects the fact we're producing the best-quality food possible." Best of What's Around produces eggs, vegetables, herbs, honey, broiler chicken, and beef. Jersey Black Giants are fed only certified organic grains grown under environmentally safe methods. Cheese, lamb, and pork are in the farm's future.

"When they bought this farm, there wasn't an animal here," Fletcher said. "These were once five separate farms. In the 1980s, John Kluge bought these farms and built an infrastructure of roads to connect them. He was farming conventionally. He had a state-of-the-art confinement feedlot. He was raising beef for big markets all over the country."

In May 2001, Kluge gave the land to the University of Virginia. The Kluge farms included homes, cottages, cattle and storage barns, silos, equipment, grain sheds, and a feed complex. Not in the farming business, the university leased the property to a corn and soybean farmer. When Matthews purchased the farms for $5.3 million, he inherited the farm buildings and nothing else around. "Not a single tool, not a single animal," said Fletcher, 38. "The Matthewses are in the process of creating something from scratch. Their challenge is even more significant because they are having to turn something around 180 degrees from conventional agriculture to certified organic. Even the ground you farm cannot be certified organic until you're three years from prohibited substances. The Matthews family does not want products on the market that aren't certified organic."

The farm's first product was multicolored eggs that became popular with regional chefs and specialty grocers. Pastured eggs, like those raised by the Fletchers, won the low-cholesterol heart of the USDA's Sustainable Agriculture and Research Education (SARE) program. No hens are ever debeaked or have their wings clipped. The farm's hens aren't confined to cages or barns. Fletcher

"ONE SWEET WORLD"
Dave Matthews Band

Nine planets round the sun
Only one does the sun embrace
Upon this watered one
So much we take for granted
So let us sleep outside tonight
Lay down in our mother's arms
For here we can rest safely

If green should slip to grey
Would our hearts still bloody be
And if mountains crumble away
And the river dry
Would it stop the stepping feet

Take all that we can get
When it's done
Nobody left to bury here
Nobody left to dig the holes
And here we can rest safely

One sweet world
Around a star is spinning
One sweet world
And in her breath I'm swimming
And here we will rest in peace

said, "The Matthews girls love to dig in the garden. They pick cherry tomatoes. They're fascinated but a little cautious about the animals. They love to pet the horses. They want to feel things; hold the eggs, touch the baby animals. Ashley always works in the garden when she has time. They're not here that much, but when they are in town they always come by the farm."

Fletcher talked in excited tones. Spring had just arrived in the quiet country. A native of rural southwest Virginia, Fletcher arose at 5:00 a.m. "Martha the donkey woke me up," she said. "We have a donkey that announces the birth of all new babies. Anyone who comes on the farm will tell you that's her job. I woke up, went out on the second day of spring, and in fact we had baby lambs. The rest of the day we had people planting potatoes and harvesting greens."

As the Matthews farm grows, Farm Aid continues to grow as a strong force. Matthews explained, "Farm Aid is paying attention to constant attempts by special-interest farms that want to get their feet in the door of organics. There has to be an awareness that if it were up to these big agribusinesses, anything that is alive will be 'organic.' There are people trying to dumb down the rules of organic."

Harper added, "You want to know what you're getting when you're buying it." Matthews continued, "Absolutely. You don't want something mislabeled.

"A push and pull has to take place," he said. "We want to push the things that are entrenched in a direction so that they are caring for the people they are serving. If we can instill the very uncorporate philosophy on giant corporate farmers that they want to produce something that will benefit the recipient—that is a giant breakthrough. At the same time we don't want them to destroy the rules of absolutely organic and healthy food. There has to be a bit of give and take. That doesn't mean anyone who is attempting to get there but not doing enough is completely evil. We have to be pushing the envelope on how good food can be, and we have to be pulling the status quo along with us. Farm Aid has been a great organization for both those things."

Dave and Ashley visit Virginia during the holidays and before the band's annual summer tour. "Since Ashley's been in school, we're here in Seattle," Matthews said. "We started our family here. This is the most grown-up part of my life, and what I'm most excited about is being in Seattle. It's an incredible community and I just love it."

The afternoon sun slipped behind a garage Matthews uses as studio space. Matthews got up and walked through the kitchen and living room to the bright front yard. Harper peeked out the kitchen window. Children were coming home from school. The sun deflected off the old fence, across the earth and into a new day. 🚜

"I am from a really small town in the Midwest, which I still consider to be my home. Three-fourths of my town is made up of farmers. They grow a lot of cotton, soybeans, and now, in the last few years, rice. I know what it means when the prices are down. And what it means to each small family in my community. My parents are cotton farmers, and I am just really glad to be part of Farm Aid. As an artist, it really propels the spirit when you are involved in something that is larger than yourself."

—SHERYL CROW, FARM AID ARTIST

Opposite: Neil Young jams with Matthews at Farm Aid 1999, Bristow, Virginia.

Farm Aid Live!

Yank Rachell, 1990

Charlie Daniels, 1993

Willie Nelson and Lucas Nelson, 2004

David Hidalgo of Los Lobos, 1986

Mary Chapin Carpenter, 1992

Texas Tornados Doug Sahm, Freddy Fender, and Flaco Jiménez, 1992

Eddie Spaghetti of the Supersuckers, 1995

Delbert McClinton, 1993

Joe Ely, 1992

Doobie Brothers, 2001

Willie Nelson and Los Lonely Boys, 2003

Jerry Lee Lewis, 2004

Larry Crane and John Mellencamp, 1985

Jay Farrar of Son Volt, 1996

David Amram, 2003

Travis Tritt, 2000

Mickey Newbury, 1993

Bob Dylan and Tom Petty, 1985

Dave Matthews, 2001

Robert Earl Keen, 1996

James McMurtry, 1990

Highwaymen Willie Nelson, Waylon Jennings, Kris Krisofferson, 1992

In Favor of Organic Foods

Marion Nestle

As a longtime analyst of the politics of nutrition, I must confess to a rather late interest in organic foods. Ironically, my epiphany came as a result of General Mills. In 2003, I was invited to give a talk on my book *Food Politics* at a meeting of the Organic Trade Association (OTA) in Texas. With "organic" in the title, I assumed I would be speaking to an audience of counterculture farmers. Wrong. I was introduced by a vice president of General Mills. At that moment, I understood that organic foods are no mere fad; they are big business.

How big a business is a matter of debate, but by some estimates, organics brought in $20 billion in the United States alone in 2004. Corporations like General Mills know that organics constitute the fastest-growing segment of the food industry. Since 1990, sales have gone up by about 20 percent annually—a rate gigantic by industry standards. Organics may amount to only a tiny fraction of total food sales—estimates range from 1 to 8 percent—but the fraction is rising. Most of all, Americans are willing to pay more for organic foods. No wonder every big food company wants to get into this business.

To consider organics a passing fancy would be a serious error. Organic farming methods constitute a principled and fundamental critique of the current system of industrial agriculture. This system wastes resources, pollutes the environment, raises animals under unsanitary and inhumane conditions, externalizes every possible cost, and is based on only one rationale: producing the most food possible at the cheapest possible cost, regardless of consequences for health or the environment. At a time when rising rates of obesity are a worldwide public health problem, the accumulation of mass quantities of inexpensive, high-calorie foods may no longer be in any country's best interest.

The Certified Organic label on a food means that its producers followed rules: They did not use any synthetic pesticides, herbicides, or fertilizers to grow crops or in feed for animals; they did not use crops or feed that had been genetically modified, fertilized with sewage sludge, or irradiated; they did not feed animals the by-products of other animals; they gave animals access to the outdoors and treated them humanely; and they were inspected to make sure they followed the rules in letter and in spirit.

Opponents of organic methods—and there are many—work hard to cast doubts on the reliability of organic certification, to weaken the standards (so there really will be something to doubt), and to make consumers question whether organics are better than industrially grown foods and worth a higher price. I cannot count the number of times I have been asked whether the organic seal really means anything. It does. Ask any organic inspector, produce manager, farmer, or meat, egg, or strawberry producer, and you immediately realize how hard they work to adhere to standards. Trust is essential, and they earn it. As for attempts to weaken the organic standards, think relentless. My interpretation: If organic standards require eternal vigilance to protect, they must be good and worth defending.

Given the potential size of the organic market, it is easy to understand why critics are enraged by the idea that producing foods organically might be better for you or the planet. They say that organic methods reduce productivity, are elitist, threaten food security, are an environmental disaster, and are unsafe. Because research on these charges is limited, they are easy to make but hard to refute.

But some questions about organics have been researched and do have clear answers. One is productivity. As early as the mid-1970s, studies questioned the idea that agricultural efficiency depends on inputs of fertilizers and

Opposite: A pear ready for picking. Above: Lettuce grown on a family farm

209

pesticides. In 1981, a careful review of such studies concluded that farmers who converted from conventional to organic methods experienced only small declines in yields, but these losses were offset by lower fuel costs and by better conserved soils. More recent studies confirm these results. Overall, investigations show that organic farms are nearly as productive, leave the soils healthier, and use energy more efficiently than conventional agriculture methods. The productivity issue seems settled. Organics do less well, but the difference is small.

If crops are grown without pesticides, you would expect fewer pesticides to get into the environment, foods to contain less of them, and adults and children who eat organic foods to have lower levels of pesticides in their bodies. Research confirms these connections. Pesticides are demonstrably harmful to farm workers and to "nontarget" wildlife, and they accumulate in soils for ages. These are reasons enough to use less of them.

Do organic methods confer special nutritional benefits? If organic foods are grown on better soils, you would expect them to be more nutritious, and you would be right. This is easily shown for minerals because plants take them up directly from the soil. But plants make their own vitamins and phytonutrients, and those levels depend on genetic strain or treatment post-harvest. The idea that organic soils improve nutritional values has much appeal, and organic producers would dearly love to prove it. I cannot think of any reason why organically grown foods would have fewer nutrients than conventionally grown foods, and I have no trouble thinking of several reasons why they might have more, but it is hard to demonstrate that the difference has any *measurable* effect on health. Nevertheless, a few intrepid investigators have compared the nutrient content of foods grown organically and conventionally. These show, as expected, that organic foods grown on good soils have more minerals than foods grown on poorer soils. They also show that organic peaches and pears have somewhat higher levels of vitamins C and E, and organic berries and corn have higher levels of protective antioxidants. In general, the studies all point to slightly higher levels of nutrients in organically grown foods. This may be helpful for marketing purposes, but is not really the reason why organics are important.

Are foods better if they are organic? Of course they are, but not primarily because of nutrition. Their true value comes from what they do for farm workers in lower pesticide exposure, for soils in enrichment and conservation, for water supplies in less fertilizer runoff, for animals in protection against microbial diseases and mad cow disease, for fish in protection against contamination with organic hydrocarbons, and for other such environmental factors. My guess is that researchers will eventually be able to prove that organic foods are marginally more nutritious than those grown conventionally, and such findings may make it easier to sell organics. In the meantime, there are plenty of other good reasons to choose organic foods, and I do.

> "You are what you eat, and Americans as a people are eating a lot of *shit*. Our band actually swore off fast food several years back. We live on the road 200 to 250 days a year and can avoid it, so it *can* be done. It's actually cheaper in the long run. No one ever believes that, but it is, and that's not even counting the financial effects of being sick from eating shit. I buy most of my groceries at the local co-op and buy organic whenever possible."
>
> —FARM AID ARTIST PATTERSON HOOD OF DRIVE-BY TRUCKERS

Opposite: An organic pepper harvest at the Knoll Farm, Brentwood, California

Restaurants Go Local

Ruth Reichl

"To tell you the truth," said Frank Dal Porto, leaning against the side of his barn in California's Amador County, "I think she's a little crazy." This was, perhaps, not the most auspicious beginning for a transaction that would revolutionize the relationship between farmers and restaurateurs. But in 1974, when Alice Waters told Dal Porto that

she would take all the pigs and lambs he raised for Chez Panisse, her Berkeley, California, restaurant, she changed not only *his* life, but that of many other American farmers. Dal Porto thought she was insane to want the animals so young, but if she was willing to pay a premium for thirty-pound piglets, he was willing to supply them. "It really makes a farmer's life easier, knowing everything is sold," he told me in 1982.

Alice Waters is just one of many American chefs and restaurateurs who realized, back in the early seventies, that technique was not enough. After going to Europe for training, these chefs returned home shaking their heads and lamenting the lack of great produce on our native soil. No matter how talented you were, they realized, it was impossible to operate a really fine restaurant without good products. "If only we could get flavorful vegetables and fruits," they sighed, "and animals that have been scratching around in the dirt."

And then they began to see that they could. What these young chefs discovered, as they drove through the countryside, was that many farmers were raising great food—for themselves. Over almost fifty years, Dal Porto had been raising everything his family consumed. And so Alice simply said, "Raise some for me." Down in Los Angeles, Michael McCarty, of Santa Monica's Michael's, had made the same discovery and was forging relationships with growers in Southern California. Mark Peel, Spago's first chef, went even further, setting up a complicated network of farmers all across the state to supply his restaurant. Meanwhile, back on the East Coast, Larry Forgione was finding farmers in the Hudson Valley and in the Midwest to supply his New York City restaurant, An American Place. These chefs were inventing a new American cuisine, one that let the food speak

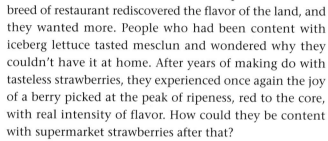

for itself, and without good raw materials they would have been lost.

Nobody at that time had any idea that they were changing the way many Americans would relate to farmers. But the diners who frequented this new breed of restaurant rediscovered the flavor of the land, and they wanted more. People who had been content with iceberg lettuce tasted mesclun and wondered why they couldn't have it at home. After years of making do with tasteless strawberries, they experienced once again the joy of a berry picked at the peak of ripeness, red to the core, with real intensity of flavor. How could they be content with supermarket strawberries after that?

And so the green market movement sprang up, spreading through America's cities, giving urban dwellers a chance to buy food from the hands that raised it. It was a small step, but it was a start.

Farmers, too, were beginning to understand that restaurants could change their lives. In 1980, Lee Jones watched his father's Ohio farm be destroyed by a vicious hailstorm. Undaunted, Jones started over. This time, however, he decided to try growing specialty produce to chefs' specifications. Chef's Garden was such a huge success that Jones took the idea one step further: A few years ago, he set up the Culinary Vegetable Institute, so chefs and farmers could work together in an experimental garden, figuring out new techniques to grow vegetables and innovative ways to use them.

Chefs themselves were beginning to understand that simply buying food from farmers was not enough. Two years ago, the Palladin Foundation, started by chefs in memory of the late Jean-Louis Palladin (his eponymous restaurant was the toast of Washington, D.C.), created scholarships to send young chefs into the field. Chefs nominate their most promising young employees for

Opposite: Organic arugula salad. Above: A chef uses fresh produce to make a delicious meal.

"[When you're eating good food], you can feel the difference spiritually. If you're eating food cooked by people who like to cook, and the food's good, and it was grown the right way, you can feel it when you're eating it. They say that people put love in the food when they're making it. It's true, I believe it— there's definitely a difference. It's more than just the food. It's the people growing the food, cooking the food. It's all connected— it's a chain. That's what people need to be more aware of."

—LUCINDA WILLIAMS, FARM AID ARTIST

internships, sending them off to spend time with the people who raise and harvest the food that they use. The idea was that by putting their hands in the dirt these aspiring chefs would become better cooks. It was just one more link in the chain connecting farmers and chefs.

Last year, with the opening of Blue Hill at Stone Barns, in Pocantico Hills, New York, the circle was finally closed. Here is a restaurant that is also a farm—and one with a mission. Stone Barns raises almost everything it serves, from the pork to the salad greens, and what it can't use, it sells. But more important, the restaurant wants to educate us while we eat.

Dining at Blue Hill is a wonderful experience, but it offers more than just a good meal. As you drive up to the restaurant, you pass fields filled with vegetables. You see chickens pecking at the ground. And as you draw nearer you might meet a pig who will one day be dinner. Here, urbanites, accustomed to vacuum-packed meat and frozen vegetables, encounter food at its source. It is a powerful experience, and for those who have never been on a farm, an unforgettable one.

The first time I went to Blue Hill at Stone Barns and saw a group of school-children looking at the pigs, I thought about Frank Dal Porto and the interview I did with him so long ago. So much has changed since then, and I couldn't help wondering if he *still* thinks Alice Waters is crazy.

Bringing Farmers and Retailers Together

Michel Nischan

My mother, born into a generations-old farm family in Missouri, was robbed of her birthright to be a farmer. Working the land was in her blood, but life and the corporate takeover of the American family farm took her to suburban Illinois, where she and my father raised us in a small house with a backyard planted with vegetables right up to the sliding- glass doors. She grew what she could, or took us to pick-your-own berry patches, orchards, and farm stands for the rest of our fruits and vegetables.

My mother's gardening and cooking abilities turned her into a neighborhood folk hero and me into a chef. And, as a chef, I bring with me the lessons she held most dear when it came to eating and cooking. They are:

- Know your food or the person who grew it.
- If you can't grow it, find someone you know who can.
- If something is good for you and is prepared so it tastes great, you'll likely eat more of it.
- Find friends who think like you do. If they don't, change their thinking, and you'll all eat better.
- You get better prices buying directly from the farmer at a farm stand.

These lessons provide the criteria for all my buying decisions, as well as the foundation for most of my relationships—especially the part about finding like-minded friends.

When I started cooking professionally, I was the only person I knew who thought this way. Over time and travels, I began meeting more and more chefs who understood that the greatest success of any good recipe begins with the integrity of basic ingredients. What began in some chef communities as minicommerce clusters to save money and support growers has turned into a collection of food communities throughout America that now include significant wholesale co-ops, farmers markets, and mail-order businesses.

Companies such as Heritage Foods USA make it possible to prepare the same kind of turkey our ancestors enjoyed at the first Thanksgiving. Because of initiatives that celebrate the cultural significance of our immigrant farm-ing communities, like the New American Farmer Initiative (NAFI) and the New Immigrant Farming Initiative (NIFI), we can now take a trip around the world without leaving home. Tuscarora Organic Growers co-op distributes fifty-five thousand cases of produce to Washington, D.C., area restaurants, and New York City residents can taste their countryside through buying produce exclusively at urban green markets.

As for the bigger picture, I developed a menu for Song Airlines that now offers fresh, organic, healthful meals to thirty thousand passengers a day. Yes, the big guys are finally coming along—and not a minute too soon. The food distribution business must become more locally focused if it is to survive the rising cost and dwindling supply of fossil fuel.

The new frontier is to move into larger institutional food-service providers (hospitals, grocery chains, schools) and also into underserved communities where grocery options are limited to highly processed snacks from small convenience stores. Midsize farmers are failing at alarming rates, yet this group is the best equipped to produce the kinds of artisan and heirloom animals, whole grains, and other foods that are being recognized by governmental agencies as essential to human health.

For those of us who have had the privilege to see soil-to-table food evolve from backyard gardening to a nationwide movement of small farm-to-table food initiatives, the simple principles of farmland mothers are the keys to making this happen. Those who really care about food quality and economic fairness have a responsibility to bring our abilities in community building and consumer education to middle Americans. They are out there, they are hungry, and they are waiting.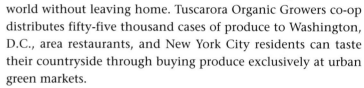

Above: A family farm–raised turkey

Gardening in the City

Carl Grimm, Director of Programs,
Garfield Park Conservatory Alliance, Chicago, Illinois

John Soto pushes red beans into the soft warm soil of his family's West Side Chicago backyard. "My father brought these beans from Puerto Rico when we moved here nearly thirty years ago," he says. "Each summer we grow enough to eat a meal every week or so all winter long, and we always plant a patch to save seed for next year." Later in the day and a quarter mile to the west, Velma Johnson stands behind two baskets of bunched collard greens talking about her favorite recipe. Her North Lawndale Greening Committee hires youth each summer to garden and grow for this fledgling urban farmers bazaar, the Chicago Home Grown Market.

There is a buzz in the air, and it's not just the bees and hummingbirds. Everyone from Mayor Daley to my next-door neighbors is talking about growing food, eating fresh, and greening the city. Some are attracted to the flavors and health benefits. Others see the power of greening to improve the quality of life, attracting people and business to the city. Some are involved to meet their neighbors and grow community, while others just like to get their hands into the soil.

There is something about touching garden soil and finished compost that is at once calming and invigorating. Medina Page, a graduate of the Growing Home job-training program, recently shared with me a realization about soil and the worms, beetles, and other beneficial organisms that live there: "It's like a city underground." Gardening in my backyard helps remind me of this incredible "city," building the soil that grows the food that feeds us all.

Grandmother Soto noticed the scarlet runner beans I planted on our common fence—bright red blossoms nodded under the weight of visiting

honeybees, while foot-long pods pulled at the vigorous vines. Before summer's end, I had traded a bag of these purple-and-black-speckled beans (that I swear are the same ones that grew Jack's beanstalk) for a bag of the Soto family red beans. Since then, we have often shared plants, food, and recipes, and the neighborhood has grown stronger and more beautiful. It's that kind of magic that makes me think a handful of beans could be worth a cow, or more.

Another kind of magic is taking place at the Garfield Park Conservatory. Velma and her friends come every few days to water their vegetable seedlings in our warm greenhouses. Volunteers plan and plant an organic demonstration garden the size of one city lot and teach visitors how to become farmers and caretakers of their own little slices of Chicago wilderness. Kids help sow and grow. Yes, there are some losses: Cucumber beetles denuded the bean plants last summer. From these losses, we learned a little of what farmers face every day.

All over Chicago and indeed throughout North America and the world, city dwellers are caught in a new fervor for flavor, food security, and environmental quality. We are touching the earth, growing gardens, and sharing our stories. And while cities are getting greener, and our bodies healthier, our personal connection to the land, to our food, to farming and to nature—and especially our connection to each other—is growing.

Opposite: A rooftop garden in San Francisco serves senior residents of this high-rise south of Market. Left: The Chicago backyard gardens worked by the author and John Soto, 2004

"The next time you sit down to a very nice meal, remember that it didn't come from a cellophane bag from Safeway. A farmer gave his whole to that meal you're eating."

~ JOHN FOGERTY, FARM AID ARTIST

Connecting Urban and Rural Communities Through Food

Zachary Lyons, Director, Washington State Farmers Market Association

The Tonnemakers have had a homestead farm on the Royal Slope in Central Washington for four generations. They grow tree fruit, mixed vegetables, and feed grasses on 120 acres. They now sell about 20 percent of their harvest at a dozen farmers markets, which generates about 40 percent of their annual income. This makes the difference between

keeping their farm and losing it. But the Tonnemakers also get to feel appreciated by their customers—something often rare in farming. Each week, at market after market, thousands of eager shoppers line up for the Tonnemakers' melons, pears, and hot peppers. They thank the Tonnemakers for what they do, and they rave about the quality of their produce. And the Tonnemakers give back. They participate in the Farmers Market Nutrition Programs, offering fresh produce to low-income families and seniors. Instead of farming alone on a hillside, interacting solely with the truck driver who hauls their harvest to the packing shed, they drive hundreds of miles to Seattle and Moscow, Idaho, to be part of a much larger community—one that not only includes the public but hundreds of other farmers from all over the state.

People in big cities and small towns alike are developing relationships with farmers through farmers markets. They are making friends with people who have dirt under their fingernails. And the next time our local government ponders building a highway up the fertile Snoqualmie River Valley, because they think it is easier and cheaper to displace farms, it will be the farmers market shoppers in Seattle fighting side-by-side with their friends whose farms will be in harm's way.

But farmers markets mean much more. Once someone visits a farmers market, he or she is hooked for life. Not only do these markets offer an extraordinary variety of fresh, high-quality farm products, but shopping there can be done outside, in the sun, wind, rain, and sometimes even snow. At farmers markets, one can run into neighbors, while watching a sleepy neighborhood bustle with life for a few hours. And there one can reconnect with a dormant part of one's soul. After all, it is only in the past hundred years in America that most of us shifted to living in big cities. Our genes are still rooted in the fertile soil, and for all the comforts and modern conveniences the city has to offer, deep down we still long for the fields.

People who support their local farmers at the market are also supporting the local businesses neighboring those markets. Instead of driving to a big box store on the edge of town to buy cheap, mediocre goods at the expense of their own local economy, they are learning the value of what it means to buy local: high quality goods; better service; and healthier, friendlier, and connected communities.

Perhaps that is why we see an explosion of farmers markets today, in every type of community, throughout our country. In the past ten years, according to the USDA, the number of farmers markets operating in the U.S. has more than doubled. And those communities that don't have them want them. When most of us cannot leave our cities to visit the farms, farmers are answering our need for high-quality, fresh food at the farmers market. And we are all better for it. 🚜

Above: The Heirloom Organics produce offerings at the Ferry Plaza Farmers Market, San Francisco

"Attention, shoppers! Buy with a conscience and save the family farm. Just go a little bit out of the way . . . look, take an extra minute to see where your food came from . . . get familiar with your food."

—NEIL YOUNG

Community Supported Agriculture (CSA)

Tom Spaulding, Executive Director,
CSA Learning Center at Angelic Organics

"Help me, I can't get this shovel into the ground!" a teenage boy begs me, as we stand in the rows of the neighbor's conventional cornfield trying to fill a bucket with soil. Frustrated, he hands me the shovel. "You do it," he says. Double his body weight, I still have trouble piercing the ground. It's like cement. With much sweat, I manage to fill the bucket,

In Caledonia, Illinois, children from Chicago's Alliance for Community Peace harvest tomatoes at the Angelic Organics farm.

and we return to the larger group of teens, all part of a hands-on inquiry into organic farming organized by Chicago teachers and our CSA farm. Crossing the property line back onto Angelic Organics, another teenager takes the shovel and easily scoops up soil from this organic field. With both buckets in hand, we spread a tarp on the ground and dump the contents out side by side. A flurry of hands works the two soils through their fingers in search of life. A few minutes later, the results are in. The soil at Angelic Organics is full of life. The neighbor's soil is barren, like a sample brought back by an Apollo astronaut. We ask ourselves, "What can this mean for the vitality and taste of the food growing in the two fields and thus our health and the health of our communities?"

HERE ARE THE RESULTS
OF OUR SOIL COMPARISON:

A BUCKET OF ANGELIC ORGANICS' SOIL	A BUCKET OF NEIGHBOR'S CORNFIELD SOIL
6 earthworms	0 earthworms
2 ladybugs	0 ladybugs
1 yellow beetle	0 yellow beetles
Tons of small white bugs	0 white bugs
2 black beetles	0 black beetles
2 ants	0 ants
Soil easily breaks apart	Soil hard as rock (kids request a hammer)
Soil is moist and dark	Soil is dry, light, and dusty

Harvesting mesclun at the Angelic Organics farm

Pondering questions like these has led tens of thousands of people over the past two decades to become shareholders in the now more than three thousand CSA farms around the nation. After the economic collapse of his conventional family farm, farmer John Peterson founded Angelic Organics in 1990. Following a 1993 phone inquiry from a Chicago family, John offered a pilot CSA membership and has never looked back. The farm now delivers weekly boxes of vegetables, herbs, and fruit to more than 1,200 area households.

The CSA Learning Center is the nonprofit educational partner to the Angelic Organics CSA. We like to say that Angelic Organics grows vegetables, and the CSA Learning Center grows people. Our mission is to empower people to create sustainable communities of soils, plants, animals, and people. Our farmers and shareholders founded the center in 1998 to handle the growing demands of shareholders, community members, and prospective farmers for direct contact with the farm that went beyond a box of vegetables. We've created diverse programs in agro-ecology education, community food security (making the local food system and CSAs accessible to low-income families), and farmer training, which now reach more than 3,500 rural and urban youth and adults annually. We touch many thousands more each year by working in partnership with community stakeholders to open civic spaces where the wider community can explore and discover the benefits of a vibrant local food system.

"You have to look at the farmer as more than just a medium to grow crops, you have to look at our future. What's disturbing to me is the fact that we're not bringing any young people into farming. My girls are not going to farm. And I don't see anybody coming in to take our place, and that's scary, not only just for black people but for people all over, white and black. What I would like to see is if we could team young inner-city urban people up with farmers and let the older farmers be their mentors."

—LEON CRUMP, SOUTH CAROLINA FARMER

Solving Hunger: Local Agriculture Lends a Hand

Bill Ayres, Executive Director, World Hunger Year

One of the biggest contradictions in America today is the prevalence of hunger and poor nutrition in the midst of surplus food production. More than thirty-six million Americans, including more than thirteen million children, live in households that struggle to put food on the table. Indeed, our large-scale industrial agricultural system has done little to solve the underlying problem of food insecurity and hunger for millions of Americans. To the contrary, factory farming has pushed countless family farmers off their land, forcing many to join the ranks of those who depend on food pantries to meet their family's needs.

Food banks have always seen themselves as part of a community as a whole. During the past decade, food banks have joined in efforts to ensure that every community has access to safe, nutritious, affordable food and that as much food as possible is grown and purchased locally to support the region's farmers and strengthen local economies. Many food banks today have their own gardens, farms, or farm stands, and many more partner with independent community gardens and farms. As a result, the hungry are getting more fresh food, while family farmers and community gardens are getting stronger.

Food banks are primarily about getting food to hungry people, but they are becoming much, much more. Through local organizing efforts with farmers and citizens alike, local food efforts are helping to build the foundation of a local, thriving food system that ensures nutritious, fresh food for all. 🚜

Teaching the Next Generation

Ben Holmes, Director of The Farm School

Schools tend to be homogeneous places where kids sit in confinement with a bunch of other kids and do what they're told. Farms are something else. They have always enabled children to learn while working with other people—farmers, foresters, builders, neighbors, retirees—whose ages, ideas, and backgrounds are different from theirs.

I was lucky enough to spend significant time on my family farm while I was growing up. Like generations of farm children before me, I was given some important skills in those fields—skills that had been basic to our growth as a nation: an ability to enjoy hard work, tenacity, a sense of duty toward something beyond oneself, and a capacity to joyfully tackle new problems every day, to name just a few.

In 1989, I founded The Farm School, based on a really simple desire to give young people something that I had been given, an experience on a farm with kind mentors. The Farm School now consists of three core programs on three hundred acres in north-central Massachusetts. Seventeen hundred visiting school children come each year in classroom-size groups and stay and work the farm for three days. The place gives meaning to the lives of children that is much deeper than I could have intended—in particular, deep meaning in the way children are educated. The proof is in the fields—our programs are solidly booked, and we are part of an emerging network of farm schools sprouting up across the country.

Why is there such a need for farm schools? Because a farm gives children the chance to take responsibility for something beyond themselves. Unlike their ordinary schoolwork, farm work embodies real responsibilities with real consequences. We ask children to be useful and contribute to the real work that needs to be done. This is a radical concept in a world that only sees this age group as an outlet for the marketing of video games and basketball shoes.

Perhaps most important, as we accelerate toward the vortex of this information age, a farm school makes sure that kids have as a touchstone a sense of the magic of reality—what it feels like to plant a seed, fell a tree, build a sturdy building. It's a crucial part of our cultural history, this work with our hands and minds. It is a part of our children's humanness. There is poetry in the feel of soil, or even the smell of a cow's breath, that cannot be duplicated on a computer screen. These are things that children need to feel to assume responsibility for the resources that will feed them. In the end, if we are to flourish, our children need to come to love a farm.

A youngster practicing agricultural skills at The Farm School

Putting "Community"
Back in the Food System

Jennifer Lamson

When Seattle's last independent milk bottler closed in August 2003, it could have spelled disaster for a small family dairy in the city's urban fringe of King County, Washington. But the foundation for a community food system was being laid there, and that network produced connections that became not only a safety net for Eric and Marie Nelson's Cherry Valley Dairy but a springboard for an expanded community food movement as well.

Today, most of the milk from Cherry Valley's herd of 170 cows travels about 25 miles to Beecher's Handmade Cheese, where artisanal cheeses are made at the nearly century-old Pike Place Market, in the heart of downtown Seattle. The cheese maker receives a fresh supply of just the kind of high-quality milk it needs and first-person knowledge of how the dairy is managed. The dairy farmer has a stable local market for much of his milk and the added satisfaction of seeing what happens to it after it leaves the farm. And the big winners are the people of greater Seattle who get to enjoy Beecher's gourmet cheese and actually see it being made at the storefront operation. They can even visit the dairy, which dates back to the 1800s, and see its operations.

A community food movement is taking shape in the Puget Sound, and in the way that all great movements are born, people are putting their heads together and pouring their hearts and souls into hundreds of enterprises designed to provide the continued abundance of fresh, healthy local food to community residents.

More than two dozen CSA farms make weekly deliveries to urban and suburban neighborhoods. King County residents can also buy locally grown produce direct from growers at twenty-two farmers markets, including one on nearly every day of the week in Seattle. In addition, citizen volunteers and seasoned farm advocates are spearheading innovative efforts to bring local produce into school lunch programs, and match up retiring farmers with "wanna-be" farmers, giving them the training they need to be successful. This movement is also supporting a community of Hmong farmers and helping them form a cooperative way to market their produce. There's a push to establish the nation's first organic farming "major" at Washington State University, and advocates are fighting to get more research funding for sustainable farming techniques. Having established and promoted a "Puget Sound Fresh" marketing program for local produce, farm advocates are organizing leadership summits to meet with farmers to identify key issues and opportunities and learn how to effectively fight for family farms.

All of this is taking place against the backdrop of serious pressures from a rapidly growing population and massive urbanization in the region. Between 1970 and 2000, King County's population increased by 45 percent, to 1.7 million, making it the twelfth most populous county in the nation. King County acreage in farmland decreased from 165,635 acres in 1945 to just over 40,000 acres today. Farmland in the Puget Sound region has been named among the most endangered in the nation. Meanwhile, Washington State ranks tenth in the nation for hunger. In 2000, more than two million visits were paid to King County food banks, more than a quarter of them to feed hungry children.

Harsh realities like these could threaten to drown out the energy of those working to build a community food system grounded in the vitality of local family farms. Yet, farmers and farm advocates in King County are tackling these challenges head-on. One key effort underway is the campaign to create a Seattle–King County food policy council. A diverse group, including local agriculture, hunger, and urban-planning experts, has launched a campaign to establish and obtain funding for the council, which will bring together farmers, food retailers and wholesalers, government officials, consumers, land-use experts, and other food system stakeholders. The public-private partnership envisioned could take a comprehensive view of the region's food systems and address challenges with innovative solutions born of previously unlikely partnerships.

Across the region, small and midsize farmers are finding new and creative ways to work together to meet demands for quantity, variety, and a longer growing season that can help get them into important local markets like restaurants, schools, and grocery stores. In the late 1990s, midsize organic farmer Andrew Stout of Full Circle Farm received some seed money from King County to determine how local farmers could work together to market and distribute their products. Now he fills his CSA basket with produce from his own farm as well as other organic farms from King County and Washington State. He employed a similar distribution system in a recent farm-to-college pilot project that provided produce to the University of Washington. And he also serves as a broker for farm supplies, helping small-scale farmers save money by purchasing for them in bulk.

Since most of the farms in King County are small, there are other cooperative efforts under way. The Sno Valley Gals are a fledgling co-op of women growers on small farms who previously marketed their produce individually to restaurants, farmers markets, and their own CSAs, and found that they couldn't offer the quantities needed to approach schools, grocery stores, and additional restaurants. Now, since they have joined together to market and distribute their products, these doors will likely remain open to them.

Small poultry farmers in the Puget Sound region found themselves up against some unfriendly regulations and a serious lack of processing facilities. By banding together to form a small co-op, Puget Poultry, they are working with legislators as well as state and county officials toward opening a new USDA-certified poultry-processing plant that will enable Seattle-area consumers to buy fresh local, organic, pastured poultry at the grocery store.

In September 2004, Seattle-area farms and farm advocates got a big boost when Farm Aid came to town and shined a bright spotlight on the area's community food movement. Two weeks of public activities with local organizations followed by a sold-out concert energized activists and farmers while spreading the word about good food grown locally to many thousands more local citizens. The events spurred the *Seattle Post-Intelligencer* to publish a series of four editorials examining various aspects of the region's food system and calling on consumers to "buy local" when it comes to food.

Energy is bubbling up across the region. A movement is taking shape. If successful, farmers and their advocates will find they have built not only a community food system but, indeed, a *community*. 🚜

"I still raise a garden. I don't have to; I just like it. And I think the stuff you get out of the garden is better than you can get in the store. And I can because I think it's better than what you get in the cans at the store. . . . I'd always rather have something homemade. If I make it myself, I know what it's supposed to taste like, and I know that I'm going to like it."

—LORETTA LYNN, FARM AID ARTIST

Farm Aid Backstage ♦ Steve Earle

Steve Earle was happy to appear at the tenth anniversary Farm Aid concert in October 1995, at Cardinal Stadium in Louisville, Kentucky. Earle was happy to appear anywhere. He had just gotten out of jail.

"That was the first time anybody saw me after I got out of jail," Earle said backstage at Farm Aid 2004. "I played 'My Old Friend the Blues' with Willie Nelson during his set. I didn't even do a set that year." In 1993, Earle was charged with misdemeanor drug possession and sentenced to a year in jail. The country-rock troubadour spent the latter half of 1994 at the Davidson County Criminal Justice Center outside of Nashville and in the Lincoln Regional Hospital in Fayetteville, Tennessee, where he detoxed.

Earle clearly had fun in Louisville. He taught Hootie and the Blowfish the deep soul riff in Wilson Pickett's "Mustang Sally." He said, "As long as they keep doing Farm Aid, I'll keep coming." Earle's commitment to Farm Aid runs as wide as the Texas plains where he was raised. (He was born on January 17, 1955, in Fort Monroe, Virginia.) Earle has played nine Farm Aids, beginning with the 1986 Austin, Texas, concert. John Mellencamp has said, "Steve Earle is a real different guy. That guy has shown up through thick and thin."

Earle wrote the hard-driving anthem "The Rain Came Down" five days before the Austin concert. There, he performed the song acoustically with Mellencamp's guitar player Larry Crane. As the song fades out, Earle snarls the words from the farmer to the auctioneer, "You can have the machines, but you ain't taking my land." Earle recorded "The Rain Came Down" in January 1987, and it appears on his album *Exit O*. "I'm one generation removed from the farm," Earle said back then. "My grandfather was pretty resilient: He never borrowed any money against his land. If farming was bad, he would just go into town and get a job with the railroad. When it got to where he could make a profit again, he returned to farming."

In recent years, American farmers have also confronted the challenge of passing family farms to the next generation. "I'm watching the farm across the road from me [in Nashville] go through that now. The oldest son didn't want any part of the farm, but he built a house on two acres he was given behind the farm. He lost it in a divorce. I bought

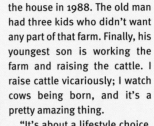

the house in 1988. The old man had three kids who didn't want any part of that farm. Finally, his youngest son is working the farm and raising the cattle. I raise cattle vicariously; I watch cows being born, and it's a pretty amazing thing.

"It's about a lifestyle choice. It's important that people who don't live in the country and don't grow up on farms understand that we're moving toward 100 percent of our food supply being manufactured by corporations, and if that happens you're not going to have as much to say about what goes into your body. You're not even going to have a choice. I pay real close attention to what I eat. Part of it is not being willing to poison myself, and part of it is a political statement."

Earle's unbending passion is apparent at every Farm Aid show he attends. He hangs around throughout the day and often returns for the encores with Willie Nelson. Earle will never forget the October 12, 1996, Farm Aid in Columbia, South Carolina, that carried over into October 13. "That was a Crazy Horse year for Neil [Young]," Earle said. "It was the first

Crazy Horse tour in a while. The following summer I ended up touring with them, but South Carolina was the first time I saw Crazy Horse in years. Me and Jay Farrar [of Son Volt] were standing on the side during their set, and I remember turning around and going to each other, '*Wooo!*' all night long."

Earle took a rare pause. Then he said, "And it was the last time I talked for any length of time with Doug Sahm [the Sir Douglas Quintet founder, who died suddenly in November 1999]. The first time I talked to him was when I got out of jail. We talked about baseball. He said, 'Man, everybody told me you can't talk to Steve—he's a San Antonio cat.' " (As was Sahm, a true Texas Tornado.)

It was nearing show time at Farm Aid in Seattle, and Earle excused himself. Someone had slipped him a copy of Percy Sledge's new CD where the Southern soul legend covered Earle's "My Old Friend the Blues." Earle walked away, holding the CD in one hand and shaking hands with the other. A few hours later, Earle would be onstage scorching through "The Revolution Starts Now." Earle had flown from Nashville to Seattle and back to Nashville in a twenty-four-hour time period.

He had to be at Farm Aid.

—DAVE HOEKSTRA

Farm Aid Program A Good Food Future

The Farm Aid mantra since 1985—"Save Family Farms!"—is being realized. Invigorated by the burgeoning good food movement that Farm Aid helped to create, we consider this development the most hopeful advance on the horizon. More and more people are reaching for family farm–identified food because it tastes better, it's fresher, and it makes us all feel connected to nature in an authentic way. Almost every community now has locally grown, organic, and humanely raised food increasingly available.

The projects that Farm Aid engages in are designed to reach out to farmers, farm groups, and consumers to increase and strengthen the connections between family farms and consumers. We know that we need to work with farmers to increase the supply of family farm–identified food and that we need to work with consumers to increase the demand for it.

On one side, we are working with farmers to take advantage of the opportunities created by a greater demand for good food. We're expanding our farm resource network to provide practical advice to farmers who want to transition to sustainable and organic growing methods. We're funding groups who provide hands-on training to farmers in these methods, including young would-be farmers. We're helping farmers learn from each other by sponsoring field days where farmers tour other farms. We're supporting research into better organic growing methods and providing muscle to the fight for good organic standards. Farm Aid backs efforts to leverage more federal dollars into organic and sustainable production research.

On the other side, we are working to spread the message to the American public that family farmers are integral to a future of good food. We have implemented the Ten Ways Campaign, which outlines ten easy, delicious, and fun ways to ensure good food for you and your family (see the poster on the inside of this book's jacket). In 2005, we sponsored the national Farm-to-Cafeteria Conference, bringing together farmers, nutritionists, and food service professionals so that children can have fresh, family-farm food in their school cafeterias. Farm Aid supports a marketing effort to encourage food buyers to "Buy Fresh, Buy Local."

Everything we're doing is aimed at adding to the number of family farmers and helping them become more successful. Farm Aid's work to give farmers the tools they need to take advantage of new markets is essential for farmers *and* consumers. Consumers will have a greater array of family farm foods from which to choose; farmers will have a better future. As farming once again becomes a viable career choice, more young people will become farmers, replenishing our country with new farmers and ensuring the availability of farm-fresh food. This is Farm Aid's hope and vision for a new American agriculture.

Onward! A Call to Action

Nobody accomplishes anything alone. You can tell from this book that Farm Aid is a web that holds all of us together in a community of action. It's a privilege to find one's place in such a community. It's a joy to throw oneself into work that is meaningful.

David Kline, an Amish farmer, has eloquently noted that when our lives are full, the work that we do becomes an intrinsic pleasure and time "not working" is more and more drawn into creative interaction with work. The lines blur between free time and work. This is not being a workaholic, but living one's whole life. That is what many of us have found working throughout the year and at Farm Aid concerts.

We visit farms with pleasure. We dig in the dirt of our own gardens. Some of us are members of local CSA farms, and all of us shop at our farmers markets. Some of us who love to cook happily share our soups and vegetables and baked goods. We all love to eat family farm food.

These experiences are available to almost everyone, no matter how urban you are, how far from the farm, how stretched your grocery dollars, how limited your time. The foraging for family farm food—the delicious discoveries, the deep satisfaction of connection to land and to soil—gives meaning to our lives.

In a world so chopped into frantic moments, when we are pushed relentlessly by marketers to purchase the most packaged, most convenient, most processed foods, it's great to sidestep all that. It can't be done all at once; it's an accumulation of many decisions over time. But simple acts can lead to groundswells of change. First, *you'll* be changed. You'll ask questions, you'll challenge yourself.

At the same time, political change is our national imperative. In a democracy, we have political choices. It's not just who we vote for. It's determining who holds the power over our natural resources and who controls the food and, if necessary, challenging those forces. Food and farming are too important to be left in the hands of a few corporations. Our government must mediate the common good so that all its citizens benefit. That challenge will take us a lifetime, and beyond—to make family farming the true basis of a fair economy and a democratic society.

Nobody can do this alone; it will take all of us. I've always found that the most fascinating people in life are curious, creative, and absorbed in a project far bigger than themselves. Farm Aid is full of characters like that. At Farm Aid, there is room for everyone. You, too!

CAROLYN G. MUGAR
EXECUTIVE DIRECTOR, FARM AID

Opposite: Dave Matthews, Neil Young, John Mellencamp, Willie Nelson, and Carolyn Mugar at the Farm Aid press conference, Burgettstown, Pennsylvania, 2002

300-Plus Farm Aid Artists

Acoustic Syndicate
Bryan Adams
Kip Addotta
Alabama
Dr. Buzz Aldrin
Dennis Alley Wisdom Dancers
Allman Brothers Band
Dave Alvin
Dave Alvin and the Allnighters
Amazing Kreskin
David Amram
John Anderson
Lynn Anderson
Skeet Anglin
Arc Angels
Jane Arden
Tom Arnold
Asleep at the Wheel
Badi Assad
Hoyt Axton
Catherine Bach
Bandaloo Doctors
Bare Jr.
Barenaked Ladies
Mandy Barnett
Roseanne Barr
Beach Boys
Gary Beaty
Beck
Bellamy Brothers
Ray Benson
Kenda Benward
Black 47
Blackhawk
Nina Blackwood
Blasters

Billy Block
Blue Merle
Grant Boatwright
Suzy Bogguss
Bon Jovi
Jon Bon Jovi
Boxcar Willie
Bonnie Bramlett
Brooks & Dunn
Garth Brooks
Karen Brooks
Aaron Brotherton
Jackson Browne
Jann Browne
T Bone Burnett
LeVar Burton
Toy Caldwell
Calhoun Twins
Deana Carter
Campanas de America
Glen Campbell
Mary Chapin Carpenter
Bill Carter
Deana Carter
John Carter Cash
Johnny Cash
June Carter Cash
Felix Cavaliere
Central Texas Posse
Beth Nielson Chapman
Marshall Chapman
Tracy Chapman
Mark Chesnutt
Dick Clark
Guy Clark
Jubal Clark

Lee Clayton
Roger Clinton
Hank Cochran
David Allan Coe
Tony Coleman
Judy Collins
Common Sense
John Conlee
John Conlee and Son
Danny Cooksey
Rita Coolidge
Jimmy Dale Court
Cowboy Ken and the Ranch
    Hand Band
Larry Crane
Crook and Chase
David Crosby
Crosby, Stills and Nash
Crosby, Stills, Nash and Young
Sheryl Crow
Cruzados
Shannon Curfman
Mary Cutrufello
Billy Ray Cyrus
Dallas Cowboy Cheerleaders
Charlie Daniels
Charlie Daniels Band
Joanna Dean
John Denver
Dixiana
Doobie Brothers
Drivin' n' Cryin'
Drive-by Truckers
Holly Dunn
Bob Dylan
Steve Earle

Steve Earle and the Dukes
Eldorado
Joe Ely
Bill Evans
Exile
Fabulous Thunderbirds
Billy Falcon
Freddy Fender
Jill and Joey Floyd
John Fogerty
Foreigner
Foster and Lloyd
Radney Foster
Pete Fountain
Kinky Friedman
Steve Fromholz
Funky Farmer All Stars
Terri Garrison
Larry Gatlin
Geezinslaw Brothers
Vince Gill
Johnny Gimble
Gin Blossoms
William Lee Golden
William Lee Golden and
    the Goldens
Tipper Gore
Gorky Park
Vern Gosdin
Grateful Dead (via satellite)
Green on Red
Pat Green
Nanci Griffith
Robert Guillaume
Guns n' Roses
Arlo Guthrie

Sammy Hagar
Merle Haggard
Charlie Haid
Daryl Hall
Hammerheads
Woody Harrelson
Emmylou Harris
Alex Harvey
Wade Hayes (videotape)
Roy Head
Don Henley
Christopher Hewitt
John Hiatt
Dan Hicks
Jim Hightower
Highwaymen
Hillybilly Jim
Al Hirt
Hogwaller Ramblers
Rebecca Holden
Peter Holsapple
Hootie and the Blowfish
Dennis Hopper
Bruce Hornsby
James House
Ray Wylie Hubbard
Timothy Hutton
Iggy Pop
Julio Iglesias
Alan Jackson
Jesse Jackson
Jagged Moon
Rick James
Jason and the Scorchers
Jayhawks
Jeff Healey Band

Bruce Jenner
Waylon Jennings
Kitty Jerry
Jewel
Billy Joel
Elton John
Don Johnson
David Lynn Jones
George Jones
Rickie Lee Jones
Keb' Mo'
Robert Earl Keen
Tom Keifer
Toby Keith
Kentucky Headhunters
Doug Kershaw
Hal Ketchum
B.B. King
Carole King
Jackie King
Knifewing
Chris Knight
Kris Kristofferson
Bobby Krueger
Jerry Max Lane
Jessica Lange
Daniel Lanois
Huey Lewis
Jerry Lee Lewis
David Lindley and El Rayo
Little Joe Y La Familia
Little Village
Living Colour
Nils Lofgren
Lone Justice
Los Lobos
Los Lonely Boys
Patty Loveless
Lyle Lovett
Rob Lowe
Loretta Lynn
Shelby Lynne

Deborah Maffett
Maggie's Farm
Tim Malchack
Richard Marx
Dave Mason
Kathy Mattea
Dave Matthews
Dave Matthews Band
Martina McBride
Delbert McClinton
Del McCoury Band
Tim McGraw
Roger McGuinn
James McMurtry
John Mellencamp
Paul Metsa
Dean Miller
Roger Miller
Minnie Mouse
Joni Mitchell
Bill Monroe
Alison Moorer
Lorrie Morgan
Gary Morris
Jonelle Mosser
Vince Neil
Billy Nelson
Willie Nelson
Willie Nelson and Family
Nelsons
Neville Brothers
New Maroons (Don Was Band)
Mickey Newbury
Randy Newman
Nitty Gritty Dirt Band
North Mississippi Allstars
Gary Nunn
Oak Ridge Boys
One Fell Swoop
Roy Orbison
K. T. Oslin
Paul Overstreet

Johnny Paycheck
Carl Perkins
Gretchen Peters
Michael Peterson
Petra
Richard Petty
Tom Petty
Tom Petty and the Heartbreakers
Lou Diamond Phillips
Phish
Pipefitters with Lou Diamond
    Phillips
Playboy Girls of Rock & Roll
Poco
Paula Poundstone
Charley Pride
John Prine
Sarah Purcell
Eddie Rabbitt
Yank Rachell
Bonnie Raitt
Mickey Raphael
Rattlesnake Annie
Red Beard
Lou Reed
Vernon Reid
Dusty Rhodes
Kimmie Rhodes
Roadmaster
Kid Rock
Rock & Roll All Stars
Judy Rodman
Johnny Rodriguez
Paul Rodriguez
Kenny Rogers
Rusted Root
Leon Russell
Jimmy Ryser
Sawyer Brown
John Schneider
Brian Setzer
Paul Shaffer

Billy Joe Shaver
Kenny Wayne Shepard
Michelle Shocked
Silent Partners
Paul Simon
Yakov Smirnoff
Anthony Smith
Son Volt
David Soul
J.D. Souther
Southern Pacific
Sissy Spacek
Spin Doctors
Nancy Stafford
Ringo Starr
Stealin' Horses
Steppenwolf
B.W. Stevenson
Allison Stewart
Marty Stuart
Jimmy Sturr
Henry Lee Summer
Sun Volt
Doug Supernaw
Supersuckers
Taj Mahal
Lee Taylor & the Rhythm
    Killers
Les Taylor
Susan Tedeschi
Tegan and Sara
Benmont Tench
Jimmy Tingle
Texas Tornados
Billy Bob Thornton
Titty Bingo
Wayne Toups
Tractors
Randy Travis
Milo Tremley
Trick Pony
Travis Tritt

John Trudell
Tanya Tucker
Unforgiven
Keith Urban
Brian Vander Ark
Eddie Van Halen
Ricky Van Shelton
Townes Van Zandt
Stevie Ray Vaughan and
    Double Trouble
Kate Voegele
Jon Voight
V-Roys
Wa
Jack Wagner
Jerry Jeff Walker
Joe Walsh
War
Don Was & Blue Maroons
Was (Not Was)
Jimmy Webb
Rusty Weir
Gillian Welch
Dottie West
Wilco
Hog Wilder
Webb Wilder
Williams and Ree
Don Williams
Lucinda Williams
Brian Wilson
Debra Winger
Winters Brothers
Wisdom Indian Dancers
Lee Ann Womack
Tom Wopat
X
Trisha Yearwood
Dwight Yoakam
Neil Young
Neil Young and Crazy Horse
Zaca Creek

About the Contributors

Bill Ayres cofounded WHY in 1975 with late singer/songwriter Harry Chapin and has been the organization's executive director since 1983.

Wendell Berry is a poet, essayist, farmer, and novelist. Among his honors and awards are fellowships from the Guggenheim and Rockefeller Foundations, a Lannan Foundation Award, and a grant from the National Endowment for the Arts. He lives on a farm in Port Royal, Kentucky.

Dr. Darryl Birkenfeld is director of Ogallala Commons, a resource development network generating commonwealth in the High Plains–Ogallala Aquifer region.

Sky DeMuro has served as Farm Aid's development associate and Web developer. She currently works at an educational farm and wildlife sanctuary in Massachusetts.

Jennifer Fahy has been Farm Aid's operations manager since 2002. She wishes she grew up on a family farm!

Reebee Garofalo is a professor at the University of Massachusetts, Boston, where he is affiliated with the College of Public and Community Service and the American Studies program. His most recent book is *Rockin' Out: Popular Music in the USA*.

Holly George-Warren is an award-winning editor and writer who has contributed to numerous books on music and popular culture. Most recently, she co-edited *The Rolling Stone Encyclopedia of Rock & Roll; Martin Scorsese Presents the Blues: A Musical Journey;* and *The Appalachians: America's First and Last Frontier*. Her writing also has appeared in the *New York Times, Rolling Stone,* the *Journal of Country Music, Village Voice,* and *Mojo,* among other publications.

Carl Grimm is director of programs at the Garfield Park Conservatory Alliance and is active in the development of composting, urban agriculture policy, and organic gardening education in the Chicago area. For fifteen years, he led programs at the San Francisco League of Urban Gardeners.

Joan Dye Gussow is the author of *This Organic Life: Confessions of a Suburban Homesteader* and is the Mary Swartz Rose Professor emerita and former chair of the nutrition education program at Columbia University Teachers College.

John Hansen is a sixth-generation family farmer from Newman Grove, Nebraska. He has served as president of the Nebraska Farmers Union since 1990. John is a co-drafter and continuing champion of Initiative 300, a successful citizens initiative placed in the Nebraska Constitution in 1982 that is the strongest and most effective anti-corporate farming restriction in the nation.

Jim Hightower is a national radio commentator, writer, public speaker, and the author of *Thieves in High Places: They've Stolen Our Country and It's Time to Take It Back*. He has spent three decades battling the Powers That Be on behalf of the Powers That Ought to Be—consumers, working families, environmentalists, small businesses, and just plain folks. Hightower also has served two terms as Texas Agriculture Commissioner.

Dave Hoekstra has been a *Chicago Sun-Times* staff writer since 1985. His work also has appeared in *Playboy*, the *Chicago Reader, Chicago Magazine*, and the *Journal of Country Music*. His profile of Steve Earle appeared in the DaCapo Press book *Best Music Writing 2000*. *Ticket to Everywhere*, his collection of travel essays, was honored in 2005 by the Illinois Center for the Book. Hoekstra wrote and co-produced the PBS special *The Staple Singers and the Civil Rights Movement*, nominated for a 2001–2002 Chicago Emmy for Outstanding Achievement for Documentary Program—Cultural Significance.

Ben Holmes blended his experience working on his uncles' dairy farm with time spent teaching middle school into the creation of The Farm School in 1989.

Sylvia Jorrin is one of two women livestock farmers in the three hundred farms of the New York City Watershed. She writes a weekly column about life on the farm in the *Delaware County Times,* and is the author of *Sylvia's Farm: The Journal of an Improbable Shepherd*.

Robert F. Kennedy Jr. is president of Water Keeper Alliance.

Barbara Kingsolver's ten published books include novels, collections of short stories, poetry, essays, and an oral history. Her work has been translated into more than a dozen languages and has earned literary awards and a devoted readership at home and abroad. In 2000, she was awarded the National Humanities Medal, our country's highest honor for service through the arts.

Frederick L. Kirschenmann, a longtime leader in sustainable agriculture, directs the Leopold Center for Sustainable Agriculture, located on the campus of Iowa State University in Ames. He continues to oversee management of his family's 3,500-acre certified organic farm in North Dakota and has an appointment in the ISU Department of Religion and Philosophy. Kirschenmann writes extensively about ethics and agriculture.

Jennifer Lamson is a founding partner of Good Food Strategies LLC, providing communications expertise to promote fresh, healthy, local foods, vibrant communities, and family farms. She is also on the board of the Cascade Harvest Coalition, working to strengthen community food systems in the Puget Sound region of Washington State.

Gene Logsdon operates a small grazing farm with his wife, Carol, in north-central Ohio. He is the author of twenty-two books, including *The Contrary Farmer, You Can Go Home Again*, and *All Flesh Is Grass*. He is currently at work on a book about art and agriculture that will be published next year as *The Mother of All the Arts*.

Zachary D. Lyons is the executive director of the Washington Farmers Market Association. He is a freelance food writer and currently serves on the boards of the National Association of Farmers Market Nutrition Programs, FORKS (Washington chapter of Chef's Collaborative), From the Heart of Washington, and the WSDA Small Farm and Director Marketing Program.

David Mas Masumoto is an organic peach, nectarine, and raisin farmer on an eighty-acre farm in the Central Valley of California. He is the author of *Epitaph for a Peach, Harvest Son, Four Seasons in Five Senses*, and, most recently, *Letters to the Valley.*

Carolyn G. Mugar has been Farm Aid's executive director for twenty years, since early September 1985.

Paul Natkin learned photography from his father, the team photographer of the Chicago Bulls. Paul shot sports in the Chicago area before becoming a music photographer in 1976. Over the years, he has photographed most of the major music stars of the last half of the twentieth century. His photos have graced the covers of such magazines as *Newsweek* (Bruce Springsteen), *Ebony* (Tina Turner), and *People* (Prince), as well as several album covers. He was the official photographer for *The Oprah Winfrey Show* from 1986 until 1993. He has been photographing Farm Aid since 1985.

Marion Nestle is the Paulette Goddard Professor in the Department of Nutrition, Food Studies, and Public Health at New York University, which she chaired from 1988 to 2003. Previously, she was senior nutrition policy advisor in the Department of Health and Human Services and managing editor of the 1988 *Surgeon General's Report on Nutrition and Health*. She has been a member of the FDA Food Advisory Committee and Science Board, the USDA/DHHS 1995 Dietary Guidelines Advisory Committee, and American Cancer Society committees that issue dietary guidelines for cancer prevention. She is the author of *Food Politics: How the Food Industry Influences Nutrition and Health* and *Safe Food: Bacteria, Biotechnology, and Bioterrorism.*

Michel Nischan is a renowned chef and best-selling author of *Taste, Pure and Simple,* recipient of the 2004 James Beard Award.

Edward "Jerry" Pennick is director of the land assistance fund of the Federation of Southern Cooperatives/LAF. He is responsible for the development and implemention of land-retention strategies for the Federation's membership, as well as for other minority landowners and farmers throughout the Southeast.

Michael Pollan is a contributing editor to the *New York Times Magazine* and a professor of journalism at UC Berkeley. His most recent book is *The Botany of Desire: A Plant's-Eye View of the World*. His new book, *The Omnivore's Dilemma: A Natural History of Four Meals*, will be published by Penguin in April 2006.

Ted Quaday is the program director of Farm Aid.

Ruth Reichl is the editor in chief of *Gourmet* magazine. She is the former restaurant critic of the *New York Times* and the *Los Angeles Times* and the author of *Tender at the Bone*, *Comfort Me With Apples*, and *Garlic and Sapphires*. She also edited *The Gourmet Cookbook* and the Modern Library Food Series.

Mark Ritchie is president of the Institute for Agriculture and Trade Policy, working to foster sustainable rural communities and regions.

Ebet Roberts moved from her native Memphis to New York City to paint but switched to photography in 1977, when she began photographing musicians. Her work has been reproduced on numerous album and book covers and featured in nearly a hundred books including *CBGB's: 30 Years of Photographs, Blank Generation Revisited,* and *The Rolling Stone Book of Women in Rock*. Publications include *Rolling Stone,* the *New York Times*, *Newsweek,* the *Village Voice,* and *Mojo,* among others. Her work is in the permanent collection of the Rock and Roll Hall of Fame and Museum; the Experience Music Project; and the Hard Rock Cafe. She has been photographing Farm Aid since 1985.

Eric Schlosser is a correspondent for *The Atlantic Monthly* and the author of *Fast Food Nation.*

Bob Scowcroft is the cofounder (in 1990) and current executive director of the Organic Farming Research Foundation. He has been an advocate for organic food and the farmers that produce it for twenty-seven years.

Mark Smith has been Farm Aid's campaign director since 2000. An avid Red Sox fan and cyclist, Mark spends as much time as possible tending his "backyard farm" with his wife and two children.

Tom Spaulding is executive director of the Community Supported Agriculture Learning Center, an educational nonprofit partner to Angelic Organics farm in Caledonia, Illinois. The CSA Learning Center empowers people to create sustainable communities and offers agro-ecology education, community food security, and farmer training programs annually to more than 3,500 youth and adults.

Martin Teitel, PhD, is executive director of the Cedar Tree Foundation. He is the author of three books and numerous articles on food and human rights.

Glenda Yoder has been the associate director of Farm Aid for fifteen years. She grew up on an Ohio family farm.

Howard Zinn is a historian, playwright, and social activist. He is perhaps best known for *A People's History of the United States*, which presents American history through the eyes of those he feels are outside of the political and economic establishment.

Acknowledgments

Writing a book by committee is not easy. It took a village, that's for sure. Paul Natkin and Dave Hoekstra hatched the idea for this book. Dave has attended numerous Farm Aid concerts as a reporter and has written many insightful stories. Paul has generously shot every show and donated his photographs. Thanks to their persistence, the idea blossomed. Thank you, Ebet Roberts, for also shooting nearly every show and donating photos. Thanks to Holly George-Warren and Ellen Nygaard, who came into the project two years ago and huddled excitedly in backstage dressing rooms as we all bounced ideas off the walls. Thanks to our book agent, Sarah Lazin, whose confidence quickly moved things forward. Thank you, Jess Rosen of Greenburg-Traurig, and also Iris Geik, who donated expert legal advice. Thank you, Mark Ostow, for the staff photo. Laurie LeBlanc kindly transcribed interviews at a moment's notice. Rodale Publishing has been a companionable partner, a mission-oriented company whose founder pioneered organic agriculture.

Thanks to all the contributors, many of whom donated their essays. Their writings sparked intense discussions and exciting new ideas. Thanks to all who were interviewed; their stories of the early days were funny, horrifying, and awe-inspiring. Valuable background information was provided by Harry Smith, Janet Corpus, Kim Buchheit, and Mike Robinson. Readers Neil Fairbairn, Will Allen, Ken Barnes, Jim Slama, David Senter, Susan Steiner, and Mark Ritchie offered valuable insights and corrections. All of us involved gained a fresh appreciation for all that has been accomplished.

Thanks to the hardy Farm Aid staff, who threw themselves into the project, and gave it their all, including good humor and crazy hours. But the star of this show was Jen Fahy, book coordinator. She took on a complicated project, communicated with a myriad of partners, and demonstrated amazing stamina to meet the deadlines. She kept hope alive.

We regret omissions and the fact that many wonderful stories from dear Farm Aid friends could not be included. Additional testimonials and stories, along with deeper reading on many of these topics, are posted on www.farmaid.org.

And finally, thank you Willie, Neil, John, and Dave. We love you and admire you.

FARM AID
JUNE 2005

Ditto on all of the above. Special additional thanks to Rodale's Margot Schupf, Andy Carpenter, Karen Bolesta, Nancy Bailey, and Jennifer Giandomenico. Our gratitude, too, to Nina Pearlman, Robin Aigner, Judy Whitfield, Robert Legault, Robin Hepler, Andrea Odintz-Cohen; photographers Jack Kotz, Lisa Hamilton, David Gahr, Michael O'Brien, George Holz, Paul Burd, Marc Pokempner, and Van Slider; and Robert Warren, Joe Ford, Paula Balzer, Mark Rothbaum, Traci Thomas, Chris Neal, Ted Olson, Mary Almond, Andy Schwartz, Jennifer Holz, Jim Sherraden, Bob Delavante, Kathy Allman, Chet Flippo, Angie Carlson, Stephanie Huguenin, Jens Jurgensen, Peter Amft, Amanda Kimble-Evans, and Karen Rauter.

HGW
JULY 2005

Farm Aid staff, 2005: Wendy Matusovich, Sky DeMuro, Ted Quaday, Carolyn G. Mugar, Jennifer Fahy, Laura Freden, Mark Smith, Katie Matus, and Glenda Yoder (from left)

Text and Photography Credits

To Malc, Soni and Joshua – M.M.
To Jeff – A.K.

First published in Great Britain in 2004 by
Frances Lincoln Children's Books, 4 Torriano Mews, Torriano Avenue, London NW5 2RZ
www.franceslincoln.com

Distributed in the USA by Publishers Group West

British Library Cataloguing in Publication Data available on request

ISBN 1-84507-039-9
Set in The Sans

Printed in Singapore
3 5 7 9 8 6 4 2

The Publishers would like to thank David and Rufus Bellamy
for checking the text and illustrations.